Praise for *Sluma*

"Slumach's gold is one of North America's most famou[...]
ADAM PALMER, expedition team leader for *Deadman's Curse: The Legend of the Lost Gold*

"*Slumach's Gold* brings together stories that have touched the spirits of my Ancestors. My mother Gail's traditional name is Kwelaxtelotiya meaning 'to be close to.' Like Slumach's canoe touching the water, these words written are 'close to' many truths about the legend of the hidden gold. My hands are raised to the authors who have recorded and shared Slumach's oral history."
TAYLOR STARR, Cultural and Heritage Monitor and descendant of Slumach

"Forget the Dutchman, Lasseter's Reef, Yamashita's Gold, and all the other 'lost mines' that are just stories. Slumach's gold of Pitt Lake may not be as well known, but it certainly has the best and most evidence—guaranteed it will make a treasure hunter out of you!"
BRIAN DUNNING, host of the award-winning podcast *Skeptoid*

"The story of Slumach's gold has been called the best campfire story ever. It's easy to see why, with its long-lost gold mine, hanging, curse and more. Even better, it's grounded in fact. Authors Brian Antonson, Mary Trainer, and Rick Antonson deftly mined the legend for this lively, important new work."
PETER EDWARDS, *Toronto Star* journalist and co-author of *Lytton: Climate Change, Colonialism and Life Before the Fire (with Kevin Loring)*

"This book is a must-read for anyone fascinated by the world of lost gold, legends about treasure-hunters, and tales of a hidden motherload protected by a curse. I know, I've been there!"
DONALD E. WAITE, author of *British Columbia and Yukon Gold Hunters: A History in Photographs*

"What makes this book stand out is the painstaking research that has gone into separating the truth from the fiction. The authors have put together a well-researched, well-written book that is rich with illustrations. Perhaps, but not likely, this edition will put to bed the false research, myth-making, and genuine lies that have surrounded Slumach and his mythical treasure."

KEN MATHER, author of *Stagecoach North: A History of Barnard's Express*

"Legend has it that old-time swashbuckling gold prospectors cried out 'There's Gold in dem der hills!' after a successful day of prospecting. Mary Trainer, Rick Antonson, and Brian Antonson have been articulately proclaiming that same message for the last fifty-two years. The ongoing passion these three have for great storytelling and accurately recording BC history is nothing short of legendary."

DAVE DOROGHY, author of *Show Me the Honey* and co-author of *111 Places in Vancouver That You Must Not Miss*

"An intriguing and meticulously researched tale of elusive gold in the British Columbia wilderness that has the heady additions of murder and a curse. As one treasure hunter says, 'If you think it's just about gold, then you are missing the truth.'"

ED BUTTS, author of *This Game of War*

"*Slumach's Gold* combines true crime, history, mystery, and memoir. A fascinating account of buried treasure and ancient curses, played out against a backdrop of backcountry justice in the wilds of late nineteenth-century British Columbia. The authors' personal connection to the story (which has fascinated them since childhood) adds to the appeal, even as they reveal the truth behind certain long-standing legends."

NATE HENDLEY, author of *Atrocity on the Atlantic* and *The Beatle Bandit*

"A great piece of research that reads like a mystery novel or a CSI episode. . .*Slumach's Gold* combines legend, myth, documentation and oral history. It's a masterpiece."

RICHARD THOMAS WRIGHT, author of *Barkerville and the Cariboo Goldfields*

"A fresh new look at one of British Columbia's enduring mysteries."

CHUCK DAVIS, author of *Vancouver Then and Now*

"Qualifies as a British Columbia classic."

BC BOOKWORLD

SLUMACH'S GOLD

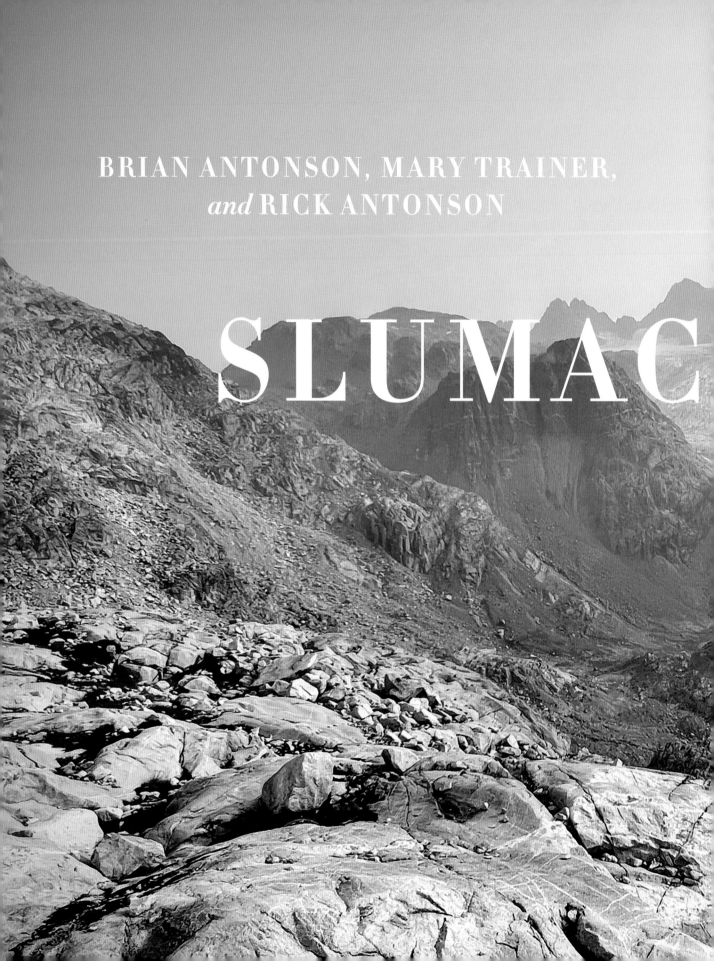

BRIAN ANTONSON, MARY TRAINER,
and RICK ANTONSON

SLUMAC

I'S GOLD

In Search of a Legend—
and a Curse

Cataloguing information available from Library and Archives Canada
978-1-77203-518-6 (paperback)
978-1-77203-519-3 (e-book)

Edited by Karla Decker
Cover design by Setareh Ashrafologhalai
Interior design by Sara Loos
Photos on front cover, frontispiece, and page xi by Adam Palmer

The interior of this book was produced on FSC®-certified, acid-free paper,
processed chlorine free, and printed with vegetable-based inks.

Heritage House gratefully acknowledges that the land on which we live and work is within
the traditional territories of the Lkwungen (Esquimalt and Songhees), Malahat, Pacheedaht, Scia'new,
T'Sou-ke, and W̱SÁNEĆ (Pauquachin, Tsartlip, Tsawout, Tseycum) Peoples.

We acknowledge the financial support of the Government of Canada through the
Canada Book Fund (CBF) and the Canada Council for the Arts, and the Province of British Columbia
through the British Columbia Arts Council and the Book Publishing Tax Credit.

28 27 26 25 24 1 2 3 4 5
Printed in China

We dedicate this capstone edition of our work to the grandchildren
of this generation's historians, ours in particular:
Brian's grandchildren, Tristin and Sierra;
Mary's grandchildren, Woods, Lake, and Willow;
and Rick's grandchildren, Riley and Declan.
What a thrill it would be if Slumach's gold is found in your lifetime.

And to our friends Fred Braches (1930–2024) and Don Waite,
sage and inimitable chroniclers of all things Slumach, with our sincerest admiration.

Contents

List of Maps

Authors' Note

THE HISTORY OF BRITISH Columbia and Canada has mostly been told from the perspective of its colonizers and settlers, and this is no different for much of the Slumach story. Racism strongly colours much of the early reporting and sensationalizing of the events leading up to Slumach's death in 1891, as well as in the years after as the legend of the hidden gold begins to gain strength. Indeed, one might also argue that the handling of Slumach's case in the early BC courts, his conversion to Christianity, and his internment in an unmarked grave are unjust acts that perpetuated the colonial enterprise.

In order to present the "facts of the day," we have laid out some of the media coverage of both the court trials and the later perpetuation of the legend in their original forms. We recognize that, although representative of the time from which it originated, the language in some of these sources, in tone and content, especially in relation to Slumach being an Indigenous person, would be considered offensive and intolerable today. Slumach was a real person, and although unbiased and reliable information about his personal life is scarce, we have tried our best to recreate an image of the man that is independent of the fancies and exaggerations of careless media and sensationalist writers of the past.

The story of Slumach's Gold occurs on the traditional and unceded territories of the q̓icə̓y̓ (Katzie) First Nation, who for thousands of years have lived, thrived, and been stewards of the lands that encompass today's Port Coquitlam, Pitt Meadows, and Maple Ridge areas, portions of other Fraser Valley locations, and the wilderness areas of Pinecone Burke, Golden Ears, and Garibaldi Provincial Parks. To this day, the Katzie People maintain deep connections to the lands, rivers, sloughs, creeks, and wetlands that run like veins through the heart of their territories. At the centre of Katzie territory are sq̓ə́y̓cəya?ɬ x̌aca? ("The lake of the Katzie") and sq̓ə́y̓cəya?ɬ státləw ("the river of the Katzie"), though we know them by colonial names, Pitt Lake and Pitt River.

Opposite Of all the images cast for Slumach, we find this one from Michael Collier's 1994 film *Curse of the Lost Gold Mine* to be the closest representation of what he may have looked like. The role of Slumach was played by Indigenous actor Norman Natrall, who passed away in 2014. Keep this image in mind when viewing other, probably inaccurate, photos and drawings of Slumach, where he is often portrayed as a young, roguish, rabble-rousing man. We would like readers to avoid the many distortions suggested over the years. Slumach was likely about eighty, had long white hair, and carried a rifle like this when he shot Louis Bee. MICHAEL COLLIER COLLECTION

Overleaf Distant clouds in "Slumach Country." COURTESY OF JAMES WHEELER

The Best Campfire Story Ever

IT WAS THE SUMMER of 1957.

Darkness and gloom hung over six young lads huddled around a campfire, the wind-driven crackle of flames making their hearts beat fast with excitement. An old woman sat on a log stump among them, captivating all of them with her ghost stories—the very stuff of summer camp. The boys shuddered in the cool evening, afraid but wanting more.

It was a weeklong boys' camp, a stretch of time spent swimming and boating and beginning to learn how to make one's own decisions about what matters most in life. Dusk's successful fishing escapade had ended an hour before and left them tired as they helped a local fisherman reel in lines and dock the boats. They'd lit a fire to fry fish and fend off the evening cold.

The fisherman's wife was also the camp cook. Her daytime friendliness turned conspiratorial in the post-dinner shadows thrown from the fire pit. She leaned toward the campfire. Her words entranced the circle of youngsters.

"There's a lost gold mine up on Pitt Lake," she began, slowly shifting her head in a westward motion, her shrug indicating the mine was close, though not nearby. "But you'll never find it—at least not find it and live." Her gaze flickered from boy to boy until she'd locked stares with each pair of wide-open, innocent eyes.

The woman continued her tale about an Indigenous man named Slumach, who was hunting deer in the rough mountain terrain when he stumbled upon a creek scattered with gold nuggets. She shivered and pulled her shawl close around her shoulders. Her voice was eerie. "There's a curse that protects his mine from discovery by anyone else."

Two of us around the fire were brothers, one nine years old, the other eight, and her words gripped our imaginations. She spoke of a mystery that would remain unsolved, she claimed, unless people like us grew brave enough to go searching for the lost gold despite the curse.

The campfire that night was on the shores of Hatzic Lake, near Mission, British Columbia, about eighty kilometres (fifty miles) east of Vancouver. Tired and ready to fall asleep, the six of us sipped hot chocolate with our feet pressed near the fire for warmth. The fisherman's wife stoked the fire back to life and continued to tell us the legend of Slumach's gold.

"That was in 1890," she said. "Slumach would bring gold nuggets into the town of New Westminster. And he'd buy drinks for everyone as he bragged about his secret creek."

Her voice was raspy yet strangely clear: "Greedy people tried to wrestle the source of the gold from Slumach, but all failed. He'd slip out of town in the night, time and time again, but would return weeks or months later with more gold."

We believed every word as her story unfolded. Slumach was real, and none of what we'd just heard seemed remotely like a legend. She took the curse seriously: "Any gold seekers who tried to follow Slumach vanished themselves on the dead-end trails leading into the mountains from Pitt Lake. There, dense fog appears without warning. Canoes tip in the sudden winds that churn the lake into nightmare waves to protect the mine from being found." None of the boys around the campfire were of Indigenous descent, though each longed for a personal link to this mysterious tale.

The storyteller tossed a cedar log on the fire. Its slivers sparked, burning bright right away. Still, we shivered. We felt fear reaching for us from the dark hillside behind her, seeking us out from the star-sprinkled sky. We knew death was out there. Six hearts nearly stopped beating when the woman came to the part about the Indigenous man being arrested for murder.

We leaned closer to the fire, riveted. "It was on the prison gallows that Slumach uttered his curse as they put a hood over his head and a noose around his neck. It happened just before the trapdoor sprang open and dropped Slumach to his death at the end of a five-strand rope." We hung on her words just as surely as if the noose had been strung around our own little necks. "Witnesses believed the curse would protect the mine from any future gold seekers, threatening the lives of anyone who went searching for Slumach's gold."

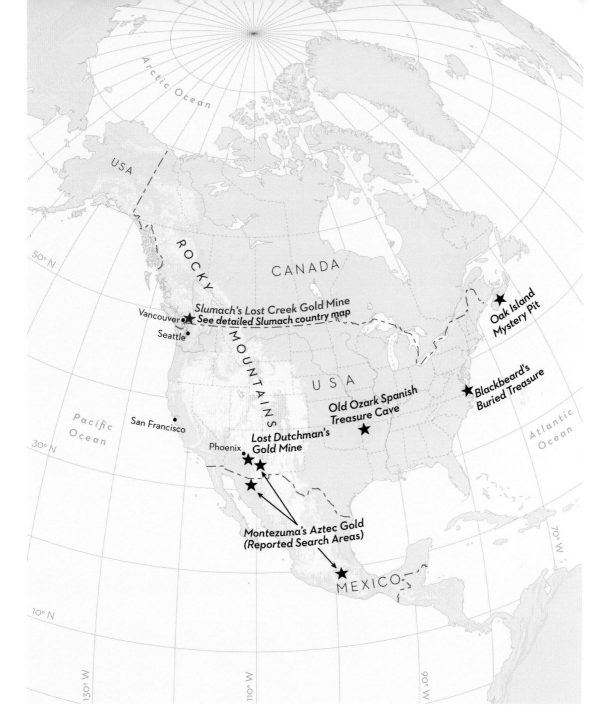

Map A: North America's most famous lost treasures—North America abounds with lost treasure stories. We authors see the five located on this map as the most compelling and interesting, and Slumach's Gold is chief among them. ERIC LEINBERGER

Opposite The glacier-fed waters of the upper Pitt River flow into Pitt Lake here. Most gold seekers pass through this region as they start their searches, no matter which route they follow. COURTESY OF DONALD E. WAITE

What story could be more gripping to the young brothers' imaginations? For years, as our family left weekend camps at Hatzic Lake and drove the narrow highway toward Vancouver and home, we'd ask Dad to slow down as we passed through Pitt Meadows and the bridge over the lower Pitt River just before it flows into the Fraser River. In the distance to the north, craggy mountains laced with ravines and home to bears and cougars bordered Pitt Lake on the east and west. The glacier-fed upper Pitt River flowed into the lake's northern end. Even from our car, we could see the mists that shrouded the cliffs so deeply as to seem impenetrable. Every time we drove by, we would look at one another in the back seat of our Chevrolet, point toward Pitt Lake, and then one of us would say to the other, "That's where Slumach's lost gold mine is. One day we'll go and find it. No matter the curse. One day . . ."

On a summer evening in 1957, beside a lake much like the one shown here, an elderly woman spoke of the legend of Slumach, his gold, and his deadly curse, captivating the minds of the young boys gathered around her. OP MEDIA GROUP

Overleaf Reflections. COURTESY OF JAMES WHEELER

On the Bank of the Pitt River

WE THREE AUTHORS WANTED this book to be called *We Found Slumach's Gold*, but such was not to be.

Picture this scene: As we bask in early autumn's warmth, a topographical map flutters in our hands, as if it's trying to grab our attention and reveal new information. The wind is up, cresting the river's waters into whitecaps and rocking a nearby canoe like a cradle. It's been misty most of the morning, with mountains playing hide-and-seek, befitting a lost gold creek tucked somewhere in their jagged folds. We gaze at them as if our watchful eyes might finally see what has eluded thousands of searchers for more than a century since a man named Slumach was hanged in 1891, the location of his fabled gold said to have died with him.

We're in "Slumach country," an hour's drive (forty kilometres, or twenty-five miles) east of Vancouver, BC.

Talking about the Slumach legend, which is said to have been born from a curse on the gallows, still brings a chill to our spines as harsh as this day's cold wind. The immense land before us—that which can be seen from here, and terrain that can only be found during days of hiking or by boating along the inhospitable shoreline of Pitt Lake, or after rigorous mountain climbing—holds answers and perhaps harbours riches, and may well protect a secret.

That's what drew the three of us together more than fifty years ago to write our first book, in 1972, about our quest to search for the legend's foundation rather than for nuggets of gold. We strove to separate fact from fiction. We'd scoured archives, researched mining data, and come to know some of the most adventurous people—contemporary and historic—who believed they could be the ones to discover what has outwitted others: Slumach's lost gold. Our fascination continued over the years, leading to an expanded book in 2007. As more years passed, even more details emerged, and we have worked to capture them in this, our third and final book.

We have written about three people who were pivotal to any credible context concerning Slumach and the legendary lost mine of Pitt Lake. The first is photographer Don Waite, who is as comfortable sifting through boxes of old files and interviewing sources as he once was hiking the mountains around Pitt Lake. Then there is the Katzie Nation's Amanda Charnley (affectionately known to her relatives and henceforth in this book as "Aunt Mandy"), daughter of Slumach's catechist Peter Pierre, who was Slumach's nephew and was present at Slumach's hanging. Finally, no one has done more substantive research about the fact and fiction of this legend than the late Fred Braches, historian, author, and creator of the websites slumach.ca, slumach.blogspot.com, and related Wikipedia pages—all of them authoritative online sources of relevant information.

A gold seeker heads into the mountain mist, hoping fortune lies ahead on the Slumach trail. MICHAEL COLLIER COLLECTION

We're older now—wiser but not richer—and that tells you we've not found gold either. But we've unearthed a heap of stories, some true and some not, about the real-life elderly man Slumach and his legacy. And we've come across a host of hints, plenty of theories, a pot-load of falsehoods, and a side dish of facts—meaning this book includes most of what someone should know about searching for the lost mine of Pitt Lake. It's about time someone had such good luck. Might it be you?

Brian Antonson, Mary Trainer, and Rick Antonson
On the bank of the Pitt River, Autumn 2024

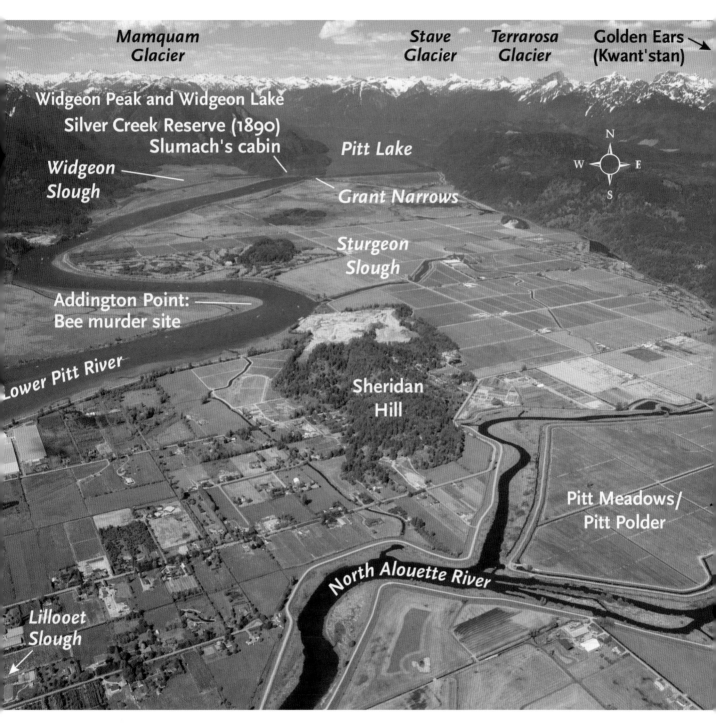

Map B: Aerial view, Pitt Meadows/Pitt Polder looking north—This is the south end of Pitt Lake, the Pitt Meadows/Pitt Polder area, looking north, providing context for Slumach country. Addington Point is now known to be the site where Slumach shot Louis Bee. The map points shown here relate to the possible site of the lost mine as well as locations key to the Slumach legend. COURTESY OF DONALD E. WAITE/ERIC LEINBERGER

Mamquam Glacier   Stave Glacier   Terrarosa Glacier   Golden Ears (Kwant'stan)

← Widgeon Peak and Widgeon Lake

Lizard Lake

Pitt Lake

Widgeon   Slough

Silver Creek Reserve (1890) Slumach's cabin

Widgeon Creek

Lower Pitt River

Grant Narrows

Map C: Aerial view looking north from lower Pitt Lake/Widgeon Creek—This is also from lower Pitt Lake/Widgeon Creek, looking north, and shows key locations in the Slumach story. In the 1880s, Slumach lived in a cabin next to Widgeon Slough. The landmark Golden Ears are to the east. COURTESY OF DONALD E. WAITE/ERIC LEINBERGER

Opposite Kwant'stan is the Salish Peoples' name for the Golden Ears, twin peaks that tower over, indeed define, Pitt Lake for aviators, canoeists, and gold seekers alike. BRIAN ANTONSON

Overleaf Golden sunlight catches the morning mist on the Alouette River in Pitt Meadows. COURTESY OF JAMES WHEELER

Chapter 1

The Legend of Slumach and His Lost Creek Gold Mine

THAT "ONE DAY" WE had mused about as children arrived when, as adults, we two brothers who had heard the tale of Slumach's gold around the campfire that night joined up with our friend, Mary Trainer, and went in search of a legend. We became familiar with "Slumach country," as some call it: the vast area around the lower Pitt River, Pitt Lake itself, and upper Pitt River, surrounded by rugged terrain with a thousand places that could hide a creek filled with gold nuggets.

Decades later, even after a handful of books had been written by ourselves and others—and after there had been well over a hundred public presentations, two television series, numerous documentaries, countless newspaper and magazine articles and radio programs, a podcast, and never-ending searches near Pitt Lake—the mystery of Slumach's gold remains unsolved and the captivating legend is very much alive.

After all our years of research, the following is our preferred telling of the legend, and we stress that *this is legend* and far removed from the facts. It embellishes the fisherman's wife's version with fiction and fantasy aplenty amid a smattering of facts, and has become the accepted version by gold seekers from around the world:

Sometime in the late 1880s, somewhere in the mountainous country surrounding Pitt Lake, an hour away as the crow flies from the bustling river port of New Westminster, a Katzie man named Slumach stumbled upon a fabulously rich "find" of pure gold nuggets.

His discovery was a "glory hole"—in the mining terminology of the day, a site where nuggets lay all about—and the bed of the creek shimmered with gold. Slumach packed some of the precious metal out to civilization and began the first of many wild tours through early New Westminster, spending freely in the Royal City's saloons and sporting houses. He tossed about nuggets and gleefully watched other patrons scramble for them. He refused to disclose any information about where he found his riches. When his supply ran out, he disappeared from town.

Again and again, Slumach returned to New Westminster, lavishly spending his gold. Then, as before, he would leave without a trace, eluding those who tried to follow him on the arduous trip back to windswept Pitt Lake and the dangerous mountains surrounding it.

Slumach often took a young woman with him when he went away—supposedly to assist him in recovering his gold. None were ever seen again. When questioned, Slumach always claimed they turned back on the trail, afraid to carry on in the hazardous terrain. He had no idea why none of them ever returned to New Westminster.

CITY OF NEW WESTMINSTER, No. 1

COLUMBIA STREET IN 1888
NEW WESTMINSTER

COLONIAL HOTEL

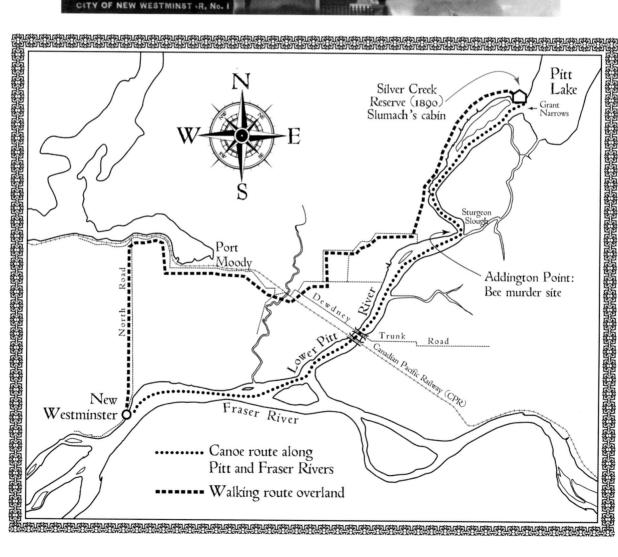

Pitt Lake

Silver Creek
Reserve (1890)
Slumach's cabin

Grant Narrows

Sturgeon Slough

Port Moody

Addington Point:
Bee murder site

North Road

Dewdney River

Trunk Road

Canadian Pacific Railway (CPR)

Lower Pitt River

New Westminster

Fraser River

· · · · · · · · · Canoe route along
Pitt and Fraser Rivers

▪ ▪ ▪ ▪ ▪ ▪ ▪ Walking route overland

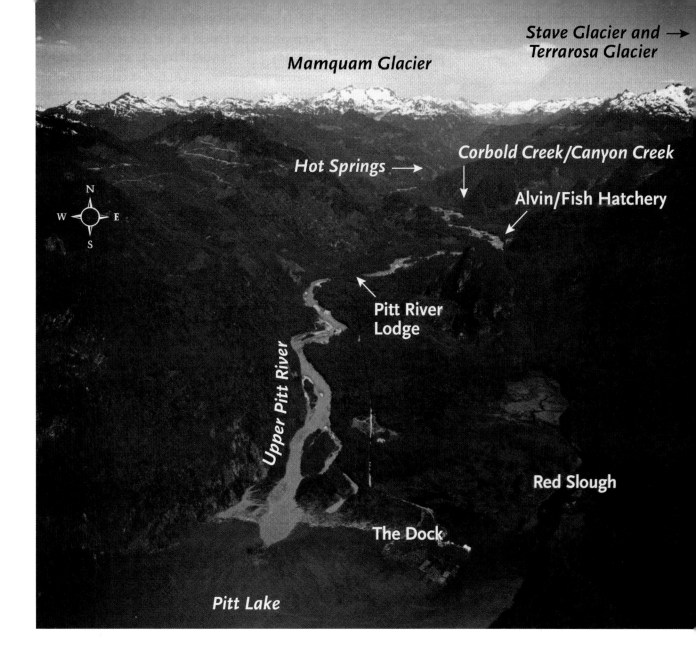

Stave Glacier and → Terrarosa Glacier

Mamquam Glacier

Corbold Creek/Canyon Creek

Hot Springs →

Alvin/Fish Hatchery

N
W ⊕ E
S

Pitt River Lodge

Upper Pitt River

Red Slough

The Dock

Pitt Lake

Map E: Aerial view looking north from head of Pitt Lake—This is the view north from the head of Pitt Lake, showing the upper Pitt River flowing into the lake at the west side of Red Slough. The river's direction was altered around 1930, before which it flowed into the lake on the east side of Red Slough. This means gold seekers in earlier times would have taken a more easterly approach up the river before moving into the mountains. COURTESY OF DONALD E. WAITE/ERIC LEINBERGER

Opposite, top New Westminster in 1888 as Slumach would have known it, if indeed he ever visited the city. Note the Golden Ears in the background, which loom over the eastern flank of Pitt Lake. CITY OF VANCOUVER ARCHIVES CVA 371-2873

Opposite, bottom *Map D: Slumach's route options from Pitt Lake to New Westminster*—If Slumach indeed visited New Westminster before he was arrested and imprisoned, he'd have either canoed a several-hour journey depending on tidal influence or walked for seven or more hours on the roads and trails available in his day, depending on the weather conditions. FRED BOSMAN

The authors, in our sixth decade of researching and admitting that finding Slumach's gold still captures our imaginations, relax near Pitt River. We acknowledge that truths and hard facts don't always win out over tantalizing fiction and the lure of a missing treasure . . . and admit the legend of Pitt Lake's lost gold mine will be with us as long as there are eager gold seekers, young or old—or until someone finds a creek filled with gold nuggets. JANICE ANTONSON

During one of his spending sprees, Slumach met an attractive girl of Chinese and Irish descent named Molly Tynan. She had arrived in New Westminster while Slumach was out of town and heard tales of his wealth and spending sprees. She announced intentions to claim this Katzie man for her own when he returned. This she did, despite warnings that naïve girls had vanished before.

Some weeks after Molly and Slumach left town for the mine, her body was brought up in a fisherman's net in the Fraser River just off New Westminster. She had been stabbed to death, and a knife was still in her heart. Slumach was questioned by police on his next trip to New Westminster. He said that when he had last seen her, she was heading on her own out of the wilderness and back to civilization. Unfortunately for Slumach, the knife taken from Molly's body had been identified as his.

On this evidence, Slumach was tried and convicted of Molly's murder. Even under sentence of death, Slumach refused to reveal the location of his mine. As he stood on the gallows, he whispered a curse on those who would seek the mine, meaning that no one would ever find his gold and live—they would die in their search. His executioner heard it, as did several witnesses: "Nika memloose, mine memloose"—"When I die, the mine dies."

The mine's location may have died with Slumach, but his curse was very much alive. In the spring of 1901, a San Francisco man named Jackson came to New Westminster on his way home from the Alaskan goldfields, and announced he was going to find Slumach's gold. He set out alone. Months later, he reappeared near New Westminster, a mere skeleton of a man, injured and shivering with pain. He told of unbelievable hardships in the mountains around Pitt Lake. And he kept his heavy packsack with him at all times.

Jackson returned to his home in San Francisco and deposited more than $8,000 in gold in the Bank of British North America there, and then died in 1904 as a result of his injuries—the first known victim of Slumach's curse. But, before he died, Jackson wrote a letter to a Seattle man named Shotwell, who had grubstaked him during a previous Alaskan venture, providing funds and equipment. He encouraged Shotwell to seek out the mine he had found near Pitt Lake and its fabulous riches. Part of that letter was a crude map identifying the location of the find.

Since Slumach's death, his curse has claimed the lives of avid searchers, casual seekers, and those struck with gold fever. Dozens have died, newspapers have reported. The country hiding his treasure is unbelievably rugged—in some places, the mountainsides are vertical, prone to sudden fog, and trails seem to disappear, leaving no way out. Landslides and avalanches are common hazards, as are winds that howl up the lake. Yet, to this day, amateur and professional prospectors search for this elusive creek, and more than 130 years after his hanging, Slumach's curse lives on to guard his secret.

Is there evidence that Slumach had such a secret find? Or that Jackson existed and left such a map? Or, is there evidence against Slumach having gold, making the legend just that—a myth? Have those who searched and those who died been chasing fool's gold? There's a bit of all of those. Over 130 years after Slumach was hanged—and nearly 70 years after the "best campfire story ever,"—Slumach's tale remains a mystery shrouded in history, informed by ongoing research, extensive documentation, fierce debates, and enchanting gossip.

Of most significance is the truth: Slumach actually lived, was Indigenous, elderly, active, enjoyed a home near Pitt Lake, and had a name easy to pronounce and equally easy to misspell. He was indeed convicted of murder and hanged in New Westminster. The deceased murder victim, however, was not a young woman but a man named Louis Bee, who died of a gunshot wound from a bullet fired by Slumach at close range at Addington Point along the lower Pitt River on September 8, 1890.

The three of us going in search of a legend must be anchored in the "facts of the matter" as they were when 1890 rolled into 1891.

Gold nuggets, the stuff of dreams for gold seekers everywhere. Jackson's letter was the first to describe his nuggets as the size of walnuts. OP MEDIA GROUP

Overleaf A double rainbow over Pitt Meadows. Could there be a motherlode of gold somewhere under those arches? COURTESY OF JAMES WHEELER

Chapter 2

The Facts of the Matter

THE SLUMACH STORY FIRST took shape in the *Daily Columbian* newspaper in the fall and winter of 1890 and 1891, starting with the killing of Louis Bee. Reporters filed sensational accounts of the murder, the pursuit of Slumach, his eventual capture, indictment, trial, and execution.

Journalistic standards were different in those days. There seemed to be little concept of simply reporting the facts fairly and accurately. The presumption of innocence as a cornerstone of Canadian law was often absent when applied to Indigenous individuals accused of a crime. Emotion figured into reporting rather than dispassionate accounts. "Just the facts" was a concept yet to emerge in journalism.

To be clear, nowhere in the newspaper reports from the 1890s is there mention of gold related to Slumach, and something like that would have been big news in the day. Nor is there any evidence that Slumach had murdered anyone other than Louis Bee. There is no reference to either such situation in the judge's bench book. Nor is there any evidence that Slumach ever uttered a curse on the gallows.

With his hanging, the day's media interest in Slumach ended. Research has not uncovered further mentions of Slumach in newspapers of the time.

The earliest account of the murder of Louis Bee says, without proof of Slumach's mental capacity, that "an insane Indian named Slumach" committed it. The description of the shooting was not dispassionate in any way, but was described step by step, loosely and clearly implying Slumach's guilt from the get-go.

Reading those contemporary newspaper reports, it feels obvious Slumach was deemed guilty in public opinion well before being charged and appearing in front of a jury. True, a guilty verdict is the way things turned out in the end, but the prejudging of his guilt by the press of the day was most unfortunate and terribly unfair. Phrases such as "The Indians are all afraid of the murderer" may have polluted any jury pool. Second-hand and hearsay information stating Slumach "has committed four or five murders during the past twenty-five years" contradict other statements that say he was "a very wonderful person."

Our initial research in 1971 took us to the BC Archives in Victoria, where we secured the bench book of Justice Montague Tyrwhitt-Drake, who presided over Slumach's trial. A bench book contains the written notes made by a judge as they sit on the bench during a trial. Drake's handwriting is a challenge to read, but his notes fill in many blanks and offer observations and asides, while confirming certain reports.

In the trial, defence counsel T.C. Atkinson applied for a delay because two people identified as "necessary and material witnesses" were not on hand. They were brought to court the following day—"Moody, an Indian" and "Florence Reed"—but they were not called to testify, without any recorded reason.

Modern jurists might blanch at the extremely short sequestering of the jury—a mere fifteen minutes—before they pronounced their "guilty" verdict. The judge then sentenced Slumach to die on the gallows in the British Columbia Provincial Gaol (Jail) on January 16, 1891.

We delved into the archives of the *Daily Columbian*. Fortunately, through a reference by the newspaper, we were able to locate the following material, initially compiled by William W. Burton for the periodical *The Native Voice* in July 1959.

The newspaper accounts that follow in the next chapter are in the prose of the day and are the most reliable accounts we have regarding the facts of the matter. We supply some commentary on these accounts to help provide insights and an understanding of the legend's unfolding. The account begins with a killing but quickly moves to tracking down the accused before covering the trial and execution, all in quick fashion that would not be tolerated today.

Opposite Could Slumach's gold be found beneath the waters of a small creek like this? ADAM PALMER COLLECTION

Overleaf Golden Ears sunset. COURTESY OF JAMES WHEELER

Chapter 3

The Murder of Louis Bee

THE *DAILY COLUMBIAN* REPORTED regularly to an anxious public, which was expecting a prompt arrest despite the difficulties faced by authorities tracking Slumach in forested areas where he was familiar with the terrain and they were not. William Moresby is mentioned frequently in the accounts of the pursuit and arrest of Slumach, and again during his trial. Moresby had been appointed governor of the British Columbia Provincial Gaol in 1877 and eventually became warden of the British Columbia Penitentiary in 1895.

The *Daily Columbian* reporting continues below with accounts of Slumach's appearance in court and his subsequent trial, but it is apparent that Slumach's guilt, without actual confirmation, was predestined in the press of the day. We were frustrated as we read these accounts, and we imagine today's readers will share a sense that such a rush to judgement was prejudicial.

In one court document, titled "Statement of the accused," Slumach is asked, "Having heard the evidence, do you wish to say anything in answer to the charge?" Various statements that seem like a "reading of his rights" follow, and then Slumach responds, "I have nothing to say."

Another court document reads,

I the above Slumagh [sic] make oath and say:
   1. That one Moody and [sic] Indian and Florence Reed are necessary and material witnesses in my behalf in the trial on the above charge and I cannot safely proceed to trial without their attendance as witnesses to depose to the following facts:
   2. (a) That the [sic] Louis Bee the deceased was habitually quarrelling with me
      (b) and that he frequently harassed me with improper language and
      (c) threatened me more than once with violence and I was in constant fear of him.

In our reading of the bench book, the distressing court statements appear to be written by Slumach's lawyer, T.C. Atkinson, and, jibing with the excerpt from the *Daily Columbian* above, were an attempt to move the trial to the next assizes, the following year. This failed. Moresby claimed he could deliver the witnesses Moody and Reed, and he did: they were in court the next morning, but they were not called to the stand for some reason known only to Atkinson.

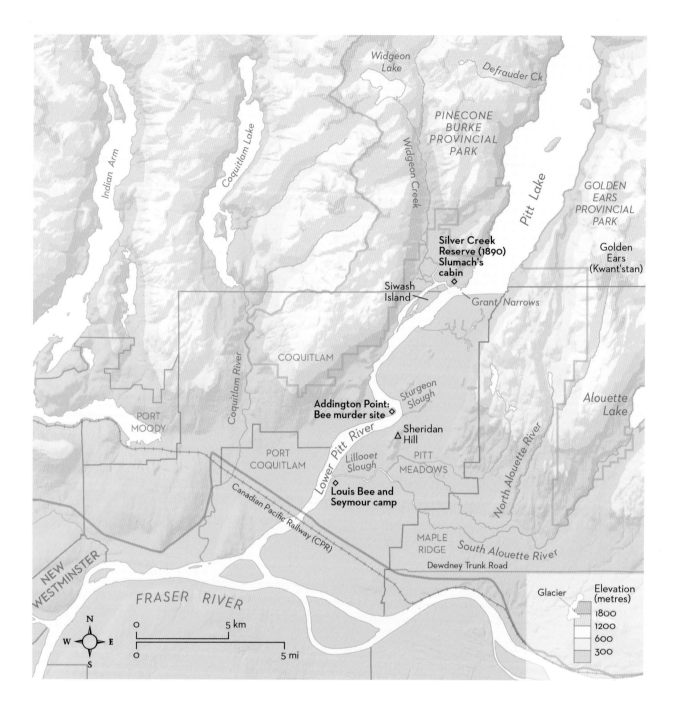

Map F: Where Slumach murdered Louis Bee——On the day of his death, in 1890, Louis Bee was camped with his friend (and murder witness) Seymour on the east side of the lower Pitt River, where today the Alouette River (then known as Lillooet Slough) enters the Pitt. Slumach shot Bee at Addington Point a few kilometres north of there, on the west side of Pitt River. Slumach escaped north toward Widgeon Creek, where he was later arrested. Seymour fled south, crossed the Canadian Pacific Railway (CPR) bridge and returned to their campsite. ERIC LEINBERGER

Top This front page of the *Daily Columbian* from March 1890 gives a flavour for the kind of media in which Slumach's story would've been reported in the fall of 1890 and winter of 1891. UBC ARCHIVES OPEN COLLECTIONS

Bottom New Westminster just after the Great Fire of September 10, 1898. Many records (including those of Captain Pittendrigh), were destroyed in this fire, some of which were probably related to Slumach's case. The central core of the "Royal City" was completely devastated. ROYAL BC MUSEUM AND ARCHIVES A-03363

This document fits with an account that Peter Pierre talked Slumach into surrendering and was with him in his final hours. Pierre's daughter, Amanda Charnley ("Aunt Mandy"), recounted that Slumach told Pierre that Bee raised his axe and thus was threatening Slumach, who, in fear of his life, shot him dead. But witness Charlie Seymour said in court that there was no threat to Slumach. Which is true? Did Seymour lie and thus thwart the success of a self-defence plea? Or was Slumach lying and trying to avoid the hangman?

A local publication called *The Truth* suggested on November 18, 1890 (after his sentencing), that Slumach ". . . grew up, as he has since remained, a man of savage instincts, with all the wild and passionate feeling of his race. He lives in this state—having reached a period of life when such a man is largely impervious to outside influences for good—until he has passed the three score years and ten of average longevity." The article suggests commuting Slumach's sentence because it really wasn't his fault that he murdered Bee; it was in his nature to do so.

DID SLUMACH MURDER LOUIS BEE? There is information that Louis Bee had been taunting Slumach before his murder by calling him a witch. This apparently was one of the worst slurs anyone could make to an Indigenous person. Might this have been what enraged Slumach to the point of murder?

One entry in the trial judge's bench book states that other Indigenous people feared Slumach, while a report in the press said they knew he had killed others before Bee. There are, however, no press accounts of Slumach's actions before he murdered Louis Bee.

September 9, 1890
SHOT DEAD

Louis Bee, a half-breed, is deliberately shot and killed by an insane Indian named Slumach, at Lillooet Slough.

A terrible unpremeditated murder was committed yesterday afternoon at a point on Lillooet Slough, not far from the Lower Pitt River, and two and a half miles above the Pitt River Bridge.

An Indian named Slumach, aged about sixty years, was hunting in this neighborhood, and coming out of the bush with his double-barreled shotgun in his hand, found several other Indians trout-fishing on the banks of the Slough.

A half-breed named Louis Bee sauntered up to Slumach and asked him in a casual way what he was shooting around there.

Without a moment's warning, or any preliminary sign of anger, Slumach instantly leveled his gun at Bee and fired.

Just before the discharge of the piece, Bee held up his hands and begged Slumach not to shoot. The distance between the two men was so short that the whole charge entered the victim's body, just under the right armpit, behind the shoulder blade.

Death was instantaneous, and Bee fell without a groan and lay weltering in his blood, while his murderer coolly proceeded to reload his piece.

One of the Indians who witnessed the awful deed immediately fled, not only to give the alarm, but from motives of personal safety. He describes the countenance of the murderer after the act was committed as resembling that of an incarnate demon.

Slumach is insane, and what he had done seemed to have kindled all the wild disorderly fancies of madness in the maniac's brain, and lit up his eyes with a ferocious gleam that boded no good to anyone whom he should encounter when his gun was reloaded.

Slumach slowly retreated to the impenetrable and pathless jungle surrounding that part of the Lillooet Slough and plunging into its gloomy recesses was lost to sight and is still at large.

September 10, 1890
THE MURDER OF LOUIS BEE

Captain George Pittendrigh, Justice of the Peace, led the team that recovered Louis Bee's body and brought it back to New Westminster. He figured in Bee's inquest and subsequently in the capture and trial of Slumach. ROYAL BC MUSEUM AND ARCHIVES A-07660

Through the courtesy of Mr. L.F. Bonson, who placed his fine steam launch at the coroner's disposal, Capt. Pittendrigh and his attendants were enabled to perform the journey yesterday from the city to the scene of the Indian murder at Pitt River, in an expeditious and comfortable manner. Long before the fatal spot was reached, the Indians could be heard chanting a loud strange death song, or coronach, for the untimely demise of their comrade Louis Bee. The party from the city, on arriving at the place where the murder occurred, found a number of Indians congregated together, and apparently suffering from fear to a considerable extent. Enquiry developed the fact that none of them dared to pursue the murderer through the bush, and their terror increased by the appearance of Slumach the day following the murder and his appropriation of the murdered man's remains. He placed the body in a canoe and set out in the direction of the lake with it.

It was suspected that Slumach's intention was to drop the body overboard in the deep water, and Capt. Pittendrigh, acting on the supposition, set the Indians to work dragging the river for the corpse. The latest news received states that the body was recovered, and was in the custody of friends in the neighborhood of the spot where the tragic occurrence happened.

The Indian eyewitness who came to the city with the first information of the crime, was taken to the city lock-up this morning for safekeeping by order of Mr. W. Moresby.

Capt. Pittendrigh and jury returned from the Pitt River last night. This morning a new jury was summoned to proceed to view the remains of Bee.

September 11, 1890
CORONER'S INQUEST

A coroner's inquest was held yesterday in the committee rooms at the City Hall upon the body of Louis Bee, the half-breed who was murdered last Monday afternoon at Pitt River by an Indian named Slumach, and whose remains were brought to the city yesterday.

Dr. Walker performed the post-mortem examination, and found the bone of the upper left arm to have been shattered by the passage of a ball, which had entered the side of the deceased, fracturing the fifth rib, penetrated the right side of the heart, and torn the lungs. The bullet was found embedded in the right lung. Death, in the doctor's opinion, must have been instantaneous.

Charlie Seymour, an Indian, was the principal witness examined by the jury.

The jury returned the verdict of willful murder against the Indian Slumach.

The body of the murdered man was coffined, and taken home by the Indians for interment at their own cemetery near the entrance to Pitt Lake. Mr. Moresby and two special officers left this morning by steamer for the scene of the murder.

They were to be met by the Chief of the Indians with a selected posse of men, and the search for Slumach will be prosecuted unceasingly until he is captured.

September 12, 1890
STILL AT LARGE

Slumach, the murderer of Louis Bee is still at large, and there is no immediate prospect of his capture, unless he is driven by starvation into the haunts of men. Mr. Moresby went up to Pitt Lake yesterday and continued the search for him, but with no success. Just before Mr. Moresby arrived, the Indians saw Slumach at his cabin, but he quickly plunged into the bush again and was not visible during the remainder of the day. On examining the cabin, Mr. Moresby found a can of (gun] powder and a large quantity of provisions, which he destroyed, and then to prevent Slumach returning there for shelter, the shack was burned to the ground.

His canoe was also destroyed.

Slumach will now have to keep to the woods until cold weather and starvation drives him in. Mr. Moresby left for Pitt Lake again this morning and may not return to the city for several days. He is determined to bring him to justice, and will, if he can, obtain the assistance required.

The Indians are all afraid of the murderer, and decline to assist in beating the bush for him, as he is well armed and has lots of ammunition. Slumach is a desperate character and is credited by the Indians with another murder, committed years ago and under similar circumstances. Although a few of the murderer's friends say he is insane, dozens of the Indians who know him, say otherwise, and declared he is only a bloodthirsty old villain.

September 16, 1890
SLUMACH THE MURDERER STILL AT LARGE

Indians who know him well, say he has committed four or five murders during the last 25 years.

His last murder, previous to the killing of Louis Bee, was committed about six years ago when he is said to have killed an Indian without any apparent cause. He fled to the mountains and remained in seclusion for a whole year, and then suddenly returned one day and took possession of his cabin and lived quietly until the perpetration of his last crime.

The Indians look upon Slumach as a very wonderful person, being able to endure the greatest hardships without apparent inconvenience. As a hunter he is without an equal, and he is adept at making fires in the primitive manner, using two sticks and rubbing the same together until the friction ignites the wood. He is said to be without fear of man or beast and to be possessed of a nature vicious in the extreme.

September 19, 1890

Mr. W. Moresby went up to Pitt Lake on the steamer *Constance* on Wednesday, returning to the city last night. Constable Anderson reported having seen Slumach the preceding day, standing on a rocky bluff afar off with nothing on but a red shirt and a handkerchief tied around his head.

He was armed with his deadly rifle, and was too far away to permit of an exchange of bullets. On the nearer approach of his pursuers he quietly retreated into the impregnable fastnesses among the stupendous precipices that frown over the lake at that neighbourhood. He has not since been seen.

September 19, 1890
SLUMACH'S ACTION

The Indians say that Slumach has always acted strangely, and at irregular intervals would withdraw himself alone into the forests that border for weeks, reappearing at the end of those periods of aberration looking haggard, and more like a savage beast than a human being. In spite of his lunacy however, the maniac never displayed any signs of hostility, nor gave indications that his freedom was dangerous to human life.

He is described as a very powerful man and is rather dreaded by his own Indian friends.

It is of the utmost importance that fishing and hunting parties going into this region, should keep a most vigilant lookout, as the murderer is still roaming the woods armed with a shotgun, and as far as can be learned, with plenty of ammunition.

The Indian who informed Mr. McTiernan, Indian Agent, of the occurrence, says that from Slumach's looks, he had not the slightest doubt that he would murder the first man he met.

Parties contemplating a visit to the spot indicated above should therefore be on their guard, as carelessness in this matter may result in a still more lamentable tragedy than that just described.

Louis Bee was a splendid specimen of the half-breed, he was tall, well-formed, and very muscular, besides having a rather handsome face. It is related of him that once, when in the city, and under the influence of liquor, six stalwarts could not hold him down, and it was only by their dogged perseverance that they at length got him to the police office.

Bee figured several times in police court, owing to his fondness for alcoholic stimulants, but otherwise he was a quiet respectable man.

Several parties of men are now scouring the woods in the neighbourhood of the scene of the murder, in the endeavor to run the desperate perpetrator of the crime to earth.

The Indians in that part of the district are intensely excited over the horrible affair, and are doing everything in their power to capture Slumach.

October 25, 1890
STARVED OUT

The Indian Slumach, who attained to ghastly celebrity some weeks ago by wantonly murdering a young half-breed named Louis Bee, has been suffering terrible privations in the mountain fastnesses around the shores of Pitt Lake, whither he retired after the murder and set the power of the law at defiance. A month ago, Mr. P. McTiernan, Indian Agent here, had a conference with the members of the tribe at Pitt Lake, and succeeded in convincing them of their duty to

deliver Slumach over to the law. From that day, no assistance was given to the outlaw, and probably on that account was he forced to give himself up yesterday to the police. Yesterday he sent his nephew for the Indian Agent, who went up to Pitt Lake accompanied by two Indian policemen, and to them the desperate fugitive quietly surrendered.

He had eaten nothing for several days, and was in a terrible state of emaciation and thoroughly exhausted.

His ammunition was all gone and his clothing in rags, and he presented a very wild and weatherworn aspect.

Slumach was at once brought to the city and placed under the care of the physicians of the Provincial jail.

At latest account today, Slumach was in a very precarious condition, his vitality being spent. The doctors do not care to express an opinion as to his chances of recovery, but it is understood that they are very small. Should he recover he will be given a preliminary trial, and then remanded for trial at the assizes in November.

November 3, 1890
DISTRICT COURT
(Before Capt. Pittendrigh, JP)

The murderer, Slumach, was up in the district court before Capt. Pittendrigh, JP, for a preliminary hearing. Several witnesses were examined, and a mass of evidence taken down, and the magistrate sent Slumach up for trial at the approaching assizes.

The prisoner has greatly improved in health since his surrender and will be strong enough to undergo the tedium of the assize trial this month. Slumach is rather an intelligent looking man of about sixty years of age. His face expressed a great deal of determination, even ferocity. He sat in court listening to the evidence this morning with the utmost apathy.

A number of Indians occupied seats and took a great deal of interest in the proceedings.

November 11, 1890
THE CASE OF SLUMACH

Slumach, the murderer of Louis Bee, now confined in the Provincial goal [sic] awaiting trial at the Assizes which opens tomorrow, is in a very bad state of health, and may not be in a fit condition to appear for trial at this term. He is very weak and does not seem to gather strength so rapidly as might be expected, considering the attention and comforts he receives from the medical superintendent and gaol officials.

Mr. McTiernan, Indian Agent, is of the opinion that Slumach will not live long in confinement, and it is a well-known fact that an Indian sentenced to a long term of imprisonment soon pines away and dies. It now looks as if Slumach will not be able to stand trial at the coming assizes, and should this turn out to be the case it is pretty certain that he will escape the gallows by death from natural causes before the spring term.

November 14, 1890
FALL ASSIZES

Court resumed sittings at 10:30 o'clock.

The crown prosecutor asked the arraignment of Slumach for murder. Mr. T.C. Atkinson, defending counsel asked that this case be adjourned until next assizes, on the ground that there were two important witnesses for the defence, Moody, an Indian and Florence Reed, who could not possibly be obtained in time for this assize, but could be produced at the next sitting of the court. The affidavits of Slumach and his daughter Mary, were produced and read . . .

Mr. Moresby said he could produce the witnesses required by the defence by 11 o'clock tomorrow, and his Lordship therefore adjourned the court until that time.

November 15, 1890
FALL ASSIZES
(Mr. Justice Drake presiding)

The Slumach murder case occupied the attention of the court today. The evidence had to be nearly all interpreted.

There were several Indian witnesses examined at length, and they gave minute particulars of the tragedy.

It came out in the evidence that Bee, the victim of the murder, was in the habit of blustering at, and threatening almost everyone with whom he came in contact. Against Slumach he indulged something like a grudge, and for a long time there was bad blood between them. The Indians who were with Bee at the time of the murder were fishing, and on Slumach emerging from the adjacent woods, a slight altercation ensued between him and Bee, with the result that Slumach shot him dead.

Justice Montague William Tyrwhitt-Drake presided over Slumach's trial in November 1890. Born in England, Drake had served on the Legislative Council of British Columbia, and was mayor of Victoria for two years. He received the designation of Queen's Counsel, and served on the Supreme Court of British Columbia from 1889 through 1904. ROYAL BC MUSEUM AND ARCHIVES A-01248

The jury retired at 3:45, and after being out 15 minutes, returned with a verdict of guilty.

His Lordship sentenced Slumach to be hanged on Jan. 16 next.

January 16, 1891
PAID THE PENALTY

Slumach, the murderer of Louis Bee, pays the penalty of his crime. Old Slumach was hanged in the yard of the provincial gaol this morning at 8 o'clock, for the murder on Sept. 8th last, of Louis Bee, a half-breed.

The particulars of the hanging are briefly as follows . . . Pierre, (the Indian catechist-medicine man) slept in the same cell with Slumach, and prayed with him day and night and it is satisfactory to know that the labor of the good priest and his assistant was not in vain . . .

The condemned man retired to rest at an early hour last night and slept well . . . Slumach awakened early and immediately went into devotional exercises with his spiritual attendants, after which breakfast was brought in and he ate a good meal with apparent relish.

A few minutes before 7 o'clock, Father Morgan baptized Slumach, who professed his belief in Christianity and the hope of salvation. Prayers were continued until the arrival of the hangman to pinion him, and to this operation he submitted without a murmur. All being in readiness a few minutes before 8 o'clock, the procession was formed and proceeded to the scaffold. Mr. Sheriff Armstrong led the way followed by Mr. Wm. Moresby, governor of the jail and the deputy sheriff, next came Slumach, supported by gaolers Burr and Connor, and followed by the hangman, masked and hooded.

Father Morgan, Pierre, Dr. J.M. McLean, Dr. Walker and a number of constables brought up the rear of the procession.

Slumach walked firmly up the steps leading to the platform, and faced the crowd below. The hangman quickly adjusted the noose, and Father Morgan commenced a prayer. Then the black cap put on, and at 8 o'clock exactly, the bolt was drawn, the trap fell, and Slumach had paid the penalty of his crime.

The hanging was very ably managed and beyond a few little twitchings of the hands and feet, the body remained perfectly still after the drop. In three minutes and fifty-eight seconds life was pronounced extinct, but it was more than twenty minutes before the body was cut down and placed in the coffin.

Coroner Pittendrigh and a jury viewed the body and brought in the usual verdict. Slumach's neck was broken in the fall, and death must have been painless. The drop was eight feet, five inches.

Over fifty persons witnessed the hanging, and a large crowd gathered outside the jail, and remained there until the black flag was hoisted. Among the crowd on the street were several Indian women, relatives of Slumach, who waited around the jail more than an hour after the execution.

SLUMACH'S SENTENCE WAS CARRIED out at the British Columbia Provincial Gaol, which was located at the corner of present-day Eighth Street and Royal Avenue in New Westminster. Today, this is the site of Simcoe Park and the headquarters of the New Westminster School District.

According to Don Waite's 1972 interview with Aunt Mandy, Slumach's daughter Mary asked for his remains so she could see that they were properly interred as his relatives wished. Her request was ignored. The prison buried Slumach, and the location was undisclosed at the time. Rumours persisted for decades as to where that might be, and historians continued to search for any hints or indications of the burial site of his remains, as would we.

The 1890s public accounting of the Slumach story ends here. The *Daily Columbian* closed their coverage, and public interest waned until years later, when rumours began that Slumach had had gold. And the legend was born.

W. T. COOKSLEY, NEW WESTMINSTER, B.

The British Columbia Provincial Gaol, the site of Slumach's hanging. For a time, it was rumoured he was buried on these grounds, but he was not. ROYAL BC MUSEUM AND ARCHIVES A-03353

Overleaf Pitt Meadows golden mornings. COURTESY OF JAMES WHEELER

Chapter 4

The Legend Is Born

SLUMACH'S WORLD IN 1890 comprised his tribal home, his family, his hunting grounds, and nearby waters that were navigable by canoe. Eventually he lived on the Silver Creek Reserve—a place and name created by Canada's government on the west side of the lower Pitt River and a designation that no longer exists.

In the years surrounding Slumach's birth early in the 1800s in Coast Salish territory—specifically, the Stó:lō Nation—Europeans and Americans were beginning to frequent and settle in the area. In 1808, explorer Simon Fraser came down the river that would later bear his name. Decades later, colonial leadership that failed to consider the ancestral rights and needs of Indigenous Peoples and were instead focused on the needs of settlers established the birthplace of the colony at Derby, on the south side of the Fraser River and on the traditional lands of the Coast Salish Peoples. In 1858, the capital was moved to nearby Fort Langley. In 1859, it was moved again to a provisional colonial capital at Queensborough (soon to be renamed New Westminster) on the north side of the Fraser, not far west from where Pitt River enters the Fraser.

If Slumach ever got to New Westminster before his arrest and trial (and we are uncertain about that), he would have found a stable and transient population of a few thousand people living along a tidy grid of streets laid out by the Royal Engineers on the traditional lands of the Kwantlen People.

During the time of Slumach's arrest and trial and in the years preceding and following his 1891 hanging, news from the wider world made its way to New Westminster and provides context for the times. Some of it was of immediate interest as new American states joined the Union, including its forty-second, Washington, the border of which was thirty-two kilometres (twenty miles) due south of Slumach's home. In 1905, forty kilometres (twenty-five miles) west, the Capilano Suspension Bridge would open as the longest suspension bridge in the world.

International events of those years were doubtless less influential in the new province of British Columbia, which joined Confederation in 1871, but they contributed to the excitement and culture on the world stage: Tchaikovsky's *Sleeping Beauty* premiered in Russia, Sherlock Holmes appeared for the first time in London's *Strand Magazine*, and basketball was invented by James Naismith, a Canadian.

In contrast with those accomplishments, and much more relevant to Slumach's situation, injustice against Indigenous Peoples was prevalent elsewhere as well as locally: in South Dakota, Hunkpapa Lakota leader Sitting Bull died while being arrested at Standing Rock Indian Reservation; the Wounded Knee massacre occurred; and the Residential School System was flourishing in BC, forcibly removing many Indigenous children from their families and culture.

Perhaps the exploitation of the Slumach legend over the next century and beyond was a reflection of some people's desire for local news to be told on a grander scale, leading to the international attention it has garnered over the years. Or might it be that gold in the region was known to exist but its location remained elusive?

IN THE WORLD OF research, provenance is important as it speaks to the origin of something, to the ability to trace an artifact, a photograph, a letter, a report, or any item of historical interest back to its creation, to confirm it is real.

Much of the Slumach legend lacks any provenance whatsoever.

For example, no actual record exists of the legendary Jackson's life, and if there was deposit information from his reputed San Francisco bank, it inconveniently disappeared in that city's 1906 earthquake. Jackson and his famous letter could simply have been invented by someone for their own benefit.

The lack of provenance takes little away from the Slumach legend, for that is precisely why a legend is a legend. Keeping the discussion alive promotes research, with the prospect of provenance appearing just around the corner.

WHAT WAS SLUMACH'S PROPER name?

The Indigenous man at the centre of this drama has been referred to as "John" or "Joe" Slumach. Aunt Mandy called him "Charlie." Throughout the court records of his trial and the documents of his execution, he is referred to as "the Indian" named Slumah, or Slumagh, or Slumaugh, or Slumogh, and Slough Mough. We also find Slum:ook, and a venerable Slamuk. William Slumach appears later, but there is no evidence that Slumach had a first name until the day he died. On the morning of his hanging, he was baptized as Petrum (Peter) Slumach. The information about him is as varied and contradictory as the legend that has grown around his life. While there are several popular spellings of his name, newspaper accounts of the day consistently used Slumach.

WHO WAS SLUMACH?

Slumach was a member of the Katzie (q̓ic̓əy) First Nation, which is part of the Stó:lō Coast Salish Peoples. Their vast territory includes Pitt Lake (known in Halkomelem as sq̓ə́yc̓əya?ł x̌aca?, "the lake of the Katzie") and the area of present-day Pitt Meadows in the Fraser Valley, near which Slumach's home was located.

Rumours surfaced that Slumach's son may have led parties into the Pitt area in a search for his supposed gold in the years after his death, but there is no proof. Nor was there any public mention of him having a son. Only a daughter is mentioned, though two names are recorded for her, Annie and Mary. There is no record of Slumach being married in any kind of ceremony.

Although he was Katzie, Slumach was not typical of his people. The Katzie reportedly preferred water travel, while Slumach is said to have been an avid hunter who mostly walked in the mountainous area at the south end of Pitt Lake. Newspaper accounts written at the time of Louis Bee's murder suggested that since winter was coming on, Slumach would run out of food, and would be forced from his hideout in the mountains. There is no formal record of Slumach's age, but speculation is that at the time of his death he was older than sixty, likely nearing eighty.

WAS THERE NEWS OF gold in the Pitt Lake vicinity before Slumach's time?

There is a legend told to us by one interviewee in the early 1970s, though we have never found an authoritative source for it:

A young Indigenous boy, in search of food, paddled his canoe into Pitt Lake and beached it on an island. When the water was low, he saw the entrance to a cavern revealed at the water's edge—he was curious and so paddled into the cavern.

As his eyes grew accustomed to the darkness of the cavern, he saw a huge serpent perched on a ledge, old and feeble, and unable to move. Before the frightened youth could find his way out, the serpent spoke to him, and told him to have no fear.

The serpent told the youth he had been expecting him. He was the guardian of this cave, and because he was old and dying, the youth must take his place. The boy asked what the cavern held that it must be guarded so. The serpent told him that deeper within the cavern there were many shiny pebbles—pebbles that must be kept from men with white skins. The serpent said that if ever such men should find the pebbles, it would bring an end to the happy life of his kindred people.

As the water began to rise in the cave, the old serpent placed his head on the youngster's shoulder. Suddenly the boy was transformed into a serpent, and before him stood an old man—transformed from the body of the serpent. The old man told the youth that he had first entered the cave as a young man, and had guarded its secret ever since. He admonished the young serpent to ensure that no man with white skin should ever enter the cave, and disappeared.

Interestingly, Pitt Lake is a tidal lake, with about a 1.5-metre (5-foot) rise and fall, a daily occurrence that gives this tale some credibility with respect to the water level changing. A marine biologist informed us that a wedge of salt water from the part of the Salish Sea known as Georgia Strait slips under the Fraser estuary and up Pitt River to the lake as this happens. If Slumach knew of this legend, it may have prompted him to search for the supposed treasure, giving birth to stories of his secret gold mine.

Could an old cave entrance like this on the shore of Pitt Lake be behind the serpent story? The entrance to an old mine shaft at lake level frames gold seekers and a view of the high country where gold may lie. Legends often have beginnings in real events. Could it be that an early Indigenous person had an experience that led to this one? OP MEDIA GROUP

BEFORE SLUMACH'S NOTORIETY, AND separate from him, there was only one reported story of gold found in the vicinity he is said to have frequented. Under the headline "Discovery of Diggings at Pitt River" on November 10, 1869, in New Westminster's *Mainland Guardian*, was this tease: "An Indian brought in a good prospect of gold a few days ago which he states he found in a little stream on the north side of Pitt Lake. He has volunteered to lead a party to the place and arrangements are being made for their immediate departure. The event has created considerable excitement in this city." No further reports on this have surfaced.

WITH HIS HANGING, THE day's press interest in Slumach ended. Research has not uncovered any more mentions of Slumach in newspapers of the time.

Yet, a scant six years later, there is a newspaper advertisement seeking investors in the "Slumach Mining Company" to find his lost gold. How and why did the revival of interest in Slumach occur? We can assume people were aware of and interested in stories of Slumach's legendary gold in 1897, perhaps earlier. But then this is significant: signatures on the share offering had connections to the Slumach case. Bartley Willet Shiles was the mayor of New Westminster; Frederick Robertson Glover was the city clerk, and had been the editor of the *Daily Columbian* when Slumach was arrested and tried for Bee's murder; Glover's brother-in-law, T.C. Atkinson, was Slumach's defence lawyer; and John Morrison was rumoured to be a farmer in Coquitlam. And if this confluence of interesting names is significant, why did this occur six years after Slumach's execution? Why not earlier? Does this bring us closer to the origin of the Slumach legend?

SLUMACH MINING CO., Ld., filed Feb. 24, 1897; capital stock, $500,000 in $1 shares; office, New Westminster.

This share offering for the Slumach Mining Company appeared in the July 15, 1897, edition of Victoria's *British Colonist* newspaper.
FRED BRACHES COLLECTION

A CENTURY LATER, AUTHOR and ardent gold seeker Daryl Friesen came across research dated Wednesday, February 3, 1897, affirming two gold mine claims by someone named Dawson and another person, J. Cromarty, staked on Stave Lake, close to Slumach country. The claims were named Golden Dawn and Yellow Jacket.

IF SLUMACH DID NOT have gold, where did the legend originate?

Aunt Mandy told Don Waite that Slumach informed her father, Peter Pierre, that Port Douglas people once gave Slumach some gold bullets as thanks for some help he had provided, and that was the only gold he ever had. However, on a separate occasion she said Slumach once slept on a rock near Third Canyon (or was it Second Canyon?—she seemed unsure in her two accounts) by the upper Pitt River and woke to see a small amount of gold in a vein in a rock face. He chiselled it out with his knife, and told Pierre that this was all the precious metal he ever had. She recounted that, two years after the hanging, Pierre led a group in search of this gold vein, but slipped and broke his hip, and he mused that perhaps Slumach had put a curse on the area to keep him— or anyone else—from finding the gold. Aunt Mandy's story leaves us wondering if Pierre just might be the source of both the gold story and the curse story, making Pierre the genesis of the legend.

IF SLUMACH HAD GOLD, where would it have come from?

The 1858 Cariboo gold rush brought thousands of prospectors to the interior of what was then the Colony of British Columbia. Taking gold to tidewater down the Fraser Canyon via the small centres of Fort Langley, New Westminster, and Victoria was a challenge. One route commonly used was known as "the Douglas Road," which involved canoeing down Harrison Lake from its northern end at Port Douglas to Harrison Mills, near where the Harrison River joined the Fraser River. (Harrison Lake and the Harrison River are both east of and somewhat parallel with Pitt Lake and Pitt River).

In 1863 the far more convenient Cariboo Wagon Road through the Fraser Canyon was completed, and the Harrison route was abandoned. One theory about Slumach's supposed riches involves the robbery in the late 1880s of a gold-laden wagon train just north of Hope, where the Fraser River turns and begins its westerly journey to the coast. Reportedly, five men staged the holdup; one was an Indigenous man. This would not be significant were it not that three of the white robbers were subsequently murdered, while the fourth white man and the Indigenous man disappeared. It was reported that the latter escaped with a sizable portion of the loot, which he buried in a secret location near New Westminster. In one version of the legend, this man was Slumach, and he made repeated trips to this cache for more gold, taking portions to New Westminster on his escapades.

WHERE ELSE COULD SLUMACH have acquired gold?

It has been suggested that Slumach headed east along the Fraser, then north up the Harrison River and Harrison Lake, winding up on the aforementioned route that many Cariboo gold-rush miners had followed to New Westminster in the 1860s—down Harrison Lake. Nuggets such as those mentioned in the legend were often taken from Cariboo deposits.

According to one rendition of the legend, Slumach would use women to waylay miners travelling along this route, enticing them with offers of physical pleasure. When the miners' attentions were diverted from their gold, Slumach would murder them, and, together with his female partner, make off with it.

Miners did disappear during the Cariboo gold rush—some simply vanished and others were murdered—although there was remarkably little violent crime.

THERE ARE NUMEROUS OTHER stories, one involving another Indigenous man known as "Hunter Jack," a Chief of the Lx'lx'mx or Lexalexamux (Lakes) Lillooet Band. On early maps of the Bridge River mining camp, there is a spot marked "Hunter Jack's Landing," close to the old Lorne Mine, which later became the Bralorne Mine. Hunter Jack lived near Shalalth and frequently made trips to New Westminster laden with gold from his diggings. Old-timers in Lillooet claim that Hunter Jack got his gold from Tyaughton Creek in the Bridge River country, an area first explored in 1858 during the Fraser River gold rush. Hard-rock claims were staked in the 1890s and eventually two mines were started, Pioneer Gold and Bralorne. Pioneer closed in the late 1950s after yielding more than

1.3 million ounces of gold, and Bralorne closed in 1971 after yielding nearly 3 million ounces. At the then-rate of $32 an ounce, this gold was worth over $120 million; today's price equivalent would be billions of dollars.

Hunter Jack was somewhat possessive about his area, and anyone who intruded could expect a confrontation. Once, a group of Chinese miners who invaded his preserve was chased out at gunpoint. To demonstrate his authority, Hunter Jack followed the miners to a river. There he charged a fee to transport them across to safety in his boat.

It is said that Hunter Jack occasionally held Potlatches at which he gave handfuls of nuggets to his guests. If Slumach was an acquaintance of Hunter Jack's and a guest at his Potlatches, he could have received quantities of nuggets. It has been speculated that Slumach cached the gold he received from Hunter Jack in a secret location near Pitt Lake, from which he drew his supply, claiming it was a secret "mine."

Even comparing facts with fiction, uncertainty remains. Could seemingly innocent accounts from speculators have led to the newspaper advertisement in 1897 publicly linking the name "Slumach" with the word "mine" for the first time?

THE LIST OF PEOPLE who allegedly died while searching for the lost mine is not well documented, and names periodically appear in articles with no sources provided for us to trace and validate. Are they irresponsible creations of spurious attribution, or could they pass the test of legitimacy? In that light, we read a report on the website beringseapaydirt.com telling of a William Snyder setting up his 1897 camp at Pitt Lake, calling it Snyder's Landing. From there he looked for gold, later saying his disappeared partner died at the hands of an unidentified assailant, an implied victim of "the curse," yet talk of such a curse did not begin until decades later.

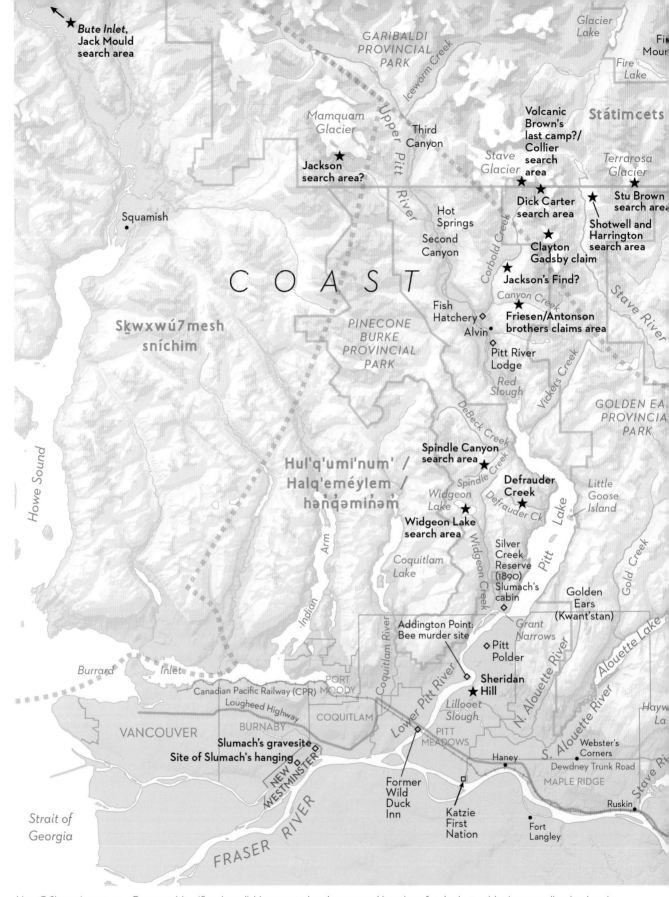

Bute Inlet, Jack Mould search area

GLACIER Lake

GARIBALDI PROVINCIAL PARK

Iceworm Creek

Fire Mou

Fire Lake

Mamquam Glacier

Upper Pitt River

Third Canyon

Volcanic Brown's last camp?/ Collier search area

Státimcets

Stave Glacier

Terrarosa Glacier

★ Jackson search area?

★ ★ Dick Carter search area

★ Stu Brown search area

Shotwell and Harrington search area

Squamish

Hot Springs

Second Canyon

Corbold Creek

★ Clayton Gadsby claim

Stave River

COAST

★ Jackson's Find?

Canyon Creek

Skwxwú7mesh sníchim

Fish Hatchery ◇

Alvin ●

★ Friesen/Antonson brothers claims area

Vickers Creek

GOLDEN EA PROVINCIA PARK

◇ Pitt River Lodge

Red Slough

PINECONE BURKE PROVINCIAL PARK

DeBeck Creek

Spindle Creek

★ Spindle Canyon search area

Defrauder Creek ★

Pitt Lake

Little Goose Island

Hul'q'umi'num' / Halq'eméylem / hən̓q̓əmin̓əm̓

Spindle Creek

Widgeon Lake

Defrauder Ck

★ Widgeon Lake search area

Silver Creek Reserve (1890) Slumach's cabin ◇

Coquitlam Lake

Widgeon Creek

Gold Creek

Golden Ears (Kwant'stan)

Grant Narrows

N. Alouette River

Alouette Lake

Indian Arm

Coquitlam River

◇ Addington Point: Bee murder site

◇ Pitt Polder

★ Sheridan Hill

Burrard Inlet

Canadian Pacific Railway (CPR)

PORT MOODY

Lougheed Highway

Lower Pitt River

Lillooet Slough

Haywa La

VANCOUVER

BURNABY

COQUITLAM

PITT MEADOWS

S. Alouette River

Stave Ri

Slumach's gravesite
Site of Slumach's hanging

NEW WESTMINSTER

Former Wild Duck Inn

Katzie First Nation

Haney

Webster's Corners

Dewdney Trunk Road

MAPLE RIDGE

Ruskin

Strait of Georgia

● Fort Langley

FRASER RIVER

Map G: Slumach country——Our map identifies the reliably reported and rumoured locations for the lost gold mine as well as landmarks that help gold seekers orient their quest. It has evolved from our 1972 and 2007 editions of this book, and now has all the necessary updates included. ERIC LEINBERGER

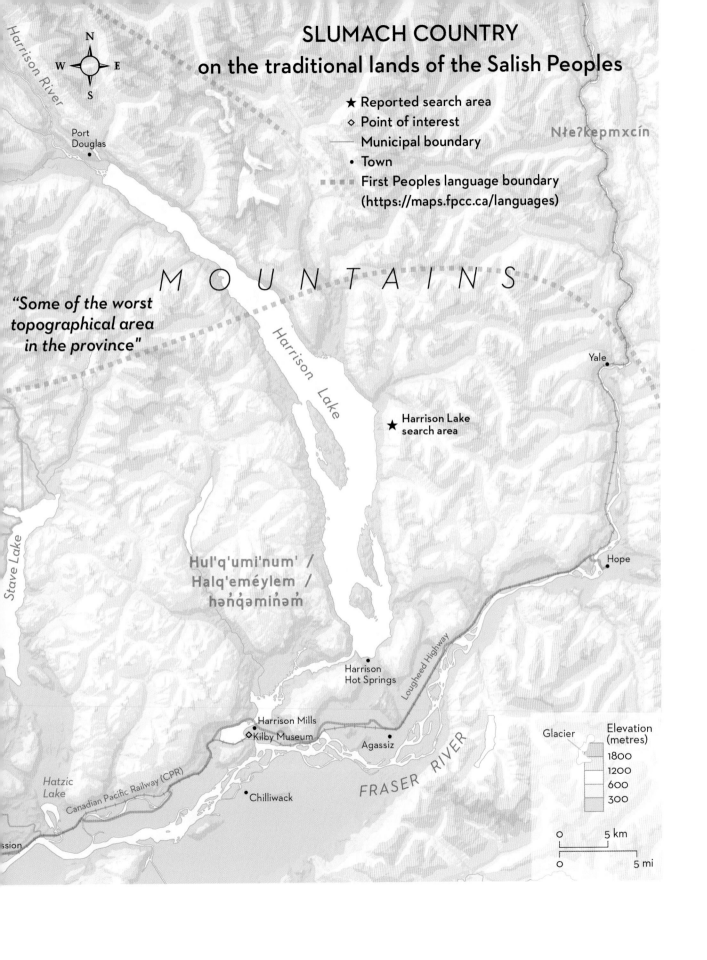

SLUMACH COUNTRY
on the traditional lands of the Salish Peoples

★ Reported search area
◇ Point of interest
— Municipal boundary
• Town
▪▪▪▪ First Peoples language boundary
(https://maps.fpcc.ca/languages)

N W E S

Harrison River

Port Douglas

Nɬeʔkepmxcín

M O U N T A I N S

"Some of the worst topographical area in the province"

Harrison Lake

Yale

★ Harrison Lake search area

Stave Lake

Hul'q'umi'num' / Halq'eméylem / hǝńq̓ǝmińǝm̓

Hope

Lougheed Highway

Harrison Hot Springs

Harrison Mills
◇ Kilby Museum

Agassiz

FRASER RIVER

Hatzic Lake

Canadian Pacific Railway (CPR)

• Chilliwack

Glacier

Elevation (metres)
1800
1200
600
300

ssion

0 ——— 5 km
0 ——— 5 mi

THERE'S THE OLD MAXIM, "Gold is where you find it." Sufficient circumstantial evidence shows there may well be a trove of gold in British Columbia's unforgiving Coast Mountain region known as Slumach country.

Author Rob Nicholson provides a primer on basic geology in his web-based *BC Prospector* magazine and what leads prospectors to expect a "find." He says,

> Gold is found in a wide variety of environments. Gold located in rock formations is commonly referred to as "vein gold." Vein gold is most commonly found in quartz veins, sulfide veins, and iron-stained rock that has been freed of sulfide. Displaced gold, commonly referred to as "placer gold," occurs when gold moves from its original host environment. Placer gold is most commonly found in creek and riverbeds. The prospector's rule of thumb for looking for the vein of placer gold is "the rougher the placer gold, the closer the vein."

WHATEVER HAPPENED, IT IS clear that hearsay and idle talk bred speculation surrounding Slumach's name and gold throughout the 1890s. The enduring legend may have been born in those years.

The legend was nurtured when prospector W. Jackson is said to have arrived in New Westminster a decade after Slumach was hanged. It took on a high profile of its own, veracity be damned.

Of course, there was competing big news from outside of BC that year: Queen Victoria died, US President William McKinley was assassinated, and volunteers were enlisting to join the Canadian army to fight in the Boer War. But the ramifications from Jackson's reputed prospecting at Pitt Lake and finding gold nuggets the size of walnuts give us the next signature date in the growing interest in Slumach's lost mine, a story that would one day itself become international news.

The year was 1901.

Opposite ADAM PALMER COLLECTION

Overleaf ADAM PALMER COLLECTION

Chapter 5

Some Say This, Some Say That

A NOVEMBER 1901 *PROVINCE* clipping introduces prospector Clifford Wellington. It tells of Wellington's harrowing experience searching for lost gold in the Pitt Lake region. The clipping is poorly reproduced and difficult to read. The date makes some suspect his quest was possibly motivated by the Slumach Mining Company share offering a few years earlier. Or, it may be related to—and conflated with—the story of W. Jackson.

The Legendary W. Jackson

Beginning in 1904, an important thread to the Slumach story emerges: the story of an alleged gold seeker named W. Jackson and an item that provides the most tantalizing bit of early chatter, the "Jackson letter."

Following the real or imagined events of the 1890s, enough of a story was circulating early in the new century to interest the legendary miner W. Jackson. According to the legend, Jackson arrived in New Westminster around 1901 and heard the Slumach stories. He declared he would find the mine or die trying.

Jackson headed into the Pitt Lake area to search for the treasure. Later, in the fall, he returned to New Westminster a sick and broken man. He spoke little, and stayed only a few days before leaving for San Francisco.

Some people noted that while he was in town, Jackson kept his packsack with him at all times. After his return to San Francisco, word came back to New Westminster that he had deposited close to $10,000 in raw gold in the San Francisco branch of the Bank of British North America (which later became today's Bank of Montreal, or BMO). For perspective, in 2024, this sum would be worth in excess of $365,000 USD, a tidy deposit indeed. Unfortunately, the great San Francisco earthquake and fire of April 18, 1906, destroyed any records that could have proved this claim.

According to the legend, Jackson never recovered from his journey into the Pitt Lake area. After three years of sickness and declining health supposedly related to that expedition, he died. But he claimed to have found gold. In a letter to a friend named Shotwell, dated 1904, he described his find. Shotwell, a Seattle resident, had grubstaked Jackson on some of his earlier prospecting trips, and had helped fund the search for Slumach's mine. Jackson's letter described the location and how Shotwell could find the mine.

A picture may or may not be worth a thousand words, but a map sure is. Jackson's map, smudged and crinkled from being shoved often into a packsack and unfolded as often, would be one of the world's prized treasure maps—if it exists.

There are today more than a few reports of ownership of the "original Jackson letter." Though it appears at least a couple of handwritten copies were made of an existing letter (legitimate or fabricated), the original has not been produced and is now presumed lost. Unless . . .

Gold seekers take in the treacherously steep and dangerous country lying between them and the potential discovery of the legendary gold. OP MEDIA GROUP

One copy of the letter, believed to have been sent to someone on May 28, 1924, is said to have been found with material belonging to a man known as R.A. ("Volcanic") Brown. May 28, 1924, was some twenty years after the original letter was supposedly written, inferring Brown had inherited the copy sent to Shotwell—or a reproduction of that. Contemporary books and numerous publications contain the Volcanic Brown version of the Jackson letter, which we can call the "standard rendition of the Jackson letter."

It appears the wording of the letter was never fully shared until nearly seventy years after it was first said to exist.

BC Historian Bill Barlee

Among the most influential voices regarding the Jackson letter was N.L. (Bill) Barlee, an inspiring high-school history teacher, historian, author, raconteur, entrepreneur, BC politician, television documentarian, and museum collector and curator. Barlee captured the hearts and minds of many as he brought British Columbia history to life in his self-published magazine and books. His *Gold Creeks and Ghost Towns*, published in 1971, remains an influential source of BC history.

Barlee claimed to have the "original" Jackson letter. (Others have made similar claims.) In a curious aside, he explained that he got the letter from his father, who had acquired it from an unknown source. In a 1970 issue of *Canada West* magazine (which Barlee edited and published between 1969 and 1982), he wrote an article about the legend. The article included the full text of the letter and Barlee's note stating that "the copy was enclosed in one of the letters from Brown which was dated May 28, 1924." Some researchers suggest that this was the first reveal of the Jackson letter. Could it be that Brown himself had shared the letter with Barlee's father?

Barlee went on to feature what we'll call the "Barlee version of the Jackson letter" in an episode of his *Gold Trails and Ghost Towns* television show, claiming to affirm the letter's existence. He read from a printed transcription, while allowing the camera to see only the signature, "Yours Truly, W. Jackson," in the lower right-hand corner. Barlee (now deceased) believed Jackson was a real character and said, "I think this particular treasure still exists."

That Barlee never showed for public scrutiny the aforementioned letter from Volcanic Brown (which the intrepid Brown had addressed to Barlee's father) nor the enclosed Jackson letter, leaves the fact of its existence open to question. We tried to find out what happened to Barlee's items, without luck.

YET A DIFFERENT VERSION of the letter subsequently emerged. It was longer and included significant new details when compared to the Barlee version. We call this more recent one the "Carter version of the Jackson letter." And that story unfolds over three generations, beginning with 1940s prospector Dick Carter, who searched for the mine based on what he understood was Jackson's original

Bill Barlee was among the highest-profile proponents of the idea that Slumach's lost gold mine was real and claimed to be the keeper of the "original" Jackson letter. His books and television shows earned huge, respectful audiences. *VANCOUVER PROVINCE*/PNG

letter, though there is no provenance on that. The Carter version of the Jackson letter follows below in full.

The preamble portion addresses Jackson's "Friend," reminding him Jackson is the man whom Shotwell had grubstaked earlier, recounting that he had gone to "Guytos," believed to be in Alaska. This expanded version of the letter then includes the familiar wording found in the Barlee version of finding gold (and highlighted as such herein). A postscript in the Carter version under Jackson's signature, lists landmarks to watch for. The core of both versions, which is marked with a blue line in the below copy, is the Jackson letter with which most gold seekers are familiar, though with slight differences. But the preamble and postscript portions are not well known and, indeed, only appear in the Carter version of the Jackson letter, and these provide interesting insights, which both help with our perception of the shorter version of the letter, and may corroborate it.

San Francisco, Feb. 10, 1904

Dear Friend

It will come to you as a surprise after all these years to hear from me for no doubt you have long since forgotten me. But you will remember the old man you so kindly grubstaked with money and provisions at Guytos. Since then I have prospected with the varied success that usually goes with the life of a prospector. In 1901 I went to B.C. and it is of this trip I want to tell, and hope you will gain by it untold thousands for your kindness to me. I heard you went broke like most everyone else at Guytos but had lost all trace of you since then except that you had gone to Washington. Well, I made a great discovery in New Westminster but after coming out for supplies and tools was taken down with a severe attack of rheumatism that ever since has left me almost bedfast until a short time ago, when I recovered sufficiently as though to make the trip again. I made up my mind to hunt you up and take you with me. In hunting over a Seattle directory I found your name and address and concluded to come to Seattle and talk the matter over with you. A few days after arriving here from my little place in the hills, I was suddenly stricken down again and the Doctors say that I will never recover and may drop off any time for my heart is badly affected. So I will tell you of my trip and what I found and direct you to the best I can to find it. It is too great to be lost to the world and I know with you it will be in good hands. Well, I arrived in Vancouver about the first of July and hired a couple of natives to take me to the headwaters of the _____ then dismissing the natives I struck out in the mountains, and they are rough ones. I prospected up beyond the lake but found nothing of importance. But the formation looked all right. I concluded to prospect back towards _____ Lake. I kept well up on the mountains but was often compelled to make long trips down before crossing could be found on the deep canyons.

I had been out about two months and found myself running short of grub. I lived mostly on fresh meat for one can't carry much of a pack in those hills. Found a few very promising ledges and some color in the little creeks, but nothing I cared to stay with. I had almost made up my mind to light out the next day. I climbed to the top of a sharp ridge and looked down into a little canyon or valley about one mile and a half or two miles long, but what struck me as singular, it appeared to have no outlet for the little creek that flowed at the bottom. Afterwards I found the creek entered a _____ and is lost. After some difficulty I found my way down to the creek. The water was almost white. The formation for the most had been slate and granite but there I found a kind of schist and slate formation. Now comes the interesting part. I had only a small prospecting pan, but I found colors at once right on the surface and such colors they were. I knew then I had struck it rich at last. In going up stream I came to a place where the bedrock was bare and there you can hardly believe me, but the bedrock was yellow with gold. In a few days I gathered thousands and there were thousands more in sight. Some of the nuggets were as big as walnuts and there were many chunks carrying quartz. After sizing up carefully I saw that there were millions stowed away in the little cracks. On account of the weight I buried part of the gold at the foot of a large tent shaped rock facing the creek. You can't miss it. There is a mark cut out in it. Taking with me what I supposed to be about $10,000 proved to be over $8,000. After three days of extreme hard traveling it would not be over 2 days of good going but the way was rough and I was not feeling well. I arrived at the lake and while resting there at the Indian Camp was taken sick and have never since been able to return and now I fear I never shall. I am alone in the world. No relations, no one to look to me for anything. Of course I have never spoken of this find during all this time for fear of it being discovered. It has caused me many anxious hours but the place is so well guarded by surrounding ridges that it should not be found for many years unless someone knew its being there. Oh, how I wish I could go with you and show you to the wonderful place for I find I can't give any exact directions and it may take you a year or more to find it but don't give it up. Keep at it and you will not fail and you will be repaid beyond your wildest dreams. I believe any further directions only tend to confuse so I will only suggest further that you go alone or at least take one or two Indians to pack food and no one need to know but you were going on a hunting trip until you find the place and get everything fixed up to suit yourself. When you find it, and I am sure you will, should you care to see me advertize in the "Frisco Examr" and if I am living I will either come and see you or let you know where to find me but once more I say to you don't fail to look this great property up and don't give up till you find

Many versions of the Jackson letter exist. Is any an original? Or are they all fabricated? This version belonged to Dick Carter around 1940. GREAT PACIFIC MEDIA

it. I am very sorry I can't give you more definite instructions. Of course I expected to have gone back long since. I have drawn a rough sketch that will help you. Success and happiness.

Yours truly,
W. Jackson
From the head of Pitt Lake and not more than 20 miles in a north westerly direction to the hidden treasure but there is no trail and nothing to guide you except that when you get within a few miles of the place you will see on a lower ridge three sharp peaks, each some 50 or 100 ft high as you face these the hidden treasure is below and to the right of these peaks,

Jackson's letter has sent many a gold seeker in search of those markers. But was this letter genuine? We have no proof beyond circumstantial evidence, such as the following observations on the fuller letter.

The "Guytos" mentioned in this version could be a misspelling of Guyots, a location in Alaska not known as a gold-bearing area.

The postscript suggests the search area should be "not more than 20 miles in a north westerly direction to the hidden treasure," which moves the focus west from the area of Corbold Creek and Terrarosa and Stave glaciers, where most searchers have sought the gold over many decades.

This version mentions a "sketch." Could that be a map?

Interestingly, this version ends with a comma, which could indicate there was more to see in the original. Or perhaps it's simply a transcription error.

One of the reasons this letter is thought to be authentic is the writer's use of terms commonly used only by those involved in gold prospecting, like "schist" and "slate formation." And, his reference to the *"Frisco Examr"* (*San Francisco Examiner*) is shorthand for one of the dailies operating in San Francisco at the time this letter was supposedly written.

Though a map was later constructed from Jackson's rudimentary directions, no map is mentioned as accompanying his original correspondence, as might be expected, and the directions are vague enough that his location could be many places north of Pitt Lake.

One rumour is that Shotwell sold Jackson's letter to a group of Seattle businessmen, who began a search for the mine. We wondered if a witness to Shotwell's actions with the businessmen was ever found.

This letter angle to the Slumach legend has become dominant for many who believe the legend is fact rather than fiction. However, there is no proof that a man named Jackson ever existed nor that he wrote such a letter, much less sketched a map.

The Mamquam Glacier area northwest of the head of Pitt Lake attracts attention mostly because Jackson said he found gold "not more than 20 miles in a north westerly direction" from the head of the lake. Mamquam Mountain lies just over thirty kilometres (nineteen miles) northwest of the head of the lake, so distance and direction fit. This is almost the same distance west from the area where Volcanic Brown searched, which was in a north-*easterly* direction from the head of the lake. If indeed Jackson's report is authentic, did he have his directions wrong when he said "north westerly"?

WHILE MANY BELIEVE THE Jackson story is myth, a *Province* newspaper report in 1906 told of a prospector named Frazier who was heading to the Pitt Lake area in search of gold. Is it possible he had the Jackson letter in hand? Perhaps Shotwell created several copies of the letter, and sold it to various fortune hunters. Since those early days, countless people have searched for the lost creek mine. Some used copies of Jackson's letter; others were armed with a "genuine" map bought or acquired from a secret source. Fraser McDonald, New Westminster's gold commissioner for twenty-two years, including during the 1960s, reported he had seen at least a dozen such maps, each pointing out different locations of the treasure. One enterprising American reportedly had printed Pitt Lake lost-gold maps that he sold for $12.50 each.

The longest version of the Jackson letter says he found gold about thirty-two kilometres (twenty miles) northwest of the head of Pitt Lake. If his compass was correct, that might put him near the Mamquam Glacier. BRIAN ANTONSON

Shotwell and Harrington

A 1911 story came our way in Charles A. Miller's book *Golden Mountains*, which nudged back known timelines with a fascinating encounter that, if true, resets expectations. The story involving Charles's father picked up on one name we knew and introduced a new one.

Government official Albert G. Miller, who was at the main Ruskin, BC, government office in late November 1911 along with fellow workers, witnessed something as the "afternoon was drawing on to early evening twilight when two men walked into the office and struck up conversation." Miller told his son Charles, "It soon became apparent one of these two men was badly used up . . . they related they had been prospecting in the Stave hills, had run out of food, had made their way under very arduous conditions to Stave Falls, where they were allowed to ride on a wagon part way to Ruskin then continued on foot to where they now were."

As the younger Miller continues his father's story, he recalls, "It was at this point that one of them said they were not exactly without means and from a jacket pocket removed a goodly sized buckskin pouch and with a melodramatic flourish untied the thong that closed the neck of the pouch, then threw a cascade of gold nuggets across the blueprints on the drafting table!!!"

One can imagine them aghast, and understandably they sought to bring the general manager into the scene, and he

made preparations for the two men to be fed and then taken to a warm room within the hotel at Ruskin. Here they received new clothing and shoes from the store and were given enough cash to purchase tickets on the evening train to get in to Vancouver. During this period the manager was doing his best to extract information as to where the gold had been obtained. Very little became known with the exception of giving their names, which were Shotwell and Harrington, that they had gone into the mountainous Stave area via Pitt Lake and were now on their way to Seattle and possibly San Francisco. Before leaving to catch

their train they gave the manager several small nuggets to pay for what they had received.

This doesn't square with earlier reports of Shotwell receiving the letter from Jackson and selling it to a group of Seattle businessmen. It actually places Shotwell in Ruskin, having himself gone in search of Jackson's gold along with a companion, and that they had found gold.

A separate 1911 Pitt Lake exploration ended in a group of prospectors succumbing to slow deaths from poisoning, except for their leader, Franklin Latimere, adding a handful of unnamed victims to the death count of gold searchers in the area. A prospector by the name of Stan MacDonald is associated with a 1932 vanishing in the mountains; he couldn't be found by a search party, and was presumed claimed by the curse. Such periodic mentions provide interesting if unverified fatal incidents, and eventually someone landed on the number twenty-three to score the curse victims total at a point in time, in the early 1960s.

We've seen press reports saying as few as eleven or as many as thirty-six people have died looking for the mine. While the figures vary, there is no question that *some* people have died during the search. If Slumach's curse is not responsible, then maybe the mine's supposed locations are. All of the suggested locales, save Sheridan Hill in Pitt Meadows, are in treacherous country. Many of those who have met their deaths while on the search may have been inexperienced people who thought they could find the mine easily by relying on their own wits, but found the task more than they could manage. Even experienced outdoor enthusiasts find the Pitt Lake mountains difficult and dangerous.

And facts won't dissuade those wanting to find gold. Even though early estimates of the treasure were as high as $100 million, geological surveys indicate the Pitt Lake vicinity is an unlikely place to find gold. Tests and studies have shown the necessary conditions for producing ore-bearing rock don't exist there, nor does the likelihood of placer deposits. If there is a mine in those mountains, perhaps it is where the gold is in the form of a vein in

The Ruskin train station in 1910. Shotwell and Harrington reportedly boarded a train for Vancouver here after coming down the Stave River from the Stave Glacier area. According to Charles Miller's telling, they reportedly carried gold with them! ROB NICHOLSON

quartz rock rather than nuggets and dust in a stream.

We've been told of stories that an Indigenous person found a mine in the area in the early 1900s, making it contemporary with Jackson. Another reports a miner took between $5,000 and $7,000 in gold from the Pitt Lake area over several years prior to 1915. Such tales are difficult to track down, making them the very stuff of legends, but they appear in various newspaper and magazine articles and should be recounted.

A *Province* newspaper report in 1910 lists as victims George Blake of Coquitlam and his nineteen-year old son George, who died at Scot Lake, crushed by a falling tree while they were searching for gold in Slumach country.

AROUND 1912, ANOTHER REPORTED search for gold involved a group of businessmen (who were not the Seattle group) believed to be operating with a copy of Jackson's letter. They employed the services of Hugh Murray, a scout, stagecoach driver, and prospector, to locate the mine. Murray led several expeditions into the Pitt Lake mountains but found nothing. He reported meeting an old Indigenous woman on one of his trips. The woman talked about once meeting a man in the same region who carried a pack full of gold. She said his name was Jackson, and her timing of the incident put the date back in the days when Jackson would have been fighting his way back to civilization after striking it rich.

Wisconsin's Wilbur Armstrong

Researcher Fred Braches discovered a 1915 article in Wisconsin's *Stevens Point Daily Journal* about someone named Wilbur Armstrong, who was embarking on his last search for "Slumagh's lost gold," saying he had been looking for the past decade. Counting back, Armstrong thus would have started searching around 1906, so perhaps he was involved with, or confused with, Frazier, who was reported to be prospecting for gold in a *Province* article in 1906. Could it be that more than one of them had a version of Jackson's letter they believed was real?

Over the following century, stories of gold were kept secret by some and shared freely by others, and eventually the legend became renowned locally and internationally. No one added more credibility to the legend of Slumach's gold mine than did Volcanic Brown.

Hugh Murray is a source of information on the Slumach legend for various writers, notably Jock Mahoney and C.V. Tench. Both include much misinformation in their stories. Should we attribute the errors to Murray? Or to "creative writing" by these writers?
FRED BRACHES COLLECTION/*MONTREAL STANDARD*, NOVEMBER 25, 1939

Tenth Trip in Search of Mine.

Wilbur Armstrong searched for gold for ten years, making his last trip in 1915. If he started in 1906, he was a contemporary of Frazier, whose search was reported in the *Province* in that same year.
FRED BRACHES COLLECTION/*STEVENS POINT DAILY JOURNAL*, OCTOBER 18, 1915

Prospector Volcanic Brown

In the 1920s, the prospector R.A. ("Volcanic") Brown began searching for the now-legendary hoard, and the legend would further build up around claims that he, at least, *did* find gold, which some suggest was from Slumach's lost mine. Of all those who have searched for Slumach's gold, Volcanic is the best known.

Brown's story came to light in the 1920s thusly: seeking refuge from a storm one night, Brown spent time with four businessmen from the town of Nelson, BC, who were on a hunting expedition. He told them that he had come across Slumach's granddaughter some years earlier, as she lay near death on a trail. Brown was known for his prowess as an herbalist, and he succeeded in saving the woman's life. To reward him, she told him the mine's secret location. (Of course, it is possible that Slumach had a granddaughter, but there is no proof this person existed.)

Brown had discovered several famous mines in the Kootenays in eastern British Columbia and is well known as an early miner in the Copper Mountain claim near Princeton. The challenge of Slumach's mine led him closer to the coast. For several years he combed the mountains surrounding Pitt Lake. There were rumours that Brown deposited several thousand dollars in gold nuggets in a Seattle bank in an account held under his sister's name, the only time a relative of Brown's was mentioned. But these rumours remain just that.

In the late 1920s, Brown went in for his annual search for Slumach's gold and was followed by two other men. He had noticed their campfire smoke some distance behind him for several days, and, when he didn't see it for two days in a row, he assumed a mishap must have overcome them. He decided to turn back, and, after a few days, found one of the men injured on the trail. His partner had left him to go for help, but Brown decided to take the injured man back out to civilization rather than leave him there. Doing so put his own search behind schedule, and he was late coming out of the mountains that year. The first snows caught him, and when his feet were frostbitten, he was forced to cut off some of his toes with his hunting knife. A search party found him and

Left This photo of Volcanic Brown appeared in the *Province* on March 20, 1932, when the paper reported on the unsuccessful twenty-seven-day search for him in November 1931. It may have been taken in 1928 following his previous rescue, since his foot is bandaged. This injury likely slowed his progress into the mountains north of Pitt Lake in 1931. *THE PROVINCE*, MARCH 20, 1932

Right The Volcanic Brown rescue party, 1928. Left to right: Herman Gardner of the BC Provincial Police; Spud Murphy; Alvin Patterson, after whom the town of Alvin, BC was named; Caleb Gardner; and Harry Corder. ROY MCMARTYN (PROVIDED BY HARRY CORDER)

carried him to safety, and a photograph of Brown from that period shows him standing with a cane and with his left foot bandaged.

Nevertheless, the dauntless prospector returned to searching in the Pitt Lake mountains in 1931. With his injury, Brown's ability to move was seriously hampered. That year, when he again failed to return, another rescue team was organized and, after twenty-seven days, two members of the search party found Brown's last camp high on an icefield near the headwaters of the Stave River. His tent, cooking gear, books, and prospecting materials were all in place, as if he had just left camp for a moment. But Brown himself was never found. Officials assumed he had gotten lost in a snowstorm or possibly fallen down one of the hundreds of crevasses on Stave Glacier.

The March 20, 1932, edition of the *Province* reported on this unsuccessful search for Brown. Among those involved

was game warden George Stevenson, who said,

> It was slow going—three or four miles a day. Our 12 by 48 [inch] snowshoes would sink to our knees, even without our packs. I've never seen it snow so thick and fast anywhere; we couldn't see a yard sometimes. Cold? Well, at night in the open we couldn't sleep much—had to keep up a fire. LeRoy [one of the searchers] was great, ready for anything and wouldn't say quit. We hoped Brown was snowed up somewhere, and so we fired single shots regularly, but everything was as still as the dead.

And now another element enters the scene: while there is no reporting of this in contemporary accounts, a legend has evolved saying the most interesting thing found in Brown's last camp was a glass jar containing eleven ounces of raw gold, proof that somewhere on his trip, Volcanic Brown had found gold. This rumour has never been substantiated, but it persists. Is it true? If so, did the searchers find this gold but kept it secret? Or, if they did find it, did they responsibly want to avoid a rush of gold seekers into the treacherous area?

The legend was further fuelled by uncorroborated stories that Brown was seen years after his disappearance leading a very comfortable life in California, creating speculation he had found the lost mine and had left his last camp as a decoy. In earlier days, Brown had had a set of false teeth made of gold, which would have made him quite recognizable.

Was Volcanic Brown another of the dozens who have allegedly died as a result of Slumach's curse, an utterance of which there is no reliable record? Was Jackson one of them? How many have *really* died while searching for the hidden fortune? Though there has never been any evidence of a mine, legend cries out that more than one person in the Pitt Lake area has found gold and met their demise shortly afterward.

Another relevant question often asked is whether modern prospectors could establish mining claims in the area where Volcanic Brown is believed to have searched. This is doubtful. The location of his last camp is uncertain. Much of the area he might have searched could be within or very near the modern boundaries of Garibaldi or Golden Ears Provincial Parks, and since no mining is allowed in provincial parks, claims could not be staked there.

The gold fever that keeps people interested was aptly summed up in an article by *Columbian* newspaper historian John Pearson: "The only thing that could kill the legend of Slumach's lost gold mine is the discovery of the elusive cache . . ."

For their own sake, however, people enticed into the Pitt River region by visions of a motherlode should proceed cautiously and heed the words of one veteran prospector: "That has to be the worst topographical area in the province."

A 1925 newspaper article by E.L. Purkins tells of the hardship survival experience of a prospector named Shotwell, featured in a suitably dire depiction in the story's header illustration. But this version of the tale mixes up the legendary roles of Jackson and Shotwell, as well as other players. It's one more spurious story amidst many spurious claims. FRED BRACHES COLLECTION/*SUNDAY PROVINCE*, AUGUST 9, 1925

Were Slumach, Jackson, and Volcanic Brown all here? The Terrarosa Glacier was another of the high-country sites combed for gold. Just east of it is the Stave Glacier. Did Slumach find gold here? Did Jackson? Did Volcanic Brown? And if so, why up so high? ADAM PALMER COLLECTION

Chapter 6

Sensationalism, Exploitation, and Escalation of Interest

The Scurrilous C.V. Tench

SLUMACH SENSATIONALISM IN THE 1930s and 1940s, much of it created by a hyped-up writer named C.V. Tench, replaced stories of serious gold seekers. Tench's wilful disinformation marred historical details, scarred any positive aspect of Slumach's reputation he may have had, and gave life to fabricated myth. This is where the legend gets a lift in popularity, albeit from a writer who garnishes his stories with salacious inaccuracies. In the rush of rumours, many journalists and sketch artists took liberties distorting the story and lead personality, on occasion humorously, but most often in derogatory ways.

Rumours of Slumach's "curse" began at this time, and the "curse" has been retroactively applied ever since, casting those who died while looking for gold near Pitt Lake as "victims," but any such references before Tench's scurrilous aspersions are revisionist history.

Writers in various publications furthered this crude "yellow journalism." In 1947, in the *Province*'s magazine, Clyde Gilmour wrote an article titled "Hoodoo Gold: Death to Tenderfeet," with a drawing by Vernon Miller showing an Indigenous man with a sack of riches spilling from over his shoulder onto a bar counter, with the caption: "Slumach swaggered into New Westminster with huge nuggets of raw gold."

Often, unsavoury writers or opportunistic illustrators took advantage of Slumach's uncertain persona, creating contrived images that harkened back to a dark side that was not factual but titillating to the public at large.

By the time Volcanic Brown's story was in circulation and Jackson's letter was thought to be credible, Slumach's story was prime picking for made-up bits and false statements made popular in the 1930s. The term "fake news" may be overused today, but it's nothing new—distorting facts, hyperbolizing stories, or puffing up malicious talk have long been ways to sell magazines or newspapers or further one's profile as a journalist or sketch artist, respect and reputation of a subject be damned.

C.V. Tench published tales in 1939 and 1941 and on through the 1950s. He had quite a track record back in the day, including writing sensational scripts for the TV series *One Step Beyond*. Tench is likely the one who started the lurid lies and gloomy distortions portraying Slumach as a nefarious, cheating, gambling womanizer. A Tench story in *Wide World Magazine* in Australia shows a sketched "Slumack" surrounded by dancehall girls. It was a time when the shameless besmirching of an Indigenous man went without scrutiny or scruples. It is reasonable to suggest Tench knew he was lying.

Slumach swaggered into New Westminster with huge nuggets of raw gold.
Drawing by Vernon Miller

Depicting a scene where "Slumach swaggered into New Westminster with huge nuggets of raw gold," this image and the accompanying story by Clyde Gilmour were loaded with false information, exaggerated and untrue, but compelling for readers of the *Province* magazine in January 1947. FRED BRACHES COLLECTION/VERNON MILLER, *THE PROVINCE*, JANUARY 18, 1947

Tench's early writings call the lost hoard "hoodoo gold," without defining "hoodoo" and letting it hang in word association with "voodoo." Things got weirder. Tench introduced fabricated names and descriptions of Slumach's supposed victims.

Fred Braches wrote to us to underline that although it was broadcaster and critic Clyde Gilmour who introduced fabricated allegations of murders of women into the Slumach story in 1947, it was Tench who created the character that Braches called "an evil twin of Slumach." Braches wrote:

Molly Tynan and her ilk were the brainchildren of Tench, who published in such periodicals as *Boy's Own Paper, Daredevil Detective Stories, Western Action, Ranch Romance,* and *True West,* to mention just a few.

His version of the Slumach story, "The Gold Mine Murders of Nine British Columbia Women," appeared in the "Annals of Canadian Crime" section of the Canadian edition of *Liberty* in July 1956. The article is illustrated with photographs supposedly of some of the victims, as well as one of a fictitious British Columbia constable, Eric

Given C.V. Tench's proclivity for concoction, exaggeration, and outright lies recounted in his stories about Slumach, there's little doubt his style would have encouraged the article's illustrator to take similar liberties when portraying Slumach as a dirty, rotten scoundrel, which he was not. WIDE WORLD MAGAZINE (AUSTRALIA), JUNE 1941

Eric Grainger, who, posing as a gold prospector, solved the case. It also includes a photo presented as that of the "slayer of the nine women, 'John' Slumach, who was hanged for his crimes in New Westminster's provincial jail. "Raw gold by the handful" says one caption, and "All his girlfriends drowned," says another.

Braches's thinking drove home points overlooked by storytellers or ignored by researchers, including willingly co-opted newspaper editors. He explained how early media claims got modified when time was taken to realize an obvious unlikelihood. Said Braches in a note to us, about an article on Molly Tynan:

> The knife was identified by Slumach's fingerprints found on the handle [according to the article]. This very statement is highly questionable. Fingerprints can survive underwater though can deteriorate quickly. However, it is unlikely that the New Westminster police would have used fingerprinting for identification in the same year the technology was introduced by Scotland Yard; therefore, in recounts of the story, Slumach is identified as the murderer when his mother recognized the knife as his, another highly unlikely suggestion.

Vancouver Sun writer Cecil Clark was dismissive of the tale in a December 31, 1954, article, calling it "wildly" told in *Liberty* by C.V. Tench and damning the distorted story and made-up personalities.

> This was a script that really went haywire, for if this was a picture of Slumach as a young man, it was taken years before photography was invented! A little research would have shown the author that when Slumach was hanged in January 1891, he was frail, tottery, white haired and . . . about 80 years old. Needless to say there never was a Constable Grainger on the B.C. Police, nor a Sergeant Hilton, nor for that matter, a Missing Persons Bureau.

Notwithstanding that facts should trump falsehoods, the names of Molly Tynan and Susan Jesner, along with Tillie Malcolm and Mary Warne, come up frequently in the stories of Slumach's mine, the sad creations of Tench's fertile mind. Tench and later unscrupulous journalists identified the victims as having died by Slumach's hand after accompanying him into the Pitt Lake country to get more of his gold. We've seen no police record of these persons, and it has proven impossible to document

These photos of Slumach's supposed victims were widely published and identified as (top to bottom) Mary Warne, Tillie Malcolm, and (bottom) Susan Jesner. To be clear, these are purported images, source unknown, and, even if known, they were used in false representation. Where these pictures originated and whether the names attached to them are correct is unknown, but research establishes there were no such murders and the names appear to be made up. Whatever the source of these women's pictures, they were not victims of Slumach. DAILY COLUMBIAN, N.D.

their existence. Even if they lived, it would be difficult to establish a connection between them and Slumach. In such stories, Slumach's reportedly repulsive countenance apparently proved to be no deterrent to young women, for they flocked to his side as he spent his gold. Some misinformed quotes say the murders stopped when he was captured after Bee's murder. Wholly unrelated women of the time had their photos printed in publications, captions naming them as the reportedly missing women.

Tench repeatedly depicted a young ruffian with a cap placed jauntily on his head and a stogie clenched to the side of his mouth as "Slummock." The face in this photo would place the date of the photograph (if it is Slumach) somewhere in the 1830s or 1840s, when photography had not even been developed very far. Moreover, while the local paper carried extensive coverage of the Slumach case and his ultimate hanging, no photographs were ever associated with the written accounts.

Tench also placed the same image in different articles to depict an Indigenous man from Nicola named Eneas George, who was convicted of a separate murder and was thus wilfully misidentified. In a 1950s update to his mischievous descriptions, Tench introduced the concept of Slumach invoking his supposed curse as he stood on the gallows, creating this myth. It was nothing less than character assassination, but it took hold as the truth.

Writer Jock Mahoney also wilfully spun falsehoods about Slumach, as did Thomas P. Kelley in his "Lost

This purported image of Slumach with a stogie clenched between his teeth has been in wide circulation since it was first used by C.V. Tench in the 1930s. It is assuredly not Slumach, as it does not fit with his age or reported demeanour, nor does it have a reliable source. It does however portray a scoundrel, in keeping with the salacious stories created by Tench. MONTREAL STANDARD, NOVEMBER 25, 1939

Gold and Murdered Maids," a 1958 article for *Cavalier*, an American magazine. There's a salacious drawing dramatizing fishermen and a policeman pulling a net from the river with a woman's body caught up in it.

Writings in *Native Voice* and other articles spread the burgeoning tale of gold nuggets on saloon floors, dance-hall girls, missing women, and the final utterance of a gallows curse.

Legend has it that a constable named Eric Grainger tried to thwart Slumach's attentions toward Molly Tynan, but there is no mention of this in court records or anywhere else. Grainger likely is the completely fictitious construct of an overenthusiastic author. *DAILY COLUMBIAN, N.D.*

Hard-to-fathom images were kept in circulation. One illustration shown on television depicts two gunmen firing pistols at one another in a bar scene as the voiceover tells of Slumach killing Bee. The subsequent scene of a search for Slumach shows a wagon train in pursuit.

Soon, most articles offered familiar media exaggerations far more often than the truth to garner the public's attention (and sell newspapers and magazines and bring viewers to screens).

AS CANADA RECOVERED FROM the "dirty thirties," a decade of drought, unemployment, starvation, and financial devastation, people aimed to get financially stable, and one way was to find gold. Whether enticed by lurid, half-baked, fabricated stories about the lost mine, or by legitimate pursuits as gold seekers, prospectors lit out. Newspaper articles from the late 1930s and 1940s reported on searches for the mine.

A 1940 item from the *Maple Ridge–Pitt Meadows Gazette* covers a search launched by Mrs. Al Jenkins, who headed up Pitt Lake to look for Slumach's mine. There is

no follow-up article to tell of her success or failure. That was frustrating for us, as was this: the same newspaper featured a 1941 article reporting that Gordon Dalrymple of Webster's Corners had found the mine three months earlier. Dalrymple claimed other searchers were "all in the wrong place," but gave no further information on his supposed find, nor proof of it. Coverage like that kept the legend alive.

Prospector Dick Carter

In the 1940s, prospector Arthur Wellesley ("Dick") Carter ventured out with his version of the Jackson letter (as recounted earlier) as his guide. He took a wider interpretation of the search area than had others, expanding his search with a number of places he marked on a topographical map, each with a large X. He covered a lot of ground in the Garibaldi area. In a country unfavourable to pack horses, searchers had to carry on their backs all the fixings required for their journey— climbing ropes, tents, supplies for the duration, and some ability to fish and hunt. Carter went loaded down with provisions.

That Carter apparently hiked and climbed his way to many of his identified sites is indicative of his returning many times, always with focus and determination, given they are not located convenient to one another, nor are they easily reached on the same journey. His photographs leave trace indicators of his route, but speculation remains about how his interpretation of Jackson's letter led him to this mountain precinct. His reading of the letter and that of Volcanic Brown's share similarities.

ANOTHER ARTICLE, THIS ONE from the *Maple Ridge–Pitt Meadows Gazette* on August 24, 1945, recounts the rescue of Joe Eaves, a prospector from Silver Creek, who became ill while searching in the Widgeon Lake area and was rescued by a Royal Canadian Air Force plane. The item also tells of a San Francisco man, John Bruno, who brought out some $9,000 in gold in 1907. This was in the same decade in which Jackson reportedly found his gold. The evident confusion in this twentieth-century reporting doubtless contributed to the plethora of mixed messages about where to search for the mine.

Adventurer Duncan McPhaden

When we learned about Duncan McPhaden's 1943 adventures, it reinforced the dangers for anyone who was captivated by legend but not properly prepared. It's not surprising that McPhaden was smitten by the Slumach legend. A former deputy registrar at the Supreme and County courts in New Westminster, he had access to the historical Slumach trial papers, which included notes made by Jason Ovid Allard, Slumach's interpreter at the trial.

After McPhaden retired in the early 1940s, the lure of prospecting became even more tempting, and he spent many summers in the Pitt Lake area searching for the elusive cache.

The often harsh and unforgiving environment certainly didn't deter McPhaden. He knew it well. In fact, in 1950 he dramatically rescued two of five forestry workers from Pitt Lake when their fourteen-foot powerboat flipped over.

The next summer, Slumach's purported curse hovered over—then took a firm grip on—the sixty-eight-year-old McPhaden. He didn't die, but he came close to dying in a terrifying scenario that unfolded one morning when a ledge near his isolated cabin close to Pitt Lake gave way under him. McPhaden tumbled over a cliff, striking his back on a huge rock.

"It took me hours to crawl back to the cabin," he recalled. "I couldn't walk."

His ordeal took a nightmarish turn. Badly injured and alone, he holed up in his cabin for two days. Then, desperate, he decided to seek help.

"I knew I would never make it if I didn't start then," he later told a *Province* reporter.

McPhaden clawed and crawled his way about 182 metres (200 yards) over rocky terrain to a rowboat at the lake's edge.

Weak and in pain, he "rowed in a fashion" to his gas boat moored offshore. His beacon of hope, Williams'

Lodge, beckoned ten kilometres (six miles) down the lake.

McPhaden would have no part of Slumach's curse. Resolute and undaunted by his deteriorating circumstances, he reached the lodge where proprietor Carl Williams whisked him to the Pitt Lake Ferry Service office in Port Coquitlam, and from there to hospital.

He survived and, perhaps emboldened by his dream of gold nuggets, lived another three decades, until 1980.

Prospector Alfred Gaspard

Reports of people disappearing while searching for gold in the Pitt River country continued in the 1950s. Among the first was an experienced prospector named Alfred Gaspard. He reasoned that one of the main obstacles to finding the mine was the rough terrain in which it was located. He felt that Slumach's curse worked so well because the terrain presented very difficult and dangerous situations that could easily lead to a "lonely death," even without help from a curse.

To avoid having to move through too much dangerous country, Gaspard instead flew into a small lake in his search area and established a base camp equipped with a radio link to the outside world. He systematically explored the valleys and mountains in the area. At one time he reported he was nearing the actual location of the mine, and should find it for certain within a few days. Shortly after this, he failed to report as scheduled. A search was organized, partially covered by an emergency search fund that Gaspard had provided to pay for helicopters in case he failed to rendezvous. The search continued for several weeks, but no trace was ever found of him, and he is suspected to have suffered the "lonely death" he had hoped to avoid.

Private Investigator Roger Gallant

In the 1950s, an unnamed millionaire from eastern Canada hired a private investigator named Roger Gallant to research the Slumach story and report to him on the feasibility of launching a search for the mine. After inspecting all available sources, Gallant returned with the verdict that the mine did not exist and the venture would not be worth the investment. Follow-up on such tight, short bits of information was nearly impossible, even though it offered a valuable perspective.

Captain Moore

Beyond Pitt Lake, other possible mine locations come into view. One frequently suggested location is up on Corbold Creek, which enters upper Pitt River from the east near Alvin, a fish hatchery about eight kilometres (five miles) north of Pitt Lake. Corbold Creek is fed from the south by Canyon Creek. It figures prominently in two searches for Slumach's mine—the 1901 search made by Jackson, and the searches made in the 1920s by Volcanic Brown, based in part on Jackson's letter. In his alleged letter, Jackson described his find as located thirty-two kilometres (twenty miles) from the lake. Parties using maps based on his letter found themselves at Corbold Creek when they began their trips. One of these parties included Captain Moore, a Victoria barrister, who gave an account published in the *Province* in 1952. Moore said he accompanied a party to Canyon Creek. His employer, W. MacDonald, had obtained a map from a nurse, who in turn had received it from a dying prospector whom she had attended in California. Some have speculated that this prospector might have been Jackson.

The map used by the Moore party must have been fairly accurate from a geographical standpoint. "Following the course laid down on the map," noted Moore, "the party turned off to follow a creek that came into the Pitt from the left. We named it Canyon Creek, as the greater length of it appeared to be between precipitous hills. But as this was shown on the map, we knew we were to follow this stream to a point where we could take our bearings from three mountain peaks." (This account is questionable because Canyon Creek enters Corbold Creek from the south, or right, as you ascend Corbold, and then Corbold enters the Pitt from the east, or right as you ascend it. Perhaps the discrepancy can be attributed to the many twists and turns the waters make in that difficult country.)

"We did so. We found the place. There correctly drawn. But, evidently the story of the gold was a figment of his imagination—probably induced by the find that carried him off. In his delirium, I fancy, he pictured the spot as being rich," said Moore.

Moore's description of his search location does not quite match the description given in our reproduced copy of Jackson's letter, but it does lend credence to the existence of Jackson and to his discovery of gold in this area.

Chief Kwikwetlem Williams claimed to have known Slumach, and his grandson, Tommy, showed various gold seekers where to search for Slumach's "glory hole" in the dangerous country surrounding Pitt Lake. COURTESY OF DONALD E. WAITE

Tommy Williams

Yet another attempt to find the mine was made in 1952, this time by reporters from the *Province*. Tommy Williams, grandson of Chief Kwikwetlem Williams, a Coast Salish man who claimed he knew Slumach, led the reporters to the supposed site of the mine. Tommy said that his grandfather had led him there years before, and that he in turn would lead a team of reporters to the same place. The area was covered with several metres of snow when they arrived, and its exploration proved very difficult and bore no positive result.

Slumach Lost Creek Mine Limited

The Slumach Lost Creek Mine Limited was formed in the early 1950s and carried out an extensive and thorough search. The company published a prospectus in the *Province* and offered 400,000 shares at a price of twelve and a half cents per share. This worked out to $50,000 capital on the first offering, with an authorized issue of 3 million shares.

In keeping with the distortion of Slumach's story at the time, there are several items therein that appear created simply for the purpose of attracting attention and do not attest to known facts. The "properties" said to be "a short distance from the west shore of Pitt Lake" could of course be many that have subsequently been explored by gold seekers. There is talk of Slumach's son and of his brother Smaamquach, yet we've never found any documentation about either. According to one newspaper account, four other men besides Slumach "actually took gold from the hidden mine." Of that account, there's simply no trace. There's the quote of "In God's truth it is Slumach's Mine," which comes across as literary invention. And none of those reputed in the prospectus to have found gold made the news of the day.

The following advice was included in the advertisement: "This is purely a speculative issue. The risk is great but it could be that the reward may be greater."

The group used helicopters and staked claims throughout the area shown them by Chief Kwikwetlem's grandson. Then, after a summer of intensive but fruitless searching, the company acknowledged its defeat in the back pages of the *Province*. Nothing further was ever heard of the group's venture.

Treasure

In 1958 a television show called *Treasure* entered the lives of the two young boys (and future co-authors of this book) who had sat around the campfire when the fisherman's wife had told them the tale of Slumach. In the black-and-white and shadowy greys of TV sets of that era, it brought these tales of adventure into our lives. The weekly series portrayed riddles kids found inspiring: a buried pirate chest still unfound centuries later despite the existence of a map; money from a daring nineteenth-century bank heist in the United States stashed in a place so secret it had never been located, despite a confession from the dying robber; hand-drawn sketches with directions to a trunk filled with valuable shares in a silver mine, still missing. The series' episode titles were fascinating, such as "Sir Harry Oakes' Lost Fortune" and "Death Valley's Stovepipe Wells." The show's host, Bill Burrud, would warn of the dangers that would-be explorers were sure to encounter if they ventured in search of these lost treasures.

The first *Treasure* episode that season featured Slumach's incredible discovery of "gold beyond your wildest dreams." Fog eventually foiled the television film crew, descending upon them with alarming suddenness and forcing them to abandon their search. The final frames from their camera captured a narrow rocky entrance fading from view as the chronicler declaimed, "There . . . is the entrance to the mine. We were that near . . . before the curse closed in."

Lewis Hagbo and Tiny Allen

We came across important research and writing on the Slumach story done in the 1960s by Alan Jay when he was a reporter and columnist for the *Columbian*. Jay's research concerned two reported victims of Slumach's supposed curse, Lewis Hagbo and Tiny Allen. By this time, any deaths of prospectors in the area were attributed not to accident but to "the curse." Jay contributed to our research and shared his findings, which included the curse's tally. Among other newspapers, the *Vancouver Sun* carried this story on July 23, 1960:

> **U.S. MAN DIES HUNTING GOLD—LOST MINE'S 23RD VICTIM**
> A vacation spent in the Pitt River badlands, hunting a legendary gold mine, ended in death for an American naval draughtsman Wednesday.
>
> [The] body of Lewis E. Hagbo, 49, of Bremerton, Wash., was brought out to civilization Friday afternoon by a rescue party led by Sgt. Jackson

SLUMACH LOST CREEK MINE LTD.

(NON-PERSONAL LIABILITY)

Incorporated under the Laws of the Province of British Columbia

A copy of this Prospectus has been filed with the Registrar of Companies, Victoria, B. C., and a copy
will be supplied to any person subscribing for shares.

FIRST OFFERING: 400,000 SHARES

PRICE: 12½c PER SHARE

Registrar and Transfer Agent:	Solicitor:
GUARANTY TRUST CO. OF CANADA	R. J. MUNRO
624 HOWE STREET	WESTERN CANADA BUILDING
VANCOUVER 1, B. C.	416 WEST PENDER STREET
	VANCOUVER 3, B. C.

Registered Office:

1016 STOCK EXCHANGE BUILDING
475 HOWE STREET
VANCOUVER 1, B. C.

TELEPHONE TAtlow 2351

This is a Speculative Investment

Top This 1952 prospectus sought investors for the Slumach Lost Creek Mine Limited. Nothing seems to have come of it, as is so often the case. FRED BRACHES COLLECTION/SLUMACH.CA

Bottom This certificate was issued in 1952 and used Slumach's name to lure intrigued investors with the prospect of gold to be found. COURTESY OF NICK ROMAN

Top This is Spindle Canyon, which was shown in an episode of the 1958 television show *Treasure* that featured the Slumach story. As ground fog closed in, the film crew had to abandon their quest to find the gold, even though they had reached what they believed was the entrance to the mine. The producers suggested the fog was Slumach's curse at work. COURTESY OF DARYL FRIESEN

Bottom This dramatic view of the Mamquam Glacier in Garibaldi Provincial Park shows the forbidding country northwest of Pitt Lake, where some say there is gold to be found. Above the tree line, rocks, snowfields, and glaciers, conditions are even more treacherous. OP MEDIA GROUP

Payne of the Port Coquitlam RCMP detachment.

Hagbo is the twenty-third man to die seeking the Lost Creek mine. Some died by accident, by misadventure, by exposure, and by murder.

The rugged jungle of rockfall and mountain north of Pitt River is supposed to hide the Lost Creek Gold Mine. It is said that the mine, in a hidden valley, was found by the Indian Slumach, who was hanged at New Westminster in 1891.

In the past 70 years, hundreds of prospectors and hopeful adventurers have hunted the gold but none have found it.

Hagbo's body was found at the bottom of a cliff; the victim of a heart attack rather than a fall. Nevertheless, the fact that his misfortune came while he was looking for the supposed mine earned him a headline. Over the years, similar headlines in other papers such as Victoria's *Daily Colonist* ("Fortune Still Elusive"), the *Province* ("The Incurable Slumach Gold Mine Disease"), and the *Winnipeg Free Press* ("Curse Guards This Lost Gold Mine"), have ensured that the Slumach legend remained in the public mind.

The other victim whose fate was recounted by Jay was Tiny Allen, who stood more than a couple metres tall and packed more weight than a healthy lifestyle would advise on his frame. During the 1960s, Allen worked year-round as an odd-job man at the Port Arms Hotel in Port Moody. Each summer, he set out on trips into the Pitt Lake area to search for Slumach's mine. With information garnered from the *Columbian*'s file, he narrowed his search. One day he contacted Jay to say that he had found the mine's location. He described the valley he had seen, saying that much of the gold was in cracks in the wall of the valley, but that most of it appeared to be down in the creek bed at the bottom. Snow and ice had prevented him from reaching the valley floor, but he was elated at actually having discovered the motherlode.

Jay noted a similarity between Allen's description of the mine and the description contained in Jackson's letter. He mentioned it to Allen, but Allen had never seen a copy of the letter. Jay showed him one, and Allen's reaction was jubilant—the two descriptions were almost identical.

The clincher in this story was Allen's 1960s description of a huge rock that can be seen inside the mine. He said it was shaped like an Egyptian pyramid— with its top cut off. Upon seeing the letter, Allen exclaimed, "That's it!" Allen was adamant he had seen the exact site as described in Jackson's letter and had rediscovered the mine so many had searched for in vain.

Allen intended to return as soon as the snow melted to allow safe access to the gold. For some reason, his journey was delayed for a year. The next spring, Jay attempted to contact him, only to discover he had died during the winter—the victim of a heart attack. A sister in Vancouver had handled Allen's funeral and had taken all of his possessions.

Jay contacted the sister, but she refused to discuss the matter of the mine. Allen had told Jay that he had drawn a map showing the route to it, but his sister denied any knowledge of the map. Jay noted some months later that he heard of a new expedition being launched to search for the mine, a search financed by three Vancouver women. No results of that search have ever come to light. Nor has Allen's map appeared in public.

Producer Hugh Creig

Jay wrote an article for *Canada Month* in April 1966, explaining that Hugh Creig, a Vancouver producer, was making a film about Slumach for television. Jay clearly indicates his own version of the tale in the article, including that Slumach had a haversack of gold nuggets and was convicted of murdering women. Jay also wrote,

> Slumach stood on the gallows with the rope around his neck.
>
> Asked if he had any last statement to make, he surveyed the watching crowd, a look of hatred etched on his face. "When I die, my mine dies with me—and all those who try to find it will die also," he snarled in the Chinook language. Three minutes and 58 seconds later he was dead, taking

the secret of the location of the mine with him to the grave.

Jay tells of Creig's respect for the curse: "I shan't actually be looking for the mine; just for a suitable location for filming in the general area, so perhaps Slumach will take it easy on me . . ." Jay noted that Creig had problems obtaining Indigenous guides, as they claimed, "It's a dead man's mine."

We've not come across any indication that Creig completed his film.

Wally Lund and Elmer McLellan

Also in the 1960s, another theoretical location for the mine emerged: Sheridan Hill, a lush, treed outcropping in the Pitt Polder area of Pitt Meadows. Although the more prominent local sites may have been Widgeon Creek and Widgeon Lake, they didn't receive as much media attention. Nor did Spindle Creek, further up Pitt Lake, which is more favourable to the tale. Still, many weekend explorers descended on Sheridan Hill.

After Dutch settlers moved into the Pitt Meadows and Pitt Polder areas, diking for land reclamation began in the twentieth century. Sheridan Hill stood in the middle of a slough variously known as Alouette or Lillooet Slough. The hill was then called Menzies Isle. It had long been a sacred place for Indigenous Peoples, and had figured in tales about deposits of gold. There is an old shaft on the hill, which led many to believe that this was indeed the location of Slumach's cache. Slumach could have stored gold there and gone back for more when he needed it. Moreover, the scene of Louis Bee's murder is directly across lower Pitt River from the hill, about half a kilometre (a third of a mile) away.

In 1961, Wally Lund, who lived in nearby Haney, "saw" the location of Slumach's mine in a dream and contacted Elmer McLellan, editor of New Westminster's *Columbian* newspaper. Lund pinpointed the location as being on Sheridan Hill, just over five kilometres (three miles) north of the Lougheed Highway in Pitt Meadows. For a few weeks, the *Columbian* ran stories about this latest search for the mine. Editor McLellan staked a claim at the site, and several hundred people journeyed to the scene on weekends to watch the goings-on. But "the stuff that dreams are made of" proved to be something other than gold. The would-be prospectors found that the hill had been worked several years earlier, perhaps in the hope that it was the mine's secret location, but searches failed to reveal any yellow metal. Today, the north half of Sheridan Hill is a gravel pit.

North of Sheridan Hill and across Pitt Lake, on the west shore, lie Widgeon Creek and, much higher up a mountain, Widgeon Lake, two other suggested sites of the treasure. And the notation reading APPROXIMATE SEARCH AREA OF LEGENDARY LOST SLUMACK MINE, pointing to Widgeon Lake, was at one time on a wall map displayed in the beverage room of the Wild Duck Inn, on the lower Pitt River in Port Coquitlam.

Staff Sergeant R. Harding

In July 1968 the *RCMP Quarterly,* a credible publication, published an article by Staff Sergeant R. Harding. As expected from such a source, it hews to the facts from the records of Slumach's trial and portrays the lurid stories as concocted, but does so with a qualifier: "So much for the facts of the case as obtained from the record, but there have been many persons who vouched that the story of Slumach's hidden gold is equally true and that the full story of his source of wealth was not revealed until after his death, being zealously guarded in order to deter would-be gold seekers."

Harding also mentioned "John" Jackson who wrote "a letter to a friend and attached a map of the Pitt Lake area," alluding to them as two separate pieces of paper.

Bernard Rover

In 1968, Bernard Rover came into the Slumach picture when two other prospectors rescued him. They found the dehydrated and disoriented seventy-one-year-old in the Vickers Creek area near the northeast end of Pitt Lake. The prospector was lying under a tarp, seriously ill after

suffering a stroke. Muddled and dazed, he talked of gold. He had crawled through sixteen kilometres (ten miles) of wilderness before being found. He recovered in hospital and became the focus of later searches.

AS THE 1970s BEGAN, history writer Tom Patterson and magazine publisher Garnet Basque produced more material recounting the legend, taking a lead on contributions in publications such as *Canadian Treasure* and *Canadian Frontier.*

In 1971, writer Mary Trainer—then twenty-three years old and having relocated to Vancouver from her home in BC's Okanagan Valley—joined two veterans of the 1957 campfire scene, her friends, twenty-three-year-old Brian Antonson (with whom she had studied in broadcasting school) and his brother, twenty-two-year-old Rick Antonson (whom she met while they worked together at a tourism bureau), with the goal of researching the story of Slumach's gold. This was the first time we three co-authors worked as a team.

It was British Columbia's centennial year of joining Confederation, and that created a growing appetite for stories about the lively heritage and fascinating personalities from within the province. Serious research was welcomed in the community, especially if it brought history alive. Feeling the contagious enthusiasm, we three history buffs went in search of the legend of Slumach's gold.

We sought every scrap of detail available in old photographs and newspaper clippings, interviewed people who claimed to know something about the mine's location, and read turn-of-the-century documents. Our objectives were to separate fact from fiction in Pitt Lake's lost-creek gold-mine story and to determine which parts of the region Slumach might have found most promising for hunting, and thus most likely to be the site of his accidentally stumbled-upon gold creek. What we discovered instead was a fabulous collection of fabrication, mistruths, and wilful embellishments, all construed into an astonishing tale. All of that was countered by uncomfortable facts and truths about an actual murder, a rush

Top From left to right, authors Mary Trainer, Rick Antonson, and Brian Antonson work on their original book in 1971. WENDY ANTONSON

Bottom Our 1972 book, *In Search of a Legend: Slumach's Gold*, captured our quest but with our own mistaken identity of Slumach, as the portrayal we offered was erroneous and based on sensationalized accounts rather than more reliable history, as we were to learn and later correct. FRED BOSMAN

to judgement, and a hanging in the unjust treatment of an Indigenous man named Slumach. It was the making of a legend.

The location of Slumach's killing of Bee was often misplaced as Lillooet Slough (sometimes called Alouette Slough) on the east side of the lower Pitt River, a spot erroneously shown on sketched maps. Further research clarified that the incident took place across the river in the marshes around Addington Point (part of today's Minnekhada Regional Park in Coquitlam), directly across from Sturgeon Slough. Slumach lived near there, and Bee died there.

Rikk Taylor, publisher of the *Columbian*, supported us in our quest. We co-authors were young and penniless; Taylor was middle-aged and successful. He fanned the embers of our interest, providing assistance and giving us access to his paper's extensive archives, which included the original coverage of Slumach's trial and hanging for Bee's murder. Taylor saw in us a youthful version of his own enthusiasm and encouraged our pursuit of Slumach's legend by covering our search activities in the newspaper. This, in turn, provided us with more leads, harder evidence, and anonymous phone calls ("I know something about the lost mine you might be interested in . . .").

One day that year, Rick was meeting with the owner of Maple Ridge Printers, who casually said he was setting up to print a book about the lost mine of Pitt Lake. He sent Rick to Waite's Photo Studio to meet the book's author, Don Waite. In August 1972, Waite published his book, which was painstakingly researched, as befitted his status as a former RCMP constable. Its title, *Kwant'stan*, is the Coast Salish name for Golden Ears, the distinctive snow-capped twin peaks of Edge Peak and Blanshard Peak, which are reminiscent of wolves' ears and appear golden when reflecting the setting sun. These peaks pinpoint Pitt Lake from a distance as they rise above its southeastern flank. Many people have speculated that Slumach's gold is hidden within the folds of those rocky crags.

Waite's book has three sections: "Lost Mine of Pitt Lake," "B.C.'s Oldest Church," and "Canada's First Train

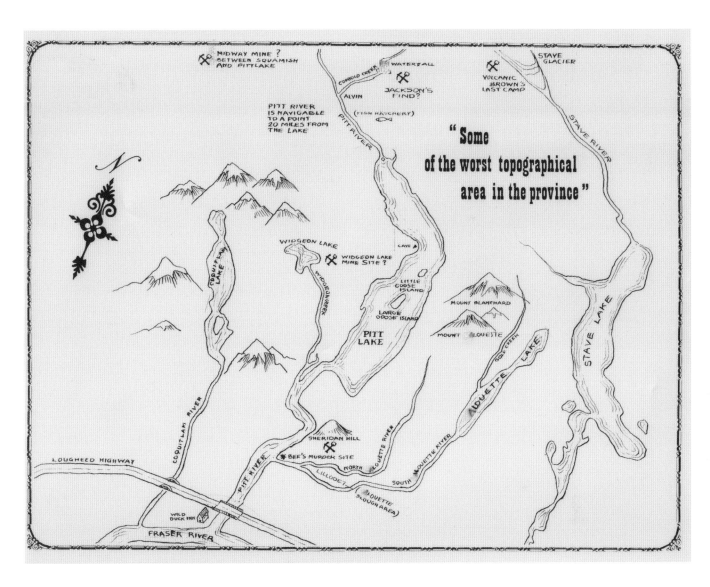

Map H: Original map from In Search of a Legend: Slumach's Gold, *1972*—Our 1972 book contained artist Fred Bosman's rendition of a map highlighting various locations around Pitt Lake where we believed, based on our research, the mine might be found, if it existed. At one point, a Vancouver Public Library employee told us she kept ordering more copies of the book because patrons would read it and, believing the map to be the real thing, return it with the map ripped out. In error, we placed the site of Slumach's murder of Bee in the wrong location in both our 1972 and 2007 editions. This error is corrected in this new edition's "Slumach country" map and storytelling. The error came from incorrect newspaper reporting in 1890. FRED BOSMAN

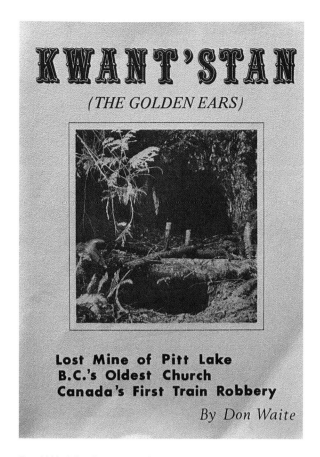

KWANT'STAN

(THE GOLDEN EARS)

**Lost Mine of Pitt Lake
B.C.'s Oldest Church
Canada's First Train Robbery**

By Don Waite

Don Waite's book came out the same summer as ours, which led to our meeting with him and becoming lifelong friends. COURTESY OF DONALD E. WAITE

Robbery." Waite's unique source of information on the lost mine legend was "Aunt Mandy," the daughter of Slumach's catechist Peter Pierre, who was also Slumach's nephew. Her oral history provided insight on Pierre spending the last night with the convicted man prior to his execution. According to Aunt Mandy, they talked of gold.

IN OUR 1972 BOOK, we gave some guiding hints for finding the lost mine and had interpretive illustrations prepared by artist Fred Bosman, who would go on to design that book.

In June of that year, the time had come to put our findings, stories, and theories into print in the fifty-six-page, saddle-stitched, self-published book we thought would put a nice cap on the Slumach tale, given it was what we thought a fairly inclusive work. Western Heritage Supply bought the first 1,300 copies and placed them in racks in drugstores, gas stations, and tourist haunts around the province.

We were not alone in thinking we'd put matters to rest. The *Province* ran a review by Fred Curtin, who noted "the authors have done a credible job in amassing all the fact, fiction, and legend about BC's most famous lost mine." He went on to say, "They have uncovered just about everything there is to know about (Indigenous man) Slumach . . ." Curtin, however, didn't underestimate the aftermath: "It is hardly likely that this little booklet will touch off another gold rush but [*In Search of a Legend: Slumach's Gold*] will stir up a lot of new interest in an old legend that just won't die."

Top According to one report, the gold lies under a mountain that appears to be the shape of a sleeping maiden, her hands on her breasts. FRED BOSMAN

Middle One rumour suggests that when you paddle north past Large Goose Island on Pitt Lake, take a look forty-five degrees to the southeast—toward Haney. On top of the mountains, you can see a man's head (from forehead to Adam's apple). Beneath this mountain is the gold. FRED BOSMAN

Bottom Yet another old rumour suggests that when you hike toward Bridal Veil Falls, look straight across the lake and see the faces of a sleeping man and woman. They appear to be lying down. When you stand so that their noses line up, you are standing on a line along which the mine can be found. FRED BOSMAN

Overleaf ADAM PALMER COLLECTION

Chapter 7

"I'll Let You Know If We Find Anything"

DESPITE OUR PERSONAL EXPECTATIONS that the Antonson/Trainer and Waite books would put the Slumach legend to rest, we were wrong. Instead, these books generated more questions. We learned about new gold seekers and came across maps and details and "what ifs" that intrigued us—as they did the public. Far from quelling interest, we'd helped create insatiable curiosity, enabled by growing media awareness—and a bit of media mischief. All this would fill the following three and a half decades with the discovery of important facts, no small number of rumours, and believable, insightful stories aplenty from (mostly) reliable sources.

In 1973 a new book appeared, *The Golden Mountains: Chronicles of Valley and Coast Mines* by Charles A. Miller. It introduced a character named Harrington whom we'd not heard of, while providing information we've recounted earlier.

FOR THE SPRING 1974 edition of *Beautiful British Columbia Magazine,* Rick wrote a seventeen-page article bolstered with extensive colour photographs taken by Maurice Borrelly of Pitt Lake and possible locations for a lost gold mine he said he didn't believe in. Brian wrote an article for *Canadian Frontier* magazine, which garnered more queries, like, "Did you consider this . . ." or, "But you've overlooked . . .." As we met genuine gold seekers over coffee or drinks, we also heard from a few cranks we confidently ignored. We made friends as we continued in search of the legend, keeping notes and digging deeper as another decade turned, and the 1980s brought more tantalizing accounts.

As but one illustration of the times, a twelve-year-old youngster read 1972's *In Search of a Legend* and was captivated. That began the lifelong quest of Daryl Friesen, who himself would later write a book about the lost gold mine, and would become a television star in a series on explorations for the treasure. And it would be Friesen's search for Clayton Gadsby's claim stake that drew attention to that prospector's name.

As another illustration, we found our book validated ideas others had, instead of dissuading them, and off those adventurers went, some into the mountains, some alongside creeks, others making films or documentaries. Along the way, they encouraged anyone willing to listen to the stories that indeed the lost-gold-mine legend was worth paying attention to and worthy of further investigation, and that it promised new findings to those who were patient. Such forthrightness made more folks want to believe that Slumach actually had gold, and that it was still there, waiting to be found by a brave soul adept at wilderness survival and willing to face down the curse. We came across many, one of whom had an intriguing claim of finding the treasure.

Prospector Stu Brown

One day in the early 1970s, G. Stuart ("Stu") Brown (no relation to Volcanic Brown) found himself in a rugged mountain canyon of fir, hemlock, and cedar. He stared down at the pond water lapping around his boots, stunned at what he saw: gold nuggets the size of walnuts, just like those described in the legendary Jackson letter. Brown reached down and lifted several nuggets out, the weight of them pulling his arm down. He knew in an instant he'd stumbled on the lost gold mine.

Brown was within the boundaries of a provincial park, either Garibaldi or Golden Ears—he was uncertain which, as they intersect in that area. Garibaldi was created in 1927, and Golden Ears was split off in 1967. But he was certain of something else: his academic knowledge reminded him that mining is not allowed within provincial parks, nor is any activity related to the removal of the nuggets he held in his hand, even if they were evidence of a motherlode. So he left the nuggets there and chose a different method for securing the treasure, one befitting his professional status.

Brown was a seemingly reliable source of information, with two bachelor's degrees and a Master of Science degree in Forest Entomology. He described himself as a "forestry service officer" who rose through positions in the British Columbian and Canadian governments. When we in the Slumach world first heard of him, in 1974, his title in full , as an employee of Environment Canada, was Supervisor of the Surveys Section, Plant Protection Division, Forestry Services.

At the time, he professed more than a passing interest in the Slumach story and studied topographical maps and stereoscopic air photos, seeking evidence of locations that might prove fruitful for searches. His role in forestry took him through many wilderness locations, and he always had an eye out for conditions that might promise gold.

In August 1974, Brown wrote to the Director of Parks in BC's Department of Lands, Forests and Water Resources. His correspondence recounted his recent "find" while on vacation, and he sought a "special permit" to legally bring out samples to prove his discovery to authorities.

Thus began a frustrating series of letters and meetings with government bureaucrats; Brown was simply trying to secure permission to do the right thing. Officials politely pointed to regulations that prohibited mining activity within provincial park boundaries; Brown already knew of those. He was not asking to mine within these confines—he just wanted to bring out freestanding nuggets to demonstrate the value lying there. He estimated a worth of half a billion dollars to 20 billion, admittedly a very broad range. His plea was dismissed again. And again. And then again.

A 1978 article in the *Victoria Daily Times* recounted these repeated attempts to get government attention, all to no avail. In the article, authorities expressed skepticism about Brown's claims. They were unwilling to commit to reimburse his expenses, even when he proposed to cover all costs prior to proving the results and only then asking for compensation. Granting permission seemed a risk the provincial government was afraid to make.

Don Waite met Brown in the early 1980s and became aware of his description that the location "is exactly like Jackson described" with minimal differences. Tantalizingly, the pool Brown said he visited was "about twenty feet across, and ankle deep in gold" and the location was "littered with large gold nuggets." In 1986, Waite, Brown, and Vic Loffler of Mission headed into the search area but were thwarted when one of them developed foot blisters from wearing new boots. Undaunted by their forced return, they focused the next day on using a helicopter to get them close to Terrarosa Lake, near Brown's claimed canyon with the pool of gold. Drastic weather had moved in overnight. Though they flew over several ravines, familiar landmarks were not visible through the low clouds, and they were thwarted again. Subsequent frustrating forays encountered more poor weather (or, some would say, a protective curse).

When they met for lunch at a restaurant in 1986, Brown disclosed to Waite a clearer description of the location of the pool he had found. Intrigued and excited,

Waite sketched the details from memory moments later, sitting in his car in the parking lot. That quickly drawn map identifies Brown's approximate location south of Terrarosa Lake, after almost a kilometre of white water. It is a description matching various locales in the area, some accessible, some difficult to approach. The more credible his discussions became, the more important was the map. That is, the more convincing his story became as it evolved, the more likely it seemed this could really be a map leading to gold.

Brown approached the mining giant, Teck Corporation, to enlist their support. A 1987 response suggested a willingness to provide $10,000 to move things forward, but no further records exist to indicate anything happened between the two parties after that date. Brown was now into his seventies and dealing with Parkinson's disease, which made him less willing or able to trek the high country than he once was.

The litany of rejections, disappointments, and dashed endeavours appeared to wind down in 1987. Gold seekers

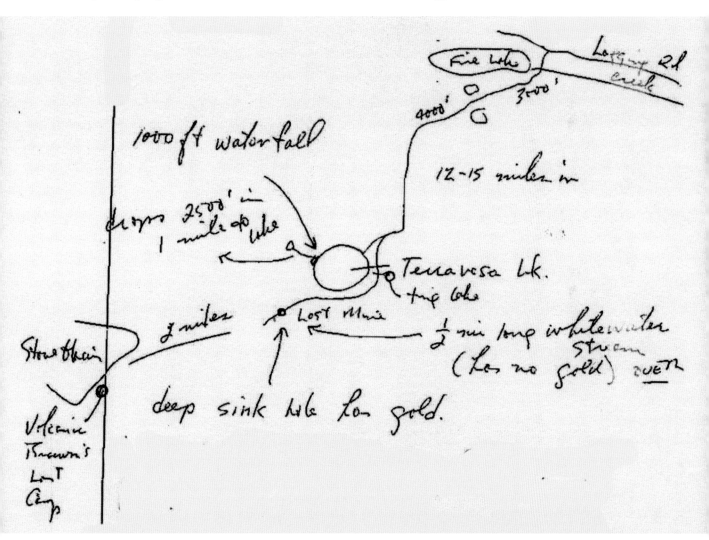

Map I: Stu Brown's reported search area as sketched by Don Waite—After lunch with Stuart Brown, and having heard him describe where he found a glory hole of gold, Don Waite rushed to his car and sketched this map with the description fresh in his mind. COURTESY OF DONALD E. WAITE

Gold seekers cross rushing water at Widgeon Creek in Slumach country. Rough water tumbles down dozens of creeks and rivers in this area. OP MEDIA GROUP

would approach him, and in the stories they told of their meetings, Brown's descriptions seemed sage and believable, sometimes motivating, though on occasion of questionable accuracy.

Brown passed away in September 2002 at the age of eighty-six, frustrated to the end by the intransigence of governments, the vagaries of weather and blisters, and the ravages of age that left him unable to successfully complete his quest for confirmation of his "find." And so, the image of a responsible and professional man, standing ankle-deep in a pool littered with gold nuggets the size of walnuts beckons those who believe in his tales. One wonders why Brown didn't bring out just one of those nuggets as evidence. He might have risked his professionalism if he had, and have possibly committed a crime, but at the same time, could he have provided incontrovertible evidence? One wonders, what value might be attached to that find today? One wonders if this was the Slumach find or the Jackson find, or neither—or both? When it comes to the lost gold mine of Pitt Lake, one is always left wondering.

IN THE SPRING OF 1981, along came publisher Art Downs. As if to kick off another decade of exploration and

escapades, he combined *In Search of a Legend: Slumach's Gold* with Waite's *Kwant'stan* into one book with a colour cover boldly splashing two words: *Slumach's Gold*. Downs, former publisher of the magazine *BC Outdoors* and the founder of Heritage House Publishing, edited it. The amalgamated Heritage House and earlier editions collectively sold over 10,000 copies (in Canada, where 5,000 copies sold is considered to be a bestseller). The book, long out of print, is now a collector's item.

Also in 1983, prominent newspaper journalist Jon Ferry hiked the high country searching for the lost mine. He wrote about it in daily reports for the *Province* newspaper, with the accompaniment of a major television broadcast about an exploratory trek, attracting new audiences to the legend while rekindling the interest of weekend gold seekers of all ages.

Vancouver television station CKVU sent a news crew of three, along with reporter Ferry and a photographer from the *Province*, into the bush. To help them, they took along a guide who was also a dowser.

Both media outlets launched concurrent series of stories in autumn of that year, smack in the middle of the broadcast ratings season. Was it a publicity stunt, or a genuine undertaking? On October 9, the *Province* sported the headline "Gold Fever! Looking for the Lost

Widgeon Lake is a favourite hiking destination for many, but is also a magnet for people seeking Slumach's mine, long rumoured to be in the vicinity. ADAM PALMER COLLECTION

Creek Mine." Reporter Ferry engaged his readers with his telling of Slumach's story and their intrepid team's plan to unearth the gold.

Each morning for a week in the newspaper, Ferry unveiled new details of their search for a stash of gold, mesmerizing readers. Each evening, television reporter Dale Robins tantalized viewers of CKVU TV's *First News* with a visual account in breathtaking narratives of their autumn wanderings up richly forested mountains and down rock-strewn valleys. They ventured to the Widgeon Lake area at the southwest corner of Pitt Lake, long rumoured to be the location of Slumach's lost hoard. Experienced Abbotsford prospector Gary McIsaac guided the team as they searched for minerals, using his dowsing skills in an effort to detect gold. His task was to show the way to the multimillion-dollar find, with television viewers looking over his shoulder in anticipation.

McIsaac once had a vision of Slumach standing in the mine, and it had driven him toward this location. Curse be damned! Two days into the wilderness, the team reported making camp "nestled beside a lake of jade and sheltered by sheer cliffs." McIsaac broke out the tool of his trade, a "dowsing bug" that contained a canister of gold and mercury. It started "to bounce around wildly." The next day's report saw the team suffering "sheer exhaustion." Undaunted, they scaled a "ladder of boulders" to a ridge leading toward Widgeon Peak.

"It's a throat-stopping sight. We are in the land of the gods. In the heavens ahead are the parapets of a celestial castle," Ferry wrote, referring to the surrounding peaks. From their perch, they could see below them a "circle of huge boulders" at the bottom of a valley, where McIsaac believed the mine might be found.

The "Valley of the Rocks," as they dubbed it, proved impossible to reach. McIsaac's dowsing bug was working overtime for the camera crew. A 244-metre (800-foot) cliff with no visible route down was their undoing. Equipment and people were wearing out, and, for their own safety, they backed off their quest, perhaps not wanting to add to the tally of victims falling to the curse that had been tabulated in the *Province* years earlier.

Their accounts cited the "thrills and perils of this dangerous mountain country," and the team vowed to return for a follow-up expedition, as they'd gotten closer to a possible find than most could ever hope to. However, Ferry later said in an interview with Brian that he knew of no team members who went back in search of Slumach's elusive mine, or of any who have died while or after searching for the gold. He summed up the trip by saying, "It was rather magical up there."

The question yet remains: what lies beneath that circle of rocks?

Norm's Tent-Shaped Rock Photo

Throughout the 1980s, revelations of all sorts kept coming our way—sometimes starkly honest, sometimes hesitatingly brief—always enchanting. One such story is this: a Mission resident we'll call Norm (no last name for purposes of anonymity) claimed he and cohorts found the tent-shaped rock—and he had pictures to prove it, but wanted to keep them to himself. At an early meeting of a Mission community group's advisory board they both served on, Norm asked Brian, "You wrote that Slumach book, didn't you?"

When Brian said yes, Norm said that he'd pored over his copy of the book many times and asked if Brian thought there was really gold "up there." Eventually, they focused on the prospect that gold may lay hidden among the peaks northeast of Pitt Lake; Brian told Norm that if there was gold in the story, that's where he thought it would be.

Norm said he and a few others knew a helicopter pilot who flew a prospector into the Stave Glacier area every year. The pilot would pick up the man a couple of weeks later, and believed his passenger's packsack was loaded with gold each time. Norm said the pilot hadn't heard from the prospector for a couple of years and thought he might be dead. Then Norm paused before continuing. "So, if the pilot doesn't hear from the prospector this year, he's going to take *us* in there!"

Brian was impressed. Norm said, "I'll let you know if we find anything."

One evening in 1985, Brian was at Norm's home for a board meeting. The two chatted. While others

This photo is very close to the image gold seeker "Norm" showed Brian in the mid-1980s. It is possibly the same rock. ADAM PALMER COLLECTION

were drinking coffee during a break, Norm motioned Brian to accompany him into a back room, where he handed him a sheaf of photographs, the top one of which startled Brian.

Brian immediately noted the "tent-shaped rock," the image bringing him back directly to the mysterious Jackson's alleged letter, in which Jackson had written, "I buried part of the gold at the foot of a large tent-shaped rock, facing the creek. You can't miss it. There is a mark cut out in it."

Brian asked Norm where he had gotten the shot. Norm grinned and said, "I took it."

The rock in the photo stood in the open, the ground around it covered in moss. In fact, it looked very much like the artist's concept drawing of the site shown in our 1972 book.

Acknowledging that Jackson's alleged gold was likely up Stave Glacier way, Norm looked intently at Brian's face before continuing: "We think it's Slumach's mine."

Brian leafed through the thick sheaf of photos. In some, people were standing near the rock, so it could be estimated at about three metres (ten feet) high. Norm had taken pictures of the site from all angles and of his partners as they stood in the middle of what they believed to be Jackson's site.

"And—did you find gold?" Brian asked him.

Norm smiled and told Brian they had dug through a foot of moss at the base of the rock and found ore, and that it assayed very high in gold.

So there it was: long after we'd first looked into the legend and found the reference to the tent-shaped rock, Brian was holding pictures of one and talking with a man who claimed to have taken gold ore from the site.

Norm died some time later—not a victim of the mine's supposed curse, but from a lifetime of smoking. His knowledge of this mine's location went with him to his grave, protected by those who, along with him, had allegedly found gold-bearing ore somewhere in the high mountains near the Stave Glacier.

Years later, when speaking with Norm's son as this new book was being prepared, it was agreed that his dad should continue to be known as just "Norm" and that

insiders in the search story will catch the reference. Norm's son commented that he knew no more now than he did when his father made his find. He also thought that the Pitt Lake area was probably "the sweet spot," as it was the only place wild and untouched enough to remain hidden "in the middle of encroaching civilization."

Documentarian Sylvio Heufelder

As we entered the 1990s, the Slumach legend finally worked its way onto the international scene in a high-profile way, enchanting European television viewers. Canada is a popular destination for German travellers, and many are attracted to British Columbia. German tourists hear the call of the wilderness like few other foreign visitors, glomming onto all things "outdoors," making them a prime audience for the legend of Slumach's gold.

"The Mystery of Old Slumach" was created at that time as an episode of the German series *Treasure Hunters*, produced and directed by Sylvio Heufelder.

In their preliminary scouting, a representative of the German film crew contacted Don Waite from Munich and asked if he'd be the intermediary between the crew and Katzie Elders in order to set up a meeting between the two parties. Waite agreed to try to make this happen and approached the Elders. First, the Katzie wanted to meet with just Waite, so he chaired a meeting with the Elders, answering their questions and asking some of his own, hoping he might bring about the requested get-together. The Elders came to the consensus that they did not want to be visited by the crew. Waite sensed they objected to non-Indigenous writers and storytellers (and filmmakers) appropriating Indigenous Peoples' history. "They tramp through our cemetery," one Elder said to Waite. "All they want is the story, and we never seem to get anything in return. We just don't want them."

Waite faxed that decision to Germany. "Don't come. They don't want you." But the film crew came anyway. They visited Waite's home and asked him to serve as historian for their project. Waite agreed to a filmed interview. "I requested written assurance from him [Heufelder] that they would not use anything that I had told them, or any footage that they'd shot of me without the express permission of the First Nations." Waite believed it was important to ensure proper stories were recorded and that this would be done only with the approval of Katzie Elders. However, because the crew did not obtain permission from the Katzie, Waite later refused to allow his footage to be used.

Yet Don Waite is a cooperative guy, collegial to a fault, and a willing collaborator—if a touch careless in trusting Heufelder's assistant from Munich, who was named Pongratz. When Pongratz arrived in Maple Ridge to talk, Waite took him to the location in New Westminster (long since modified by time) where Slumach was hanged. Their relationship became cordial.

By this time, Waite had compiled an impressive collection of archival notes on Slumach. He kept everything in a manila envelope. This included his journals from trips to the headwaters of the upper Pitt River and records from a trip into Fire Lake with Stuart Brown. There were also copies of correspondence from gold seekers and long-ago newspaper clippings about the legend. It represented the most comprehensive assembly of research anyone had, much of it irreplaceable. Thus the manila envelope contained a researcher's treasure trove.

Waite agreed to let Pongratz have the folder of material as background for the German film crew's trek. They organized everything in chronological order from the first entry of August 9, 1925, through to October 31, 1987. They numbered the pages, the last being 223. Two new photocopied binders were made by Waite at a photocopy shop: one for loaning to the filmmaker on the promise it would be returned, and a second binder for himself. The original material in the manila envelope was mistakenly left behind at the copy shop.

Around the same time, the German production crew contacted Archie Miller, the former curator at the Irving House Historical Centre (now the New Westminster Museum and Archives). As one of the more knowledgeable people about local history, Archie provided the film crew with cautions as well as insights, hard truths, and rumoured half-truths.

Archie Miller appears in the resulting television show delivering this emboldening line about the gold creek, "There are people who say they've found it." The film crew departs civilization, heads to Pitt Lake, and sets about searching for the motherlode with a storyline tailored to eager German television viewers.

As their episode unfolds, a local guide leads them up Pitt Lake in canoes. Eventually, they head out on foot into the lush woodlands surrounding the lake, a forbidding and dangerous step. They have fine August weather, and follow established trails. Around bends they discover crumbling miners' shacks, prod at quartz veins, dip into hot springs, and contemplate creeks rich in spawning fish.

Heufelder's crew seek what might have been Volcanic Brown's route but, several days in, they realize Brown's find was likely higher up the mountain than where they'd been able to reach. Belatedly, they decide to take a helicopter into mountain territory above 1,830 metres (6,000 feet). Despite a thorough reconnaissance of this high country, they find no trace of Brown's camp. (With almost 115 years having passed before the German crew's visit, it's not surprising that it would be gone.) Their helicopter search for Jackson's valley bearing a stream with no beginning or end and a tent-shaped rock also proves futile but is visually gratifying for the cameras, as the landscape is extraordinary.

Having been rebuffed by Don Waite, the filmmakers tracked down British Columbia historian and politician Bill Barlee. Waite explains, "Barlee knew about the Jackson letter, and he blew it up to make it look like, yeah, he found gold up there." We asked Waite if he thought Barlee believed Slumach ever had gold. Waite replied that he didn't think so.

The interview with Barlee lends credibility to the show. On German television, Barlee talks of Jackson's letter. "The original letter was date-stamped from a government office . . . I examined it very closely . . . it uses certain phrases only used in the 1880s and 1890s." He further notes, "It's not like other letters . . . this is a genuine letter . . . and the terminology makes it genuine and the date stamp makes it more genuine." For a

Icefields in Slumach Country. ADAM PALMER COLLECTION

historian of Barlee's stature to judge the letter that way adds tremendous weight for any researcher delving into the Slumach jungle of myths and truths. Barlee further claims, "There's no doubt Slumach had something to do with it." For German viewers, that would be like American viewers hearing from CNN's Anderson Cooper that the lost mine story is true.

Miller's wrap-up on the show leaves no doubt about how the filmmaker wants the viewer to feel: "I think it exists . . . we just haven't found it yet." The gold mine remains lost.

And that's not all that became lost. Waite never heard back about the archive binder he'd loaned to Heufelder's assistant. Waite believed it had been taken to Munich after the filming. His overtures for its return were ignored.

And in what sounds like a calamity of errors, the only other copy in existence (given that he'd left the original at the photocopy shop in error) was Waite's personal photocopy of the precious, irreplaceable research. It disappeared

around the same time, due to an unauthorized borrowing. Years of effort were lost for Waite and other researchers who had come to see him as the primary source for details, dates, and critiques. What we will call the "Missing Waite Binder" appeared at the time to be as lost as Slumach's gold.

Suspicious Jack Mould

Elizabeth Hawkins's 1993 book title, *Jack Mould and the Curse of Gold: The Slumach Legend Lives On*, leaps from the book's cover festooned with skulls, a hangman's noose, and glittering chunks of raw gold. She milks the hype in her blurb: "He lives on the edge—of life and of the mine." And between the covers lies a romp—a rollicking tale about a questionable rogue's lifelong quest for Slumach's gold.

Reading the book, one soon wonders if the gold Jack Mould has sought is at all connected with Slumach, for Mould focused his search at Bute Inlet, over 200 kilometres (120 miles) to the northwest of Pitt Lake. That said,

Slumach's story weaves in and out of Mould's. Hawkins calls him "larger than life." Throughout years filled with prison terms, toiling in logging camps, unlucky romances, families torn apart, episodes of sabotage, an attempted suicide, and a constant feeling of "What could possibly happen next?" Mould's unwavering focus was to find the gold guarded by Slumach's supposed curse.

The Spanish were very likely the first Europeans to explore British Columbia's coast, and Mould and his father Charlie found evidence of their workings in the mountains at the head of Bute Inlet. Did the Spaniards take gold from this part of the mainland? Did they leave any behind? Have others—perhaps Slumach—found it since?

This is the meat of Mould's Slumach search. His father searched the inlet in vain for gold, but found plenty of evidence that others had been there before him. An old, carved cedar door, bearing images of Spanish soldiers, stood as mute evidence of their presence here. Had Spaniards carved the door? Was it perhaps the Coast Salish People who had encountered them as they moved along the fjords, nudging their boats in near shore, slipping into the wooded hillsides in search of any treasures the land might have to offer? Whatever its origin, the door was there, and Mould saw it.

Then there was the iron bucket and the pulley block-and-tackle rig. Other evidence spoke volumes to the young Mould as he learned at his father's side to thirst for this elusive shiny metal and the promise of incredible fortune.

What would any story of Slumach's gold be without its own tent-shaped rock? Jackson's original description of his rock has fuelled imaginations for well over a century, and Mould's story locates it high in the snows of the Bute Inlet area. It looks down over the inlet from its perch, or rather, it did: a photo taken in the 1990s shows Jack Mould with the rock at his home. The object in the photo looks more like a thin climber's cairn than a rock shaped like a tent. It's tall and slim, and sits atop a collection of other roughly hewn rocks of similar shape. The actual rock is perhaps one metre (three feet) high at maximum and doesn't convey the image of a tent, but it's Jack Mould's version, and it fits with his story.

Although he didn't want to believe in Slumach's curse, Mould's life had taken many untoward turns, and his attempts to find the hidden trove had been defeated by disaster, weather, and mishaps of his own or others' making. He did admit to video producer Michael Collier in the 1990s, "definitely I stronger and stronger believe [sic] there had to be a curse."

And there was more to come in Jack Mould's story.

Mysterious Donna

Another gold seeker crept into our research in the middle of the 1990s in stories we found in a newspaper report. Donna did not want her surname disclosed by the reporter. Her tale led us to a simple question with a complex answer: Might someone find Slumach's mine, only to realize the gold is already gone? Donna, an Alberta farmer, claimed that was exactly what happened to her in 1994.

Readers of the October 10, 1995, edition of the *Vancouver Sun* enjoyed a lengthy article by reporter Mark Hume that recounted the Slumach mine story, reminding the knowledgeable and luring the novice.

In it, Hume also told of how Donna and her husband studied aerial photographs of the Pitt Lake region, using Jackson's letter as a guide. She told Hume, "We were able to determine there was only one place it could be. I guess you might call it a detective job." Clues from Jackson's 1901 letter, including a description of the hidden valley, the white colour of the creek's water, no visible entrance or exit to the creek, and the tent-shaped rock, all pointed Donna to one valley north, beyond the head of Pitt Lake.

Even determining a spot within Garibaldi Park meant winnowing down 1,950 square kilometres (over 750 square miles) of speculation. Garibaldi Park has many trails and is full of popular hiking routes, many arduous. But Donna and her husband were heading where no one else would go, or so they thought. Featuring rugged land beneath peaks that tower and intimidate, their route was not for the faint of heart.

Having identified their foremost hunch, they attempted to reach the location overland on foot. That first backpacking trip into the wild country proved too much for the couple. Named for Mount Garibaldi (itself named after Italian revolutionary Giuseppe Garibaldi), the park is a challenge to traverse. Indigenous Peoples used the disparaging name Nch'kay ("Grimy One") because of a nearby river's gloomy waters. The foreboding name was apparently overlooked by the would-be gold seekers.

The provincial park had been established seventy-five years before Donna and her husband first set foot on a path within it. As a result, any mining in it would be illegal, however honourable one's intentions. Despite such knowledge being common, the couple returned to the park a year after their misadventure, chartering a helicopter to deliver them to their search area.

Sure enough, they found the tent-shaped rock and the creek running with white water, with no visible entrance or exit to the valley; this was what they believed to be the location of Slumach's and Jackson's hoard.

What they found next brought their search to a disappointing halt: the site was riddled with deep pits and tailings, the obvious leave-behinds of a mining operation, albeit small. Someone had been in to the site with heavy machinery, likely brought in by helicopter. Whoever had been there had dug the pit, left the tailings where they fell, and departed. If there ever *was* gold in this hidden valley, there was none left for Donna.

Contacted nearly thirty years after his article first appeared, journalist Mark Hume said, "I doubt Donna's failure to find the gold will dampen the enthusiasm of other treasure hunters. We don't know who was there, or what they found, or if Donna's sleuthing had taken her to the right place."

Hume offered an irrefutable insight: "I think until someone steps forward and provides proof they found Slumach's gold, there will always be those who believe a hoard is still out there somewhere, just waiting to be rediscovered. And so the legend lives on."

Newspaperman Rikk Taylor

In the early 2000s, long-retired *Columbian* newspaper publisher Rikk Taylor, whom we hadn't seen for nearly two decades, telephoned to arrange a get-together, as he had some startling news. A week after his call, on a fine autumn day with colours changing everywhere, Rick Antonson, now middle-aged, and the now-elderly Rikk Taylor settled into a booth at The Keg restaurant in Burnaby, and a scene unfolded quite unexpectedly.

Struggling with the degenerative aftermath of a stroke, Taylor spoke in a halting voice. He told Rick that he'd kept an eye on the Slumach story after he had left the newspaper business. Then, he made a remarkable gesture: he held up a large Ziploc bag that contained several small samples of quartz, and a rock the size of a man's fist. As he pushed the parcel across the table toward Rick, he paused to open it and reach inside with a jittery hand. He retrieved two dusty sheets of paper that had been tossed around with the rocks. "It's an assay report," he said, shaking dirt off the pages.

Rick was puzzled.

"I want you to have all this," Taylor said. "The rocks contain a lot of gold." Then Taylor began to tell his story in earnest.

"They've found Slumach's lost mine . . ."

Rick was awed by the bag of quartz, the glinting dust, and the validating assay report.

Taylor grinned. "See for yourself," he said, as much a dare as a direction.

"Where?" replied Rick. "When?"

"I'll get to that," he said, "because it's not where you think it is. It's not where people have been looking."

Rick tested the heft of the rock in his hand. "Could this be from Stave Glacier? That's where Volcanic Brown spent his last trip, and he found gold."

Taylor smirked. "Brown was wrong. Miles wrong. He was mountains away from where Slumach found gold."

"Brown *had gold*," said Rick. After all, reports said eleven ounces of gold had been found in a glass jar in his last camp.

"Some nuggets," clarified Taylor. "He just had some nuggets."

True. Brown could have had gold along with him from elsewhere.

"Brown was high up on the Stave Glacier," said Taylor,

who then pointed at the gold on the lunch table, "Certainly not where this came from."

Rick asked, "Where'd you find this?"

"First off, I didn't find it. Oh, I did chisel out these rocks, and kept some for myself. But I accomplished that climbing around a finished mine site. They didn't leave much. It was cleaned out pretty good. Gold makes people thorough," he said. "Crazy, but thorough."

The two clinked glasses in a toast: "To Slumach."

"Who are 'they' who found the mine?" asked Rick.

Taylor hesitated a few moments. "I got a phone call."

Oh, how many of our own tips or stories had begun that same way. "Late at night?" Rick asked with a laugh.

"Yes. Late at night," said Taylor.

Taylor began his story. "A fellow I know dabbled in mining all his life. We've grown old together, periodically swapping Slumach tales and guesses. He never gave up looking. Never stopped believing. He got a lead from two miners who'd found a vein—a profitable vein. That was several years ago. Then they went quiet on us."

The restaurant was noisy, so Taylor leaned across the table as Rick hunched over to hear his whisper.

"Harrison Lake," he said.

"Harrison?"

Taylor nodded repeatedly as Rick whispered the list of likelier sites. "Not Corbold Creek? Not Stave Glacier? Not Pitt Lake?"

"Harrison Lake," Taylor affirmed.

It turned out that when Taylor's miner friend next heard from the two prospectors, they told him they'd cleared their find of gold-bearing rock. They had crushed and carted away what they wanted and then processed it into flat bars of gold. They'd left the area as one might expect: untidy and untended, since it no longer held value for them. So they told Taylor's old miner friend where it was. The two of them ventured out one weekend in a four-by-four to the east side of Harrison Lake, to a point on a logging road where, clued by a landmark, they tried to get off the road and into the mine site. After three aborted attempts, their scratched vehicle forced its way through brush, veered around a large tree and onto a barely passable trail that showed old tire ruts.

"It was there all right," Taylor continued. "Dug, carved . . . indications of some blasting, a foot of deep and notable tire tracks from a grinder left rusting under a tree—everything else was washed by rains, smoothed by a few winters' snows."

Rick was in awe: gold in a Ziploc bag, a dated assay report, and a man known for his integrity—all at the same table.

"We chipped away all weekend, certain we were in Slumach's footsteps," Taylor said. "Jackson never found this, nor did Tiny Allen. Volcanic Brown may have trekked near there on his way to the Pitt, but if he'd found traces, he'd have pitched his tent, prospected a while, and lived a wealthy life."

That prompted the next question: "How much?"

"Millions," Taylor replied. "The gold mine was worth millions."

"You should go there," Taylor said after a pause. He was visibly tiring from his post-stroke weakness and the animated conversation. "Camp overnight at the mine," he said. "If nothing else, you'll feel the presence of Slumach's ghost. We did."

Before he got up from the table to leave, Taylor did something both Slumach and Jackson would have admired. He picked up a napkin and set it between them. When he removed a pen from his pocket, Rick knew a special moment was about to unfold. Then Taylor said, "Let me draw you a map."

After this memorable meeting, the two old friends would never see one another again. Taylor died in 2003.

He would have been dismayed to have learned years later that Rick misplaced the plastic satchel containing Taylor's proof of gold, either in the process of a home move, the donation of boxes of books, or perhaps—most hopefully—was it in one of the containers of Slumach archive materials acquired by the Simon Fraser University library?

Overleaf Perhaps Slumach's legendary gold remains hidden in a cave such as this? ADAM PALMER COLLECTION

Chapter 8

An Aviator Flies into Pitt Lake Looking for Gold

FROM 1998 TO 2006, bush pilot John Lovelace hosted the popular TV series *Wings Over Canada*. The series showcased stories about Canada's gold-mining towns, deserted places, and wilderness areas. Intrigued by the Slumach legend, Lovelace envisioned an episode that would tantalize viewers by combining stunning images of British Columbian mountains and lakes with a compelling search for gold.

"You can't lose when you're dealing with a gold story," he recalls. "A cache of gold stirs the imagination for everybody."

The producers agreed, and in 2002, Lovelace, accompanied by mining engineer Tom Morrison and a production crew, piloted his Cessna 185 Amphibian into the vast wilderness around Pitt Lake. Flying the bush plane over log booms beside mist-shrouded mountains, the crew landed at the head of Pitt Lake, where the upper Pitt River flows into it. They were determined to at least find some fun behind the Slumach legend, if not gold.

"There's no question that the man existed historically and that he found gold. None at all. How much is unknown," he says.

In the resulting documentary, "Lost Gold Mine of Pitt Lake," Lovelace tells viewers he is perplexed that no one has discovered the lost treasure, since the area it's supposed to be in is only twenty-five kilometres (fifteen miles) by air from Vancouver.

"There are two storylines. The first is that he had a cache and that he found all this gold and hid it. And the second story is: where did he get it? And that's the angle we took. We weren't looking for his cache, but we were exploring the streams and valleys to find out what kind of mining he would have encountered," says Lovelace.

Morrison serves as their guide and says that here they'll find copper, nickel, and maybe gold. But he sets the crew on alert right from the start when he advises, "Gold will make a fool of you, every time." Morrison is familiar with the haphazard thinking that leads people astray in search of gold. "In these mountains, that could get you killed," he says. "You can take at face value that gold exists around here," he adds, and that, given the extent of mining in the 1880s, most of the creeks in this area would have been searched. "That some gold made it through here is history," he says, and he believes that persistent rumours of it continuing to be found suggest that ". . . the stuff has to come from somewhere."

The show goes on to describe Slumach as a "wily miner . . . adept at hiding his mine." One old-timer claims that Jackson's gold looked like it came from bedrock, and while there *is* lots of bedrock about, it is covered by overgrowth and protected by thick bushes that block out sunlight, causing heavy moss growth that reduces visibility. And, at best, such places are often located in streams that are "here one year, and gone the next."

The camera pans around to reveal the landscape. From beautiful shots of huge timbers fallen over creeks and gushing waterfalls cascading into rocky caverns, one gets the impression that these creek beds are filled with water much of the year and certainly too dangerous to approach. Rushing streams twist back on themselves, and some of these waterways act like "nature's sluice" according to the narrator. Gold panners work hard to separate gold from gravel, often running water over the rocks, yet here it happens naturally as the rough waters twirl and grind the stones.

This forcefulness calms eventually, opening up new areas for prospectors to kneel and ply their trade. Indeed, because "all the good ground has been panned over and panned over," it is *only* when rough water carves new routes for creeks and opens up new gravel beds that fresh opportunities arise. That must happen with some regularity, we must surmise, since we're told this is where "prospectors come in all the time."

Because the region is accessible only by boat or seaplane, the adventurers hike where there are no roads. Both sides of the upper Pitt River once had homesteaders, but they gave up long ago. Now there are only ruins and overgrown old logging roads, evidence of broken dreams.

The film crew does find one local resident, however: a fisherman living in a cabin, who confidently claims that Jackson "climbed up the highest point" in this area and that it was from there that he spotted gold in a stream below. But, he says, "streams disappear," referring to the constant changes in the landscape caused by fluctuating weather conditions and shifting water levels, changes that have made following Jackson's lead such a challenge to would-be gold seekers. Lovelace, Morrison, and the film crew eventually come upon the Geraks, who built and own the Pitt River Lodge. They set out together to find a particular creek in what Danny Gerak calls "the hidden valley."

On the way there, the excitement is palpable when the pilot and his crew see a stream roiling through bedrock and just out of reach. They speculate that this is exactly the type of difficult place where Slumach might

have spotted his gold: a narrow passageway would have required a small, thin person to be lowered down to pan for the gold, retrieve it, and be pulled back up—all grist for a legend about a man who killed his female helpers in order to keep the source of his gold a secret.

Lovelace and Morrison, clearly excited, follow Danny to this seldom-seen creek, one that Danny says has little exposed bedrock and so much overgrowth it helps to "keep the place secret." He says this is the "one creek that shows gold," but that all the other gold seekers who come looking here for Slumach's gold miss it because the water is usually too high.

At the end of his first episode on Slumach, Lovelace is shown relaxing alone on a riverbank. Looking out over the water, he asks no one in particular, "Is there gold in the Pitt River Valley?" He pauses for just a moment before answering his own question. "You bet there is—beyond your wildest dreams."

"The Lost Mine of Pitt Lake" was one of 172 *Wings Over Canada* shows, and one of the most popular. "After the show aired, we could have run people in there every weekend. The phone rang off the hook," says Lovelace. The DVD of the show sold well and is still available at wingsovercanada.ca.

Although Lovelace planned a return trip with equipment to film under water, the years passed and it never happened. He is now retired after forty years of flying commercially. But there's a spark in his voice when he talks about the legend.

In a 2023 interview, Lovelace mused about how he would approach the story today. Climate change, he says, has affected the natural sloughs that exist in the area. Glaciers are receding and the water table is changing, two factors that would change his view on where to search. He adds, "It's a story that will never have an ending. I think it may have been found. There could have been caches that have been hidden."

After all these years, this pilot–adventurer still believes there's gold to be found in Slumach country.

WHEN OUR SIGNIFICANTLY REVISED book *Slumach's Gold* was published in 2007, it included what can now be seen as only preliminary versions of what we've just retold here in fully refreshed and expanded content. Obviously, any sense we authors had of being done with the Slumach legend in 2007 was premature, once again. That book was greeted with considerable media coverage, launching an onslaught of yet more gold-seeking endeavours that would be continually brought to our attention in the ensuing years, always challenging our assumptions, providing new facts, testing our theories, and revising our storytelling for the better.

After all our years of research, we still enjoy sharing one of the soundest renditions of the Lost Mine of Pitt Lake mystery—a classic telling under the direction of filmmaker Michael Collier, evocatively titled: *Curse of the Lost Gold Mine.*

Upper Pitt River joins the lake in a broad delta, while fabled Corbold Creek joins the Pitt from the east, near Alvin, about eight kilometres (five miles) north of the lakehead. Gold seekers often take this route into the high country, where they believe Jackson and Volcanic Brown found their fortunes. COURTESY OF DONALD E. WAITE

Overleaf The rugged terrain of the mountains around Pitt Lake would have been challenging for even experienced gold seekers to navigate. ADAM PALMER COLLECTION

Chapter 9

Curse of the Lost Gold Mine

IF YOU HAD TO choose one show to immerse yourself in the lore and legend of the lost mine of Pitt Lake, it could be with this television production. Brew steaming cups of tea to keep you warm in the snowstorm scenes, have pen and paper handy for jotting down memorable lines, and snuggle up in a comfy chair to relax with the storyteller, the "old prospector," played wonderfully by Donnelly Rhodes. The Slumach tale is an alloy of truths and wishful thinking. A signature telling, with a wonderful juxtaposition of fact and fancy, is this 1994 docudrama *Curse of the Lost Gold Mine*.

Michael Collier is the film crew's expedition leader. Collier remembers, "As a kid, living on Pitt River Road in Coquitlam during the 1950s, our family bought produce from an old farmer, and it was he who told my parents about Slumach and the lost gold mine. I stood nearby, absolutely enthralled—a kid no higher than the farmer's tabletop." As an adult, he researched Pitt Lake's prospects for gold for fifteen years.

That created a curiosity and a motivation that would never leave him. He devoured our *In Search of a Legend: Slumach's Gold* and Don Waite's *Kwant'stan* in the early 1970s. Hooked again, he began his own research. He built a cabin on Pitt Lake, spending family vacations there and exploring the area. "I always kept an eye out for the tent-shaped rock," he says. Over the years, Collier canoed many miles along the rugged shoreline of Pitt Lake, and refers to it as wild and unforgiving. Yet discovery of a site eluded him. Having climbed many of the region's mountain peaks, he says that the lost gold mine "could be right in front of you, but you'd never know it."

In the 1970s, the young Collier began a documentary about the lost mine, and filmed his own first expedition into the area. "We were young and inexperienced both as gold seekers and as business people. I wasn't able to raise the financing necessary to complete that Slumach project." At that time—and this serves history well—he filmed an interview with Aunt Mandy, preserving important parts of the Slumach story she'd first disclosed to Don Waite. He kept the rights to this footage for use in the documentary he would eventually make.

Does he believe Slumach had gold? "I'm skeptical," he says. Then he smiles and recalls, "But Aunt Mandy said Slumach had gold, and that couldn't help but fan the flames."

By the 1990s, Collier was an established filmmaker with international awards. He secured funding for his long-dreamed-of film based on the legend of the Pitt Lake mine. This allowed him to devote himself full time to his research, which included many days spent at newspaper archives, museums, and libraries around British Columbia. He sought out old-timers in addition to contemporary gold seekers.

Gold seekers traverse one of the many snowfields and glaciers blanketing the area and possibly concealing Volcanic Brown's last camp.
MICHAEL COLLIER COLLECTION

His near-two-week expedition into the area in 1994 is featured in his filmed retelling of the legend. This thoroughness extends to how the production crew set up the film's storyline. Early on in the film, the investigation team is shown in the New Westminster Public Library, going over newspaper accounts and assorted documents and topographical maps. They describe their approach: they will hike into a specific area and try to locate Volcanic Brown's last camp. Their premise? If gold was found in the camp and Brown had indeed found a motherlode, then somewhere within half a day's walk should be evidence of a mine or workings.

The thrills in Collier's movie do more to encourage future gold seekers than to dissuade, though the dangers of gold seeking are apparent throughout. The film weaves two narrative threads: one from a distant past full of myth and legend, as told by veteran Hollywood actor Donnelly Rhodes, the other chronicling the present-day expedition, led by Collier, into the rugged Pitt Lake mountains. Historical footage and contemporary interviews round out the characterizations.

Rhodes plays an irascible, pipe-smoking pioneer at home in his log cabin, seated in front of a river-rock fireplace. As the logs flame, he looks to the viewer and promises, "I'm going to tell you a story . . . only thing I will ask of you: don't ask me to say it's true. You know how stories go . . . "

Rhodes's character puffs thoughtfully on his briar pipe and winks mischievously. Then the re-enactment of Slumach's murder of Louis Bee begins—on the sepia-toned film of the early days of cinematography. The film's soundtrack features the chanting of Indigenous Peoples.

Slumach is depicted as a white-haired elderly man. All reliable information suggests he was around eighty years old when he came to his sad end, and the actor in the film matches that image. (As a note about the veracity of Collier's research, this portrayal of Slumach is as close to accurate as any recreation in art, sketch, or description has likely come—the actor has the bearing that a Katzie man of his reported age and activities could well have had. It is a refreshing, believable glimpse of the man, unadorned with glamour. The role of Slumach was played by Squamish actor Norman Natrall, who passed away in 2014.)

In the film's action, Slumach encounters Bee, who is seen getting out of a canoe. Slumach is quick to murder him, though in later replays of the scene, as details evolve, other versions of the Slumach–Bee encounter are also re-enacted, providing a sense of how word-of-mouth in the day distorted the truth, even before magazines played loose with it half a century later. Bee's threatening and Slumach's hiding are portrayed believably in a good balance to other versions saying a blunt, forthright murder happened. Eventually, Bee is seen as a provocateur carrying a "one-bit axe" and yelling threats at Slumach.

Rhodes as the old prospector, sporting a scruffy beard and peering over the top of his glasses, leans back in his chair before goading the viewer: "So, if you're thinking of taking off half-cocked into Slumach country, there's something you should know." He then talks about the curse, building on the legend. In gravelly tones, he tells about the alleged murders of various victims (three white women, five Indigenous women), focusing particularly on Molly Tynan, who he says was a waitress at the Sasquatch Cafe.

He goes on to talk about the disappearance of other ne'er-do-wells who followed Slumach in hopes of stealing his gold. They faced "deadly hardships," and always got lost when Slumach disappeared "as if he dropped through a tear in the universe."

As Rhodes tends the crackling fire to help dry his wool socks hanging in the background, he talks of "expedition after expedition." The story is soon following Collier's three adventurers in modern times, one of whom is a reliable mountain guide. Their eleven-day trek, starting

Veteran actor Donnelly Rhodes plays the old prospector in Michael Collier's 1994 docudrama *Curse of the Lost Gold Mine*.
MICHAEL COLLIER COLLECTION

with a helicopter drop-off, follows, after a fashion, the last known route of Volcanic Brown. It also replicates a better-documented routing of the search party sent to find Brown. As they venture into menacingly foggy surroundings, Rhodes's voice warns the viewer, "There's still danger in Slumach country."

The hikers spend much of their seventy-kilometre (forty-five-mile) treasure hunt hypothesizing about "ol' Slumach." They flash newspaper headlines from the *Province* showing lost-mine stories from 1906, 1910, 1939, 1951, and on to 1983 and 1989, each either claiming more victims of the curse or reporting on daring searches.

The sharing of fresh insights is left mostly to the old prospector, authentically portrayed by Rhodes in his long-sleeved shirt, vest, and loose tie, and with a tendency to peer across the top of a kerosene lantern when he's got a point to make, like this one after Slumach was charged with murder: "No witnesses for defence were called," he says of the trial. And "Slumach was never asked to tell his side of the story." He says Slumach even "wept a bit" as his trial progressed, though no reporting confirms this.

Noting emphatically that "gold fever was an epidemic at the turn of the century," the prospector offers his take on the motivation behind all the searches for Slumach's lost mine: "It's greed [that] describes the never-ending tale of human tragedy, natural-born greed. Well, that's as good as a curse any old day of the week."

In the mix of recreated scenes, modern searchers, and the prospector's storytelling of this legend of Slumach, the facts remain elusive. Over the decades, since the hanging of Slumach in 1891, the rumours and fabricated elements of the story live on to this day, changing with each telling of the story. Some questionable and demonstrably false events include:

- The report that on the day of Slumach's hanging, a woman appeared with a canoe full of gold to pay for Slumach's release;
- The suggestion that Justice Drake, who sentenced Slumach to hang, offered to commute

Members of Michael Collier's team take five during their quest for gold. MICHAEL COLLIER COLLECTION

his sentence to life imprisonment if he divulged the source of his gold;

- The claim that Jackson killed a companion, which appears nowhere else;
- The reference to *John* Jackson. Jackson's alleged letter was, in fact, signed "W. Jackson." (This error in Jackson's first name could perhaps be attributed to our 1972 book *In Search of a Legend: Slumach's Gold*, wherein we also used the same incorrect first name).

Surprisingly, the docudrama tells of Slumach passing his secret on to a son, who reportedly took a helper along to search for his father's mine. Since the film claims that only the helper returned, it seems to suggest Slumach's "own son" was the first victim of the curse.

Intertwined with the hikers' mist-shrouded climb through the difficult terrain is the story of how Volcanic Brown, on one journey into Stave Glacier, sensed he was being followed and then turned back to find his stalker dead, having fallen over a cliff. Here we find another conflicting story: the version that tells of Volcanic turning back and finding an injured man on the trail is well known, but we were unaware of this version, which speaks of yet another hapless victim of the curse.

Partway across the mountains, the film's adventurers find the remains of a campsite at an elevation of 1,830 metres (6,000 feet) and set about determining if it might have been Brown's. Collier remembers that as they dug below the moss, they found charred wood from a long-ago campfire, "left as though a marker." This is all above the tree line, and overlooking the spectacular Stave Glacier.

And, partially hidden under the lip of a large boulder, they find a crucible that they estimate must have been there for nearly eighty years. Mining experts confirmed that experienced prospectors used such crucibles around Brown's time and later also confirmed this particular metal canister of a suitable age. Collier says, "Only sophisticated prospectors of those days would have carried one of these. They'd use it to grind at the quartz to loosen the mix of gold and start the separation process." It could not be confirmed as Brown's, but it was a "very, very old indicator" that at least one serious gold prospector camped at the head of Stave Glacier around that period. If it wasn't Brown, Collier asks, "Who else?"

The members of Collier's expedition are well equipped, professionally guided, and comforted by having radio contact with the outside world. Even so, when they move on from what they believe is Brown's last camp farther into the Stave Glacier area, they become trapped in a sudden snowstorm. Wind gusts nearly rip their tents from their grounding pegs, and they are stranded on the mountainside for three days. It was as though Slumach's curse, long blamed for nasty winds as a protective measure of the mine's location, was about to end their quest in disaster. Collier remembers, "The whole tent was trying to be airborne. We were lying inside it, just trying to hold it down. Death was very near."

At the end of the film, Rhodes's character comes into view again, resting near the warmth of a cedar fire in his log cabin. He offers a final warning to those who would

Gold seekers hunker down for the night in glacier country. Traversing glaciers and snowpacks is dangerous business, and searchers must be prepared for winter conditions at all times. MICHAEL COLLIER COLLECTION

be "lacing up your boots, picking up a shovel and a map, and heading for these hills." He cautions, "They say that Slumach guards the entrance to his mine to this very day."

In 2024, Michael Collier offered this summary:

There is no proof that Slumach ever found any gold. But he was a real person and was hung for a killing that may have been self-defence. There was no mention of gold at his trial or in the newspapers of the day. Yet years later, rumours circulated in the press and the seed was sown for the legend as we know it today. Each writing of the story has often been embellished to entertain the public and to sell newspapers, magazines, or books. As people took the legend for fact, they began to die in the wilderness seeking this elusive gold treasure. When the renowned Canadian prospector Volcanic Brown did find gold in the

Pitt Lake mountains, he unfortunately disappeared along with his knowledge of its secret location. My advice to any present-day prospector would be to ignore most of the legend and try to follow the route of the rescue party that found Volcanic Brown's camp.

Curse of the Lost Gold Mine was broadcast Canada-wide on the Canwest Global Network. Winning silver awards at both the New York Film Festival and the Worldfest Charleston International Film Festival, it brought the Slumach story increased international attention. Collier told us he continues to get requests for copies of the production from across North America and Europe: "Whether these are from armchair enthusiasts for Slumach's legend or eventual gold seekers who may one day find something remains to be seen!" The video is available today on YouTube.

Collier's gold seekers set up camp in glacier country. MICHAEL COLLIER COLLECTION

Overleaf On the precipice. ADAM PALMER COLLECTION

Chapter 10

Search for the Truth?

THE TITLE OF THIS chapter is a conundrum: after learning all the available facts by autumn 2007 and still proceeding in their Slumach expeditions, were gold seekers really interested in the truth? The year became yet another milestone for quests—ours and those of others—in search of a legend.

Many among those still searching had helped establish truths around the legend's origin story. However, most of those now pursuing the legend were actively looking for gold, some ignoring evidence that suggests there's no gold to be found. That quandary would weave throughout our conversations with gold seekers and researchers, believers and non-believers.

Only one thing cast a pall over our research for the book, and that was the missing Waite binder, as neither of the absconded copies—the one loaned to the German research assistant or one that Don loaned to another person later—had reappeared. The contents would have sparked debates and ideas and new places to search for the lost gold. All that meant missed opportunities for us to have chronicled.

Slumach's Gold: In Search of a Legend (note the main title and subtitle were transposed) included all the information known on the subject up to that moment. The book spent twenty-three weeks on the *Vancouver Sun*'s BC Bestsellers List between 2007 and 2008. Its popularity sparked fresh interest in the legend by believers in the curse, hordes of eager prospectors, a rash of reported finds, deeper research, more facts uncovered, and more disputed memories.

Slumach's Gold was published around the same time as a feature in the *Province* encouraged both those with gold fever and those who were skeptics. A new constant emerged: often, as new research disproved old myths, so, too, did new theories hint there actually could be (or may have been) gold in "them thar hills." A series of coincidences ensued in a short period of time.

In a happy coincidence with our book's September 2007 release, the *Province* reporter David Spaner phoned Rick and asked, "Is there anything you can tell me that's new information about the lost gold mine at Pitt Lake?" The newspaper ran an entire feature in its *Unwind Sunday Magazine* on things to do with the family during the upcoming Labour Day long weekend. The newspaper created a map and a fresh frenzy of interest when showing likely locations for the gold in a five-page feature titled "Slumach's Gold; The Search for the Truth."

Then, Jack Mould disappeared the very week our book was published.

Mould was dead. But he was very much alive when our account about his search was published just days before. He likely never read it. The following report on slumach.blogspot.com appears under the headline "Jack Mould Missing?"

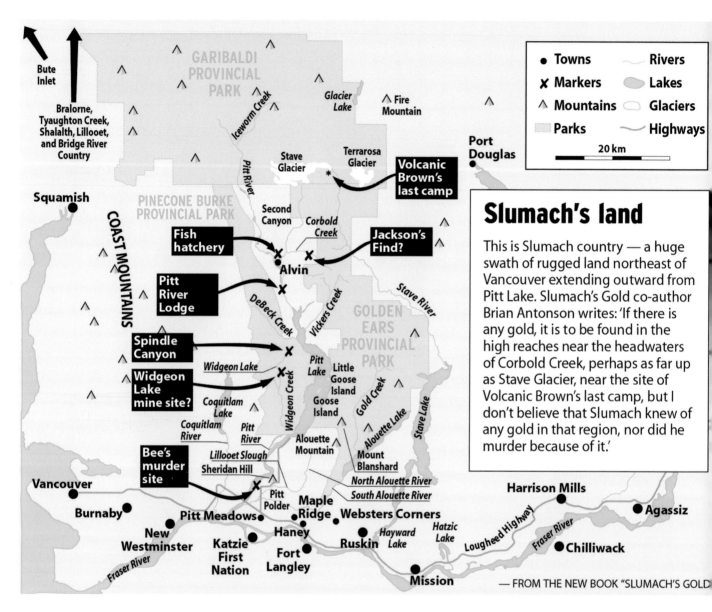

Slumach's land

This is Slumach country — a huge swath of rugged land northeast of Vancouver extending outward from Pitt Lake. Slumach's Gold co-author Brian Antonson writes: 'If there is any gold, it is to be found in the high reaches near the headwaters of Corbold Creek, perhaps as far up as Stave Glacier, near the site of Volcanic Brown's last camp, but I don't believe that Slumach knew of any gold in that region, nor did he murder because of it.'

— FROM THE NEW BOOK "SLUMACH'S GOLD"

Map J: "Slumach's Land"—The *Province* newspaper has a long history of chronicling the Slumach legend and brought fresh coverage with a 2007 feature that included this map, noting the entire area as "Slumach's Land." VANCOUVER PROVINCE/PNG

"In September, the *Campbell River Mirror* reported the disappearance of 71-year-old prospector Jack Mould while gathering fresh water from the Southgate River. A source close to the investigation tells that when the search started, his dog was still waiting for him and that Jack's gun was leaning against the car, but he was gone."

One reporter observed that Mould's body may have been swept under log booms nearby at the time. Mould's remains are unlikely to ever be found. With him went his absurd claims about Slumach's gold. Well, mostly.

NEAR ENOUGH TO THAT timing, Garth Dinsmore, a friend of Brian and Rick since childhood, called Brian to say, "That picture you have in your book of the tent-shaped rock has a helicopter in it and that got me thinking about a friend of mine who has flown his helicopter into Slumach country. He's Dean Russell. We should all meet up for breakfast and he'll tell you about his flights into the Pitt Lake area—sometimes with gold seekers."

Not only did Brian and Rick meet them within the week, Garth brought along his son Mike, a student in Capilano University's film program, who, sensing an unfolding story, documented that and subsequent breakfasts. Years later, Mike became the lead filmmaker for the reality television series *Deadman's Curse*.

Dean Russell was clear: "It's dangerous up there. Sudden downdrafts. About five years ago I asked Daryl Friesen, who you write about as a gold seeker, to come along with me up to Pitt Lake in my Robinson R44 helicopter."

Russell's motivation that sunny August day was to pinpoint a Mitchell B-25 crash from long ago—that, and to identify possible sites for the lost mine. "A fierce gust of wind forced my chopper to crash. An outcropping held us back from a horrendous descent into Pitt Lake." Fortunately, no one was hurt. Sometimes the curse just teases. "No doubt this was Slumach's warning to 'stay back,'" quipped Friesen later.

Rick asked Russell if he knew any specifics about the stories we had heard of prospectors taking gold out of locations only a helicopter could access.

"Rumours," replied Russell. "Pilots are good gossipers but closed-mouthed about specifics when it comes to clients. There's no one bragging they've bought themselves a new helicopter with gold nuggets."

(A postscript: Russell would have better luck when he headed to Yukon's goldfields a few years later and reworked an old mine, recovering gold once deemed not worth the effort by earlier mine owners. When he showed Brian a photo of a baker's scale laden with nuggets, Brian was amazed. Russell admitted the rough reality of the business: "Two million in, one million out.")

THE MOST IMPORTANT CHRONICLING of the Slumach story in terms of hard facts began Monday, May 21, 2007, when Fred Braches posted the first items on his slumach.blogspot.ca and initiated the slumach.ca website, the digital repository of virtually every word ever published about the Slumach legend. If ever in the long arc of Slumach mythology there was someone dedicated to searching for the truth, it has been Braches. Whonnock resident Braches was a Slumach "truther," a stickler for detail and for proven facts. He created the website to hold written accounts that date from the time of Louis Bee's murder through to the present.

Braches searched out all written material, both fiction and fact, that surrounds the tale. Magazine and newspaper stories, information on books and video productions, the bench book kept by Judge Drake at Slumach's trial, testimony from Aunt Mandy and many others who carried knowledge and background information—all ended up on the sites.

The work of Fred Braches—researcher, skeptic, historian, author, and linchpin in all-things Slumach—informs everything we write and the escapades of anyone serious about the legend. Sadly, Fred's great, skeptical eyes closed forever on February 1, 2024, at the age of ninety-three.

As part of a five-page feature in the *Province* newspaper, Rick, Mary, and Brian appeared with an enlarged promotional copy of their thirty-fifth anniversary edition of the updated *Slumach's Gold: In Search of a Legend* in 2007. VANCOUVER PROVINCE/PNG.

IT WASN'T LONG AFTER our new edition was selling briskly in bookstores, general stores, museums, and gas stations around the province and online that West Vancouver resident Jim Carter contacted Brian. Carter had a background that included senior positions in the educational and government fields. For a time, he was president of the West Vancouver Historical Society.

Jim's father, Dick Carter, had made expeditions to the Pitt Lake area in the 1940s, using Jackson's written guidance. Dick passed along what he believed was a copy of the original Jackson letter to Jim, who shared it with Brian. We came to refer to it as the "Carter version of the Jackson letter." Jim told Brian that this was "at best" a copy of the original, but even that couldn't be proven. Jim was clear in his thought that his father might have written out this copy himself. Brian alerted Fred Braches, who met with Carter and published the letter on slumach.ca. Jim Carter passed away in 2021 at the age of eighty-nine. This was the version of the Jackson letter that we shared earlier, annotated.

LATER IN 2008, A man carrying a plastic bag with a parcel in it showed up at a bookstore where Don Waite was signing copies of his new book *Maple Ridge & Pitt Meadows: A History in Photographs*.

"I'm Greg Henderson," the man said to Waite. "I think this might be yours."

Henderson handed Waite the "missing Waite binder," one of the two missing photocopies of the 223-page compendium of diary notes, articles, newspaper clippings, and correspondence Waite thought had been taken to Germany and never returned, or perhaps lost when he had loaned it to a worker building Pitt River Lodge.

His face a mix of shock and flabbergasted smiles, Waite asked, "Where the hell did you get this? I thought it was lost forever."

Henderson explained that he buys access to storage lockers whose renters have skipped town or not paid the rent for six months, after which the lockers have lapsed into the custody of the building's management. He pays a fee and gets whatever contents have been left behind. Having explained that to Waite, he continued, "I got this locker. Not much in there, actually. Then I saw this. My first thought was to put it on eBay. Man, there's a lot of great information here. I didn't even know about the lost gold mine until I read all this stuff of yours. When I realized how important it was, I tracked you down. I'm giving it back to you."

The upshot of what happened here is twofold: many of us now have a copy of the "missing Waite binder," and, of note, the incident spurred Henderson to become a serious Slumach gold seeker in his own right.

SLUMACH'S GOLD: IN SEARCH of a Legend triggered a letter from a reader in Florida who'd been born in the Fraser Valley. Tucked inside was a photo of the September 9, 1952, share certificate in the Slumach Lost Creek Mine Ltd.; this was information we did not have. He'd purchased eight hundred shares for one hundred dollars, which he claimed was "money down the drain or down the creek."

INTERNATIONAL INTEREST IN THE Slumach story ran high when a German film crew was rumoured to be in the Pitt Lake area. At first confused by some as Heufelder redux, it was not, but perhaps that confusion is why it didn't appear as a separate piece in our 2007 book, though it had taken place two years earlier. The details were sketchy at first—there were passing mentions of searchers gone astray, or their intentions being unmet and their legacies mixed. This became known as "the Lennartz Expedition," after the filmmaker. A few years later, they made the local news, and later still their movie was produced.

The German film *Auf Slumachs Spuren* (*On Slumach's Trails*) was released in 2010. It recounts a search for the mine, and appears tied to a 2005 expedition as well as a follow-up in 2010 to enhance the documentary with contemporaneous footage. With good cinematography and great storytelling, the film reportedly received very high ratings on German television.

This team had gone into the Pitt Lake area two or three times. Strikingly, their good fortune turned (there's the curse again!). The story begins with an ending, as reported the evening of September 10, 2010, on Radio CKNW and News 1130. This is one audio transcript:

Seven German documentary filmmakers are safe and warm again after being rescued around 7:30 Friday night (10 September 2010). They set out September 1st to scout a location northwest of Harrison Lake for a film they were making.

[Rescue coordinator] Jones says they had a malfunctioning satellite phone, which they charged with a solar panel to call for help. "We launched with two helicopters right away when we got called. We were requested directly by the regional manager from the Provincial Emergency Coordination Centre so it was an emergency request."

He [Jones] adds [that] with fading light and bad weather rolling in, the timeline for saving the men was tight, but thankfully it went off without a hitch.

Tim Jones with North Shore Search and Rescue says the men didn't bring waterproof jackets, "In the last three days they started to get soaked and couldn't keep warm. Their sleeping bags got soaked, they didn't have tents, they had two tarps, one of which got damaged in a storm, and so they had one tarp left between the seven of them. They were now starting to get mildly hypothermic."

Rob Nicholson, who coordinated the rescue of Lennartz and his fellow explorers, confirmed Lennartz' presence.

In one example of Slumach-induced prattle, rumour spread that a crew member had a seriously injured leg, requiring his "extraction," but then television footage showed the same person walking around with no problem at the landing point once they'd been choppered out. That, and a general unease, led to speculation the "rescue" was an assisted transport out of the bush. Its unintended consequence was a legacy of mistrust—it may well have been a legitimate need, though off-handed assessments by others who had hiked the area inferred the group may have been poorly prepared for such eventualities, resulting in an unorganized situation requiring rescue from the exploration site.

FOR OVER ONE HUNDRED years, countless rainbow chasers who began their research in the comfort and safety of libraries and their homes decided to take the next step and venture physically into dangerous "Slumach country."

We wanted to know more about these people who staked their reputations on finding a lost mine, making public their quests and opinions. And we wanted to know what motivated individuals to put themselves at risk. Many added to our findings or found information we missed, or, better yet, came up with possibilities we'd never contemplated. Some have created controversy. Yet by taking risks, they have furthered the truth. And where truth was not available, they provided careful assumptions, fair analysis, and heartfelt (albeit biased) theories about Slumach's gold.

We respectfully call these worthy adventurers "gold seekers." One wonders how this legend would have evolved without characters like Friesen or Carter or Lennartz.

These gold seekers have enjoyed ongoing escapades, curious revelations, the development of friendships, and a willingness to disclose enough secrets to confuse one another. Yet they've displayed an eagerness to collaborate when partnership didn't get in the way of competition. Time has tested the stories of many who have been around awhile—and added newly minted gold seekers as well. As it happened, one way to keep track of them all grew out of Don Waite's idea to gather everyone together periodically, right up to the publication of this book, nicknaming the group "The Lost Mine of Pitt Lake Society."

Opposite One of many tent-shaped rocks. ADAM PALMER COLLECTION

Overleaf ADAM PALMER COLLECTION

Chapter 11

The Lost Mine of Pitt Lake Society

THE OCCASIONAL GATHERING OF gold seekers and skeptics, called together on a casual basis to exchange secrets and false leads to divert one another, happens under monikers such as the Lost Creek Gold Mine Society or Slumachers' Society, but remains formally named as it began: the Lost Mine of Pitt Lake Society. At heart, gold seekers are rumour mongers, and they trade in half-truths. Each time the group convenes, it brings together the quirky habits and quick wits of eccentric individuals, clever TV series personalities, and serious researchers in an atmosphere of unquenchable curiosity celebrating the quest to find Slumach's gold.

Don Waite launched the society in April 1987, first calling for a gathering of stalwart Slumach aficionados Danny Scooch and Vic Loffler—who brought topographic maps and a 3D magnifier. Geologist Len Werner, Mike Boileau, and Rob Nicholson showed up. Waite hung a large welcome sign outside his home.

Though all involved saw one another on occasion, it was twenty-two years before a quasi-formal second meeting of the society was convened in January 2009, expanding the callout. Hosted on woodsy acreage in Whonnock at the home of Fred and Helmi Braches, it was notable for attendance by members of Slumach's extended family: Willie Pierre, Cyril Pierre, Stuart Pierre, and his wife Alida. (Their ancestor, Peter Pierre, was with Slumach when he died. Aunt Mandy was Peter Pierre's daughter.) The group gathered on the couches and floors of the Bracheses' cozy home. Also at that meeting were Greg Henderson (who'd found the photocopy of the "missing Waite binder"), Mike Boileau, and Daryl Friesen, along with Brian and Rick Antonson, and Don Waite.

Then came a wonderful surprise in May of that year. Cyril Pierre and family, of the Katzie Nation, invited the society to the Swan-e-set Longhouse. Among those attending for the first time was a colleague of Michael Collier, whose 1994 film was shown. Also on the screen was the episode from the 1958 television show *Treasure,* which featured Spindle Creek as the lost mine's location. The hosts shared a salmon caught that morning and barbecued on site, bannock made earlier in the day, and friendship. There were discussions about freeing Slumach from the legends, potentially righting the wrongs against this man due to the unfair application of laws, in what has been characterized as insensitive, racist "white man's justice." Researchers Archie and Dale Miller were there too. Archie is the former custodian of New Westminster's Irving House Museum and the city's archivist.

When the fourth meeting took place, the attendees included Willie Pierre, Cyril Pierre, Greg Henderson, Don Waite, chronicler Fred Braches, and newcomer Claus Andrup. This occurred near the 120th anniversary of Slumach's hanging, in 2011.

By the May 2014 gathering, Braches and Waite had met and worked on a TV series with the mountaineering duo Adam Palmer and Evan Howard, whose participation enlivened every conversation with doubt and facts, suspicions and certainty—all from their first-hand experiences from trekking in the high country. Daryl Friesen had become a regular at these events, and the tension of debates and controversies began to inspire the making of a video.

A new television series, *Curse of the Frozen Gold*, was created in 2013 and 2014, and several of the gang enjoyed lots of occasions spending time together as they became television stars.

As time elapsed, there remained a willingness to keep a wider batch of gold seekers engaged. In July 2018, it felt like it was time for a reunion. Waite and his wife, Tina, invited everyone to their home for a potluck dinner. Mountaineer Evan Howard was there with his mom, and Lance Willett attended, sharing the tragic story about his late daughter's fatal car crash, which he feels guided him in a dream to a mineshaft near the Stave Dam in search of Slumach's gold. This was portrayed in one of the series' episodes where a mine shaft was discovered, but it proved not to be related to Slumach.

Greg Henderson was a regular now. Fred and Helmi Braches graced the event with a sense of being elders among sometimes contentious, often mischievous adventurers.

In August 2022, members of the society—still an ad hoc group—were encouraged to meet at the Fort Langley Seniors Hall as part of the filming for a new television series, *Deadman's Curse*. The producers and crew invited all manner of researchers and gold seekers, as well as the show's cast, the week before the series launched on the History Channel. The day before the meeting, producer Tim Hardy asked Brian if he could chair the evening, which Brian agreed to do.

After welcoming everyone, Brian said, "We want to catch up with what's new in the legend with everyone, so let's start with Don Waite, the founder of this Society." Waite deferred, saying there were others in the room with

more current experiences. Palmer was cool and cautious and knowledgeable, Braches revealed a few pieces he was about to disclose on his blogspot, and the evening unfolded informatively.

This was being filmed for a later episode of the television series, and that's when the producers brought in a dark horse—a guy no one else had ever met, and only heard of recently—David Muise. Given the floor to tell his story, Muise claimed he'd been in the mine, and said, "the tent shaped rock exists." He recounted a story he wanted others to believe, saying, "There's a deep hole below one side of it where the nuggets were buried by Jackson and now have been dug out."

Palmer challenged Muise. "You take me in and I'll tell you whether you have something or not!" Muise's nod was that of agreement. One could catch the knowing glances of the film crew and producers realizing they were on the brink of another escapade of tension and hard hiking.

Debate raged in the room as Friesen challenged whomever he disagreed with, handling it well. Braches's skepticism confronted others with his calm commentary. New on the society scene, George McGuiness stood to tell his story, hesitant at first. He seemed to have information he didn't want to share. He claimed to have been in the mine, but in a totally different location than Muise cited. Relaxed by conversation and perhaps emboldened by the night's storytelling, he said, "I'll be right back," and with that, he was gone from the room. Minutes later, he returned from his car, holding a clear plastic box of material. Opening it, he rummaged a bit within and pulled out a rock. He handed it around and when Waite held it, his hand lowered. "This is heavy . . . it has gold in it."

McGuiness's eyes said it all: he knew where he'd gotten this, and it was from searching in the Pitt Lake area. To silence or further the murmur in the room, we're not sure, he said, "There's more."

As Brian was walking out the door at the end of the evening, Michael Francis of the producing team thanked him, and his next words confirmed suspicions that the drama between Muise and Palmer was partially in aid of setting up a forthcoming episode. "We're going in tomorrow with David and Adam. We leave at 7 AM."

DON WAITE WAXED PHILOSOPHICAL in early 2024, noting that when he first started the society in the mid-1980s, he had no idea that down the road a few decades, his work would have been fundamental to numerous things: books, television series, podcasts, websites, more society meetings, and online discussions. The legend truly has a life of its own.

Many of the members of the Lost Mine of Pitt Lake Society deserve attention individually, as their searches have been unique, often compelling. And, much to the benefit and enjoyment of everyone "in search of a legend," most of them took their personal quests to new heights when they appeared in *Curse of the Frozen Gold* and/or *Deadman's Curse*. Their stories are told in the following chapter.

The Lost Mine of Pitt Lake Society members met at the Swan-e-Set Longhouse in Pitt Meadows in 2009. *Back row, left to right:* Don Waite, Garnet Pierre, Dick Hamilton, Martin Lindgren, Stuart Pierre, Dale Miller, Archie Miller, Daryl Friesen, Fred Braches, Cyril Pierre. *Front row, left to right:* Trenton Pierre, Greg Henderson, Katlyn Henderson, Andrea Lindgren, Alida Pierre, Brian Antonson, Karen Chan, Rick Antonson. HELMI BRACHES

Overleaf ADAM PALMER COLLECTION

Chapter 12

The Gold Seekers

"The key to finding lost treasure is a good map—and a lot of luck."—Anonymous

Don Waite

The Slumach legend's longest advocate began his career as an RCMP constable who found the last living connection to Slumach. Now in his eighties, Don Waite remains a staunch believer that there's much to credit the legend and also much to discredit it, but he's not willing to give up the search. Waite was one of those who encouraged us in recent years to take a closer look at Mike Boileau's story, for example, leading to a fuller gold-seeker profile about him. Waite put a focus on Charles Miller's 1973 book *The Golden Mountains*, guiding us to the story of Ragnar Bergland and Louis Nelson, which we recount later in this book. That just touches on his influence on our writing, an influence he's had since we were first-time authors with competing 1972 books about the lost gold mine, *In Search of a Legend: Slumach's Gold*, and *Kwant'stan*. This competition led to amalgamated storytelling and friendships. "Don knows more buzz about the lost mine than the three of us put together" was a recurring refrain among us as we got to know him.

Waite's intrigue with Slumach, and his research into the legend, is now in its sixth decade. In the late 1960s, Waite was trained in solving murders—finding missing people, tracking clues, and substantiating evidence. At twenty-two, the wavy-haired rookie was the youngest detective at the Burnaby detachment—prone to taking risks and exceeding expectations. He had been designated as "plainclothes," and made privy to the elite investigative minds within the force. He honed investigative skills and a sense of justice that would serve him well in later years as a writer, historian, and gold seeker.

After a transfer to the New Westminster detachment, Waite was assigned duties at the old courthouse building, the RCMP's base in New Westminster at that time. The historic site meant little to Waite until one day, the corporal-in-charge changed his life with a simple request: "I need you to help me move out some case-file boxes from the old vault."

When the corporal unlocked the vault's padlock and flicked the light switch, the single light bulb revealed a circular staircase climbing three levels against walls stacked with dusty files. Waite recalls the musty old-paper smell that overwhelmed him. As the two men entered the high-ceilinged archives, Waite touched a wooden crate to his right and wondered what purpose this old room had served in the distant past. As they moved boxes around, the ever-curious Waite peeked through some files. He pulled out mildewed papers and saw for the first time the handwritten word "Slumach."

Seeing what Waite was holding, the corporal told him, "This is where they hung old Slumach."

"Who?" asked Waite.

"The Indian. The murderer. January 1891. Put a rope up there, over that beam," said the corporal, pointing high above them.

Waite recalls his captivation. "Even though I later learned Slumach was in fact hanged not in that room but at the provincial jail, some blocks away, that moment launched me on a lifelong quest for the truth behind the Slumach story."

Less than a year later, Waite was posted to Maple Ridge, in the Fraser Valley, close to Pitt Lake. Soon he met residents of the Katzie First Nation, whose handed-down recollections of Slumach's mistreatment under the law only eighty years prior were still very much alive. Because of the injustice they felt he had been subjected to (a court of British based laws, a rush to judgement, and a pattern of racism and indifference towards Indigenous Peoples), they viewed Slumach almost as a hero.

Constable Waite arrived at the Katzie reserve one day as part of his orientation to the area. Seeing a middle-aged man walking toward him carrying two huge fish over his shoulders, Waite introduced himself. Chief Joachim (Joe) Pierre set the fish on the ground and extended a scale-coated hand in greeting—the first of many between the two men and a sign of their early bond. Trust grew from their honesty with one another. Mutual candour grew into mutual respect. Their friendship brought with it a link to Slumach that Waite would otherwise never have had. Yet their times together ended sadly and too soon. When Joe Pierre, his mother, and his son died in a tragic car accident in 1971. Waite served as one of the six pallbearers, and the only one who was non-Indigenous

Prior to that sad event, in 1970, Waite got to know Pierre's aunt, Amanda Charnley ("Aunt Mandy," as she was known), through Pierre's wife, Agnes. He'd heard that Mandy knew stories about Slumach, so one day when he was off duty, Waite and Agnes drove to Mission for a visit with Aunt Mandy, who would forever anchor his perceptions about the legend of Slumach's gold.

This first meeting with Aunt Mandy and her husband, Clinton Charnley, was the beginning of Waite's multi-year relationship with the elderly couple, a relationship rich in historical anecdotes of Indigenous Peoples and settlers, Mandy's Nation, and life on the reserve. Most importantly, he learned about her deceased father and Slumach. Mandy's father, Peter Pierre, had a reputation that was widely respected. In 1936, he shared details of the traditions and beliefs of the Katzie with Dr. Diamond Jenness, who wrote an interpretation, published in 1955 in *The Faith of a Coast Salish Indian*.

When Waite visited the couple, Clinton would often greet him as he walked up Charnley Street. It became Waite's custom to visit Mandy.

Invited into their home one day, Waite sat across the kitchen table from Aunt Mandy. He was impressed by how his host would smooth her vinyl tablecloth and pour coffees—attentive and competent, despite blindness from an accident in her youth. Waite had a notepad before him on the table and his pen at the ready. He knew he was about to be let into Aunt Mandy's confidence. She had decided to trust him to retell Slumach's story properly to others. She began, and Waite started scribbling notes: "Here is what my father told me about Slumach, the killing of Louis Bee, and the gold that Slumach found in the Pitt country."

Waite's years of investigative work made him sense he was about to hear the truth, a truth that placed gold in Slumach's hands. Aunt Mandy's rendition is what has made her the default source of assumed fact, settled folklore, and believable oral history when it comes to Slumach.

Aunt Mandy continued:

My father, Peter Pierre, a catechist from the Roman Catholic Order of Mary Immaculate at Mission and a medicine man of the Katzie Indian Reserve, was Slumach's nephew. Father said that Charlie Slumach at the time of the shooting of Bee was closer to eighty than to sixty, and that he was a crippled and harmless old widower who lived at the bottom end of Pitt Lake in a shack that was on the abandoned Silver Creek Indian Reserve. He was part Katzie and part Nanaimo Indian [Snuneymuxw]. He had a brother, *Smum-qua*, and a married daughter, Mary, living at Cowichan on Vancouver Island.

My father spent the last week of Slumach's life with him in prison, teaching him religion and preparing him for the hereafter. It was during that week that Slumach told him what had happened at Alouette Slough. He said that he had been heading up the lower Pitt River in his canoe to his cabin when he spotted a deer. He shot at the animal from his canoe and then pulled in to the beach to see if he had hit the animal. Seeing blood, he ventured into the bush to look for the wounded animal. After a lengthy and futile search, he was returning to his canoe when he saw two Indians in a canoe out on the water. One was Louis Boulier,

The friendship between Amanda Charnley (Aunt Mandy) and Don Waite lasted many years. Her family memory of Slumach's story figures large for students of the legend. TINA WAITE

a half-French, half-Kanaka man, often called Bee for short, and the other was Charlie Seymour, an Indian from Harrison Mills.

Slumach told my father that Boulier held a grudge against him and, stepping ashore, came at him wielding an axe and shouting, "I'm going to chop your damn head off!"

She went on to say that Slumach told Pierre that he had raised his shotgun out of sheer fright and fired point-blank at Boulier, killing him instantly. Seymour, the only witness, disappeared into the bush.

Slumach placed Boulier's body in the victim's own canoe and set it in midstream to drift down to the [Boulier's] fishing party. Slumach did not accompany the body because he feared Boulier's friends might mob him. He then got into his own canoe and paddled upstream to his cabin.

The following day, a boat came out to Slumach's home. The occupants or posse merely fired shots into the house, which resulted in Slumach escaping out the back door and hiding under a fallen tree. The group aboard the boat disgusted Peter by the irresponsible manner in which they carried out their duties. To ensure that Slumach would not return to his home for shelter, they burned it to the ground.

It was to Peter that Slumach eventually surrendered. Peter persuaded his uncle to give himself up to the Indian agent. My father went into the bush after his uncle without a gun, despite warnings from the posse. Peter told them that he was going to see his uncle and not some wild animal. He found Slumach half-starved, hidden under a fallen tree.

According to my father, there was only the hangman, Father Morgan, and himself that actually witnessed the hanging of his uncle, although a great many were present outside the gallows. When the hangman was placing the hood over

Shown here are Peter Pierre, a Katzie medicine man and Slumach's nephew, with his family. Pierre's daughter Amanda (Aunt Mandy) is in the front row at right. Pierre was with Slumach when he was hanged in 1891. MAPLE RIDGE MUSEUM P08993

Slumach's head, the old Indian asked him in Chinook to not waste any time. At that moment, my father closed his eyes and began to pray with Father Morgan. When he opened his eyes all he could see was the dangling rope.

Mandy paused. Waite realized she was emotional about what she was going to tell him next. "Slumach was buried in an unknown grave in the prison cemetery in Sapperton, despite attempts by his daughter to get possession of his body to give him a proper burial."

Waite recalled that he got up to get the coffee pot. Silence settled as he poured Aunt Mandy and himself another cup. He told her how much it meant to him that she was telling him all of this, and assured her that he would treat it with care and portray it accurately.

She thanked him, and then began to tell him about Slumach and how he found gold. Waite later recounted her story word for word in his book, *Kwant'stan*.

Aunt Mandy said,

It was during my father's stay in prison that Slumach told him about finding gold in the Pitt country.

Slumach told my father that only on one occasion did he ever take gold out of the Pitt. He said that he had met Port Douglas Indians [Xa'xtsa Peoples] from the head of Harrison Lake coming off Glacier Lake and down Patterson Creek into the upper Pitt Valley. They told him that they had taken horses partway, but had driven them back towards Port Douglas and had crossed Glacier Lake on foot. They gave him a handful of bullets moulded from gold that they had found in Third Canyon.

Slumach spent the night in the canyon and slept on a bench-shaped rock on the west side of the river. The rock was covered with a rust-coloured moss. When he awoke around 5 AM, he could scarcely see the sun coming over three mountain peaks for the east wall of the canyon. During this time he was still shrouded in darkness. As it became lighter, Slumach could see in his own surroundings. Peeling the moss off his rock bed he saw a yellow metal. He dug out some gold from a small quartz vein with a penknife and half-filled his shot bag with them. He sold the half-filled bag, which was about the same size of a ten-pound sugar bag, to a storekeeper in New Westminster for twenty-seven dollars. The storekeeper went back to England a short time after the purchase.

That, claimed Slumach, was the only gold that he ever took out of the Pitt country. Sitting on the cell bench, Slumach drew a map for Peter of the location where he found the nuggets. Peter memorized the drawing and then destroyed it. Years later he redrew the map. His daughter traced out three copies; however, the original and the copies were destroyed in the 1930s in a house fire.

Slumach skeptic Fred Braches later posted an important counterpoint to this story on his blogspot: "The only plausible reason why Pierre would have drawn this map and had copies made was that they were intended for sale or to impress gullible prospectors." Seen in that light it seems unlikely that the map drawn by Slumach ever existed, in our view. For Pierre, with his intimate knowledge of the lay of the land, a few pointers would have been enough—he did not need a map.

Aunt Mandy was finished. She'd told the story as it had been told to her, faithful to the account as best as one can be with oral history.

Glacier Lake, where Aunt Mandy reported that Slumach had been given "a handful of bullets molded from gold by Indigenous people from Port Douglas at the head of Harrison Lake." ADAM PALMER COLLECTION

One of many tent-shaped rocks investigated by gold seekers searching for Jackson's "find." Many such rocks, of varying sizes, have been reported in a number of search areas. COURTESY OF DONALD E. WAITE

For Waite, this version of Slumach's story did not reconcile with the legend and stories that were circulating in the popular journalism of recent decades. Instead, it rang of truth. By this stage of his studying records and testimonies, Waite knew that there was no documented reference to Slumach finding "nuggets as big as hen's eggs." It was increasingly apparent to Waite that legends about the lost mine of Pitt Lake had begun long after the death of Slumach and were subject to embellishments, loose connections, and made-up inferences. Yet, at its base, it seemed the legend might be rooted in what he'd just heard.

As Waite put it in *Kwant'stan*, "The accounts did, however, portray the Caucasian man's attitude toward Indians and crime by showing the pathetic fashion in which the poor chap, Slumach, got railroaded to the gallows." In Waite's view, newspaper accounts of 1890 and 1891, by giving a one-sided account, sent Slumach to the gallows long before he had even been captured.

Waite had also learned there had been numerous expeditions over the years into the Pitt country to rediscover Slumach's mine, and that they had often met with devastating circumstances. What led people to take such risks? From where had come stories of Slumach and gold and

a curse to protect it? To Waite, an anecdote from Aunt Mandy about the first such expedition may well be what the legend of Slumach's curse is based on.

"Two years after Slumach's death," Waite retells from his notes about that session with Aunt Mandy, "Peter Pierre and Dave Bailey, a half-Scottish, half-Kwikwetlem man, set out for Third Canyon in search of the gold vein that Slumach had described to Peter Pierre. The map scrawled by Slumach in his jail cell was etched in Pierre's mind."

If one takes that to be accurate, then the following is not at all hard to believe, nor is the interpretation Waite takes.

"While attempting to cross a creek on a fallen tree, Pierre lost his footing and took a bad spill, breaking his hip. He had to be carried out. He never went back."

Waite smiles at what may be the genesis of legend. "Aunt Mandy told me her father, Peter Pierre, jokingly suggested that his Uncle Slumach 'must have placed a curse on the area.'"

In pondering this, Waite grew sombre as he recalled that over thirty people reportedly died in the past hundred-plus years as a result of Slumach's curse, something tracked by supposedly reputable news outlets

like the *Province*, though tallying such dramatic (and suspect) figures stopped in recent decades. We wonder—as does Waite—is this episode told by Peter Pierre to Aunt Mandy the source of a rumoured "gallows curse"? Or did Pierre tell half-heartedly of a reputed "curse" in order to keep people away from the site where he believed Slumach might have touched gold?

In the world of legends and lost treasures and hearsay, it is hard to refute this shorthand: Slumach, gold, curse—three interlinked words that all need a reputable source to connect them, and Waite believes that source is Aunt Mandy.

DON WAITE REMAINS AN inveterate gold seeker. Once he retired from a second career as an aerial photographer, he continued writing books, passing the dozen mark, including *The Cariboo Gold Rush Story, British Columbia and Yukon Gold Hunters,* and an autobiography, the latter heavy with Slumach adventures. "Fascination with Slumach led to my writing of books, and sparked my first interest in gold hunters," he says. "We never know where relationships will take us. Life is like that."

So is death. Around 2006, Waite sat in the Simon Pierre Longhouse on the Katzie lands as a roaring fire burned in the rock pit, its smoke rising through a gap in the roof. He listened to the deputy commissioner of the RCMP deliver a eulogy for Agnes Pierre, who had become the Katzie Chief years earlier upon the death of her husband, Joe. Many dignitaries attended, and RCMP officers in formal red serge tunics were on hand. Waite was again among the pallbearers as they walked the cedar coffin around the lodge two times, and then to a waiting hearse. Later, standing at the cemetery in swirling snow, Waite eased the rope through his hands as he helped lower his friend's casket into the ground.

When the television crews began filming *Curse of the Frozen Gold* in 2014, no one was a more logical choice to consult, among credible gold seekers, than Waite. His Pitt Lake adventures by boat and on foot, from casual hot-spring visits to demanding hikes, his campfire storytelling, and the visits in his home are all renowned.

And he can be cutting about those he feels make claims that don't meet his expectations. Despite Waite having sketched a map of his conversational directions from Stu Brown and despite the two of them having journeyed to look for Brown's purported "pond of gold,"

Gold seekers triangulate with a topographical map, deciding which route to take to the high country and perhaps gold. Many trails, creeks, and glacier routes offer tempting opportunities, but which to follow presents a quandary. OP MEDIA GROUP

his eventual summation about Brown is not charitable. "Brown never had gold. His story is make-believe."

WHEN WAITE FIRST INVITED fellow travellers to the Lost Mine of Pitt Lake Society, it was not for a lark, but to gather together an informal group of fellow enthusiasts. His goal was to encourage the swapping of tales, to introduce gold seekers to one another, to deliver firsthand accounts of daring escapades to writers, and to ensure the legend lives on through establishing facts and challenging myths. And later, as he hosted the gathering again, he continued to nurture the good that came from tale swapping. The meetings set the stage for delivering possible truths to fellow seekers, and for the forging of friendships. Many who came to those meet-ups left with new ideas of where to search—or left behind trail tidbits they hoped might lead others astray, away from where they believed only they would find gold. The following are descriptions of these other gold seekers; their stories are often a legacy of Waite's.

Daryl Friesen

Daryl Friesen is among the handful of serious Slumach gold seekers: those with a commitment to research, an openness to fresh ideas, and a penchant for great storytelling. (The latter quality landed Friesen a lead role in some popular television documentaries.) It could be that today's two most tenacious pursuers of Slumach's lost gold mine are Friesen and his friendly nemesis, Adam Palmer. Friesen says of their relationship, "I hate being in his shadow."

Friesen willingly wades into a discussion about little-known facts he's sussed out, such as in his taped phone conversation with Bill Barlee about the Jackson letter, in which he tells Barlee, "You were the first person to ever publish a story which contained the Jackson letter. I was kind of wondering where you got it from."

Barlee replies, "Volcanic Brown gave it to my father."

"Really, the old prospector who died on Stave Glacier?"

"That's right, my father showed it to me when I was twenty and I made a copy," says Barlee.

"Where is the letter now?" asked Friesen.

"My father sold it to a collector, some rich American, I believe."

And there you have it—a frontline conversation between two avowed believers in Jackson's letter.

However, Friesen is not shy about other observations that cast doubt on an area he wishes held a clearer truth. "Jackson's 'three peaks' landmark is common for lost treasures," he says. It shows up in the Lost Dutchman's mine tale, Inca lost treasure stories, and even King Solomon's mine."

When Friesen talks about a quest for the truth—about a man as much as a mine—he says, "the map is the beginning." He reminisces about his first time spreading open a topographical map of Slumach country across a kitchen table. "When you start placing topo maps together, the epic quest comes alive. The treasure map!"

But not everyone had a map. One man had a dream. And in that dream, he saw a huge tent-shaped rock exactly as described by Tiny Allen. If there is one dead prospector Friesen is fixated on, it is Clayton Gadsby. To start at the end of the story, here's Friesen talking today: "I have staked Clayton Gadsby's old claim now." And here's the shortest version of the story that leads to that.

As readers will remember from a previous chapter in this book, in the 1960s, Tiny Allen talked about a tent-shaped rock with the top knocked off (perhaps by other falling rocks, we may assume, or perhaps cascading into that position on its own). As Friesen is the first to admit, "Now, there are tent-shaped rocks everywhere. But not with their tops off." Gadsby flew in a Cessna over rugged landscape near Pitt Lake, searching for and finding an area to explore: he saw the rock in question. Gadsby was a boater and hiker and found his way to Pitt Lake often, and in those times street talk recounted Allen's exploits, so that influenced Gadsby's finding and staking a claim—one he said produced gold.

"I met Clayton," Friesen told us, recounting a visit with the man before he passed away in 2007. "He showed me a slide show of his claim." Then the stickler for privacy said, "I can't tell you what he showed me." (There's always more left unsaid with these gold seekers.)

"I believe the Clayton Gadsby location might be where Jackson left gold . . . it fits well," said Friesen. It became his quest to find Gadsby's claim. His chance came when the *Curse of the Frozen Gold* TV show took him into an otherwise difficult (read: expensive) place to get to. And he says he had to fight to get the rumoured location into the show. "The TV guys want a story and then [to] move onto the next episode. I wanted to find gold." He got only partway there, as they found no immediate evidence of gold there, but he plans to go back. "I found Gadsby's stake and tag," he said. (The tag identified the claim.) "Absolutely this location relates to Tiny Allen. There's no spot like it." Remember, this claim comes from someone who has actually been to dozens of other reputed spots. "You can see the rock from the ledge as Tiny described. As Jackson described. The rock is gigantic. Can't be missed." And, he stresses, it's not within the provincial park boundaries.

Such "finds" have been a long time coming. Friesen's 1984 excursion with his dad to an abandoned silver mine in the hills near Yale, BC, sparked a lifetime passion for treasure hunting in the twelve-year-old, and he took up the quest for Slumach when he was nineteen years old.

Enamoured by the thrill of the chase and inspired by a local library file about lost mines and our 1972 book, the curious boy began a relentless, lifelong search for Slumach's gold. Friesen wrote the 2006 book *Seekers of Gold*, which chronicles his tenacious search for the mine up to 1991. He is currently completing a sequel.

There's a certain Slumach stamina required, even when fuelled by the reckless perseverance associated with youth. In his teens, Friesen and his buddies explored, hiked, camped, tramped, helicoptered, sea-planed, drove, crawled, and otherwise blitzed their way around every boulder, canyon, stream, and river in the upper Pitt Lake and Garibaldi Provincial Park areas. His book describes

Daryl Friesen has been chasing the elusive lost gold mine for decades, diving into dense forests, climbing high mountain peaks, and starring in numerous YouTube videos and two television series. KAREN CHAN

how nerves became frayed after one soaking-wet hike up DeBeck Creek that involved tripping, falling, and pushing through treacherous terrain. But even unpredictable weather, steep slopes, and prickly devil's club couldn't squelch Friesen's unflappable spirit.

"My dad . . . was the one person I thought believed in me, because when I was young, he took me up to that lake and up to those mountains and he made me believe that the gold was there. He made me believe I could search for it, and anything was possible."

On one of his first trips, Friesen met an elderly Indigenous man known as Houseboat Harry, who told him that there was no gold in the upper Pitt region; rather, it was behind the head of DeBeck Creek. Friesen remains committed to the notion of gold in that vicinity, where Spindle Creek flows into DeBeck, and he has an old map that shows the area marked for mineral exploration. "Mike Boileau found gold on the upper Spindle," he says. But he has other ideas as well. "People, like TV producers, try to pin me to one spot, but I see many potential places. The search is gold for me."

Friesen was also mesmerized by an audiotape made in 1969 and given to him by a Mrs. Smittberg, who owned a cabin on the shore of Pitt Lake, right next to the mouth of DeBeck Creek. On the tape, Smittberg talked about a group of prospectors who, in her absence, had broken into the cabin to find shelter after their boat sank in Pitt Lake. They left a map in the cabin that was marked with an X on top of a small canyon (later identified as Spindle Canyon) just north of Widgeon Lake. "There's something there," Friesen said recently. "It could be where Slumach himself found gold."

"So you believe Slumach had gold?" one of us asked.

"Yes, but how much is the question. It's like a fish story. The size keeps getting bigger with each retelling."

The threat of Slumach's curse lurks in Friesen's book: "Once you would get close to where you wanted to be, some weather factor would always get in your way and crush your plans. It really makes you wonder if what they say about a curse on this place is true."

Sometimes Friesen and his prospecting partner, Shawn Gryba, seemed to come deliciously close to the gold. During one backbreaking day of panning in Spindle Canyon, success appeared to be at hand: "I couldn't believe what I saw resting within the black sand at the bottom of my gold pan. I was staring at one very small piece of gold about the size of the end of my fingernail. I screamed in ecstasy as I brought it out of the water. Here was truly a sign there may be something in this canyon after all."

Friesen later acknowledged the sample was simply too insignificant to get assayed.

Intrigued by Don Waite's writings, Friesen interviewed Stu Brown, who claimed to have found the mine in the Garibaldi or Golden Ears Provincial Park area in the mid-seventies. Their visit occurred in 2000, three years before Brown died.

Friesen began politely, yet curiously, asking, "When was the last time you went up there?" Brown told him it had been in 1980. Then came the real question: "Did you ever find gold?"

Brown's casual response, "Yeah," was frustratingly short.

"How much?"

"Considerable," he replied, continuing the evasion.

Friesen tried another approach. "Would you ever talk to anyone about where you went?"

"I am a little leery about it all. I'd not go back at my age. And to tell about it would be endangering people's lives. No one in their right mind would ever go in there with that terrain."

Friesen pressed for details: "Is it anywhere near Stave Glacier?"

"Well, that's a matter of distance. But I can say it is generally east of Terrarosa Glacier, near Stave Glacier."

"I guess you would not be able to show the area on a map, would you?"

"You have to know the country . . . "

Like gold-smitten prospectors 130 years ago, Friesen is dedicated to finding his strike. Decades later, he remains inspired by his father. He climbs in dangerous territory

This aerial view of Slumach country gives another perspective on the treacherous topography north of Pitt Lake, including Corbold Creek. Did Jackson and Volcanic Brown explore these many creeks? Did they find gold? HERITAGE HOUSE COLLECTION

deceptive. "Pyrites is the most evil stuff in the world," he laughed. "I hate it."

His take on the map Don Waite scrawled after his visit with Stuart Brown is this: "Stu being Stu probably gave Don a little good information, just a little off," in order to keep his secret. Being coy and a tad unspecific, Friesen says the map that Waite hurriedly drew is accurate—if moved south a couple of miles, "nearer Stoney Creek," as "that's where Brown's canyon is."

To prove the authenticity of his beliefs, Friesen says, "Stuart wrote a letter and paper-clipped a photo to it showing the site. I now have that rusty paper clip, [the] brown, crinkly letter, and the photo. It is my most holy Lost Mine relic"—a relic he keeps to himself.

Friesen's writing in the *Lost Journal of a Wandering Prospector* always strikes us as reliably insightful, often pithy, as in this snippet:

> I have chased cursed gold in bedrock cracks under clear mountain streams. I have been on TV networks around the world because of a quest. But this quest has suddenly stalled. Was it all just the dust dream of a lingering childhood? Unfortunately, one can be forced by reality to grow up. I have no choice but to keep faith and keep searching. The quest goes on.

Friesen's ambitions today reflect a more mature but no less subdued determination. "What's the truth? That's what I want to find," he concludes. "It's possible that the Browns, Slumach, and Jackson all found gold, but in different locations."

But it's more than that, as part of his poetic waxing reveals:

> If you think it's just about gold
> Then you are missing the truth.

"The truth is," says Friesen, "Pitt Lake likes to break your heart."

that most men his age would avoid, even if they had his physical wherewithal.

He is still driven but is more analytical before trotting off into dangerous places. "I fully believe what Stuart Brown told me is true," he told us before this book was written. "But there's lots of pyrites in the area, and pyrites looks like gold. But Stuart, he's a smart guy and would know the difference. If you hold pyrites, it's light, and a similar handful of gold would bend your arm." (Indeed, pyrite is known as "fool's gold" because real prospectors know the difference immediately.)

But, he adds, "Prospectors look for rust and red earth, as they are an indicator of iron pyrites." He says the Italian word for red earth is Terrarosa. Yet it can be decidedly

Spindle Creek flows into DeBeck Creek, which empties into Pitt Lake from the west. Author Mary Trainer and gold seeker Danny Gerak ponder this possible route to the legendary gold in September 2023. RICK ANTONSON

Danny Gerak

Danny Gerak says he and his father fished the upper Pitt River since "I was six or seven years old." Now in his sixties, he recalls that the legend of Slumach's lost mine was talked about while casting lines and shared with new friends brought along in search of steelhead, salmon, and bull trout. The curse was discussed around campfires as shadows loomed. The gold was real, and maybe even the curse. And would be found near the upper Pitt River, in Gerak's mind.

An old fellow from the area ran into them when Gerak was young and told them about his great-grandfather meeting Slumach onboard a skiff taking them across Pitt Lake, southward from the north shore. This would have been around late summer in 1890 at the latest. Slumach had come out of the woods and "had a giant gold nugget, which he showed to my great-grandfather on the boat ride," said the man, placing Slumach, upper Pitt Lake, and gold together. To Gerak, it is but one testament of where the gold came from.

There's another. "An old woman who'd long before worked at the fish hatchery nearby brought us a picture of Volcanic Brown," said Gerak. "She said he used to come down to the fish hatchery, and came in from not far behind their location." He'd been mining just in the back of a logging camp. That reinforced the proximity of gold in Gerak's mind, as did her saying, "Volcanic Brown was in the woods mining and would every once in a while come out and dress up proper and go to the city, and then he'd return. And go prospecting again."

Those who say Brown trekked "way back up Stave" dismay Gerak: "He didn't go as far as people think. No way a seventy-year-old was walking across that glacier." Loggers would have known roughly where he was going, and he seemed to be near enough to their work sites. "But there's no damn way he'd be carrying a big backpack of supplies up onto a glacier."

Gerak has yet another testament: "My aunt had a neighbour who'd prospected not far from where our lodge is today," says Gerak. "I met him. He'd gone down into a narrow valley and brought up a couple gallon pails of dirt from around a pool of water. He panned it and found colour. I've still got a vial of this gold." Gerak laughs, "It gets smaller from all the handling because I keep taking it out to show people." He knows the potential is significant. "The prospector only took dirt from the edge of a deep pool. He never got back. There's more gold there."

All those stories lead to Gerak's "hidden valley," where he'd taken pilot–adventurer John Lovelace. The creek remains nameless.

"My whole theory is that people don't realize the main upper Pitt River where it nears the lake was altered. In the late 1930s the logging road was rebuilt to run down the opposite side." Gerak explains that the upper Pitt used to flow into the lake on the east side, before diversion, where "Red Slough" is now.

From there, you could easily go up and over a mountain and be into Canyon Creek, Corbold Creek, and this nameless creek area. In Slumach's time and Jackson's day, and for Volcanic Brown, one would have canoed up the river, though it was tough. You'd park the canoe and head out. A day hike with a backpack is a lot of work today, but then it would have been even more difficult.

Rick, Mary, and Brian aboard Dan Gerak's boat on Pitt Lake as this new edition nears its 2024 completion. JANICE ANTONSON

The only way is right up a valley. Yet there it is, a ridge and a look down at Jackson's find.

Gerak has been there. "It's a crevasse that goes down 150 feet. It's so narrow that when I've flown over it you can't see it from a helicopter." He describes it as a little channel no more than ten feet wide. "There are giant trees all over. The trees grow tight over both sides of the creek."

Gerak says the nameless creek feeds into Corbold Creek. "Others say gold was found up Corbold, but Corbold flows the other way. I've panned the creek in the hidden valley when water was low, low—in August." Believing this is the same place worked by Slumach and Jackson and Volcanic Brown, he adds, "I'm not the only one who found gold there. Users have long called the nearby logging road "Golden Road." Ask yourself why." There's a pause. "In all my years following Slumach's legend, this is the only place I know anyone has found gold."

Some forty years ago an old-timer with property along upper Pitt River wanted to sell, and Gerak's dad bought it. Eventually they built what is today the Pitt River Lodge, a mecca for serious sport fishing. And a comfortable setting to muse about a motherlode being within hiking distance.

One wonders if prospecting might be an equally or more tempting endeavour than fish guiding, especially if one believes the source of the legend is close at hand. When asked if he believes, Gerak is emphatic. "Yup, one hundred percent Slumach had gold. And Jackson had gold. And Volcanic Brown had gold. And that hidden valley is where they found it."

Mike Boileau

Will Slumach's gold ever be found? Mike Boileau says, "No. The legend will generate tourist dollars, but that's all you'll ever get out of it." His opinion is based on years of seeking the gold himself, without a positive result.

Boileau's early experience in hiking, camping, and hunting led him toward many adventures. He partnered with Ragnar Bergland (known as "Berg"), who had been searching for the gold near Pitt Lake since the late 1920s, and felt he knew the most promising areas. Berg and his earlier partner, Louis Nelson, had an original focus on the Widgeon Creek area. They came upon one of the many tent-shaped rocks in the area, even before knowing about Jackson's description in his letter to Shotwell, and found signs of previous visits to the area—axe cuts, blazes on trees, etc.

When Boileau and Berg took up searching together, they covered a lot of treacherous ground, including the Spindle Canyon area. In the mid-1970s, they stumbled upon pieces of twisted aluminum, obviously out of place in the dense bush. This led them further uphill, where they came across the wreckage of a Mitchell B-25 bomber, which, it turned out, had crashed in 1953. Rumours had circulated that the B-25 was carrying $800,000 in cash and another $800,000 in gold bullion. The wreckage was a mere eight metres (twenty-five feet) below the crest of the mountain. A slight change in elevation, and the crew would've reached their Vancouver destination safely.

Water in the Widgeon area flows downhill to two locations, the Coquitlam Lake reservoir and Pitt Lake. If there is gold in that area, he believes it will be in a vein. "I'm not sure about placer gold," Boileau says, as the conditions for it were just not right. And he wonders about Spindle Lake, high above Pitt Lake. He's explored all these locations without success, but suggests there is much he might have missed.

Boileau has seen rockslides that cut through the forest of trees, and suggests one of these may have swept over any location where Jackson and others may have found a tent-shaped rock. This location is distant from the Jackson letter description of his search area being north and west of Pitt Lake, but the mountains on that west shore of the lake have become favourites for true believers.

At one point, Boileau found some quartz showing traces of what might be gold, so he had this assayed by Crest Laboratories in Vancouver. Before giving him the results of the assay, a lab employee asked him, "Where did you find this?

He answered, "Up in the mountains."

"No, exactly where was it?"

"Up in the bush."

"Can you be more precise?"

"No, not really, why?"

"Well, if you can access this, you have a substantial find on your hands." Boileau said the results showed the possibility of four ounces of gold per ton of rock, with three ounces of silver.

This find resulted in great interest from two other people he does not name, and Boileau finally agreed to take them to the location, based on an agreement the three signed. The deal went sour when one of them declared, "I already have this area staked." Boileau felt he had been used. Subsequently, one of the two drowned in Pitt Lake, and the other was killed in a plane crash in Yukon Territory. He checked claim records and found their paperwork had been filed two weeks after he had showed them the suspect location, proving he had indeed been deceived. He was unable to return to the location, in any case, so no further proof of the claim was possible.

Boileau has concerns about televised discoveries of small items like a jackknife or picks being associated with Slumach or Jackson, as they could have been left there by anybody. He supports the idea that there is no evidence whatsoever that Slumach had any gold. In fact, he expresses indignation at how Slumach was treated by the criminal justice system in 1890, and maintains that the evidence showed he shot Louis Bee after being threatened with an axe that was about to be thrown at him—in other words, he killed Louis Bee in self-defence.

Boileau answered a knock at his door once to find the young Daryl Friesen standing there, looking for some

A lake at the foot of Stave Glacier. Volcanic Brown's last camp may have been found in this area. ROB NICHOLSON

advice on searching for the elusive gold. He admires the many YouTube videos produced by Friesen as he chases clues and rumours that might lead to a find and has followed Friesen's career, written work, and television appearances with great interest.

Along the way, Boileau has written of his own adventures, and his summary of them, entitled "Forbidden Treasure," is available on the slumach.ca site. Newspaper articles and interviews by filmmakers have figured in his pursuit. Long retired, Boileau speaks fondly of his days seeking the treasure, but insists Slumach never had anything to do with it.

Rob Nicholson

For Rob Nicholson, decades after the first of eleven searches, the mine still proves elusive. Nicholson's personal journey as a gold seeker began long ago, and his interest has continued all these years. His e-book, *Lost Creek Mine* (2003), his extensive website, his searches for the mine's location, and his willingness to share all he knows about the legend attest to his lifelong dedication to searching out the truth about Slumach and his gold.

Nicholson's research began in earnest when he worked in a logging camp at Alvin, on the upper Pitt River. Over the decades, he's made seven helicopter trips and four hiking expeditions into sites in Garibaldi Provincial Park

(the southern half of which was renamed Golden Ears Provincial Park in 1960). Along the way, he has struggled with the harsh territory and personal health challenges, but he packed much material into his publications.

He reports seeing, on one of his trips into the rough country at the head of Pitt Lake, a huge boulder that may be Jackson's tent-shaped rock, though it seems its dimensions would have warranted a note in Jackson's letter. Nicholson's text reads:

> The particular "Jackson" rock to which I refer is in fact huge. It sits alone on a bench not far from Iceworm Creek and definitely seems to be out of place in its surroundings. It is similar in appearance and somewhat larger than the native "standing rock" west of Keremeos, BC.
>
> The "Jackson" rock measures approximately 100 feet by 100 feet at the base by 70 feet in height. It has a slight overhang or lean in a southerly direction. On the ground a few feet out from the base but still just under the peak of the overhang are several very old fire pits spread out to form the shape of a semi-circle or arch.
>
> At the base on one side of the "Jackson" rock is an obviously old depression measuring approximately 4 feet by 3 feet by 1 foot in depth. The depression is not a natural occurrence. The ground cover that has re-established itself over the depression suggests that the hole had been dug many decades earlier.
>
> About 30 feet to one side of the "Jackson" rock are two slabs of rock leaning together that definitely give the appearance of a pup-tent. These slabs measure approximately 8 feet by 8 feet in length by 5 feet in height. One can actually crawl inside this natural rock structure.

What captures the attention of any Slumach aficionado is Nicholson's assertions about this being the rock whereof Jackson wrote,

I am fairly confident that this rock formation is the tent shaped rock that Jackson was referring to simply because of the hundreds of tent shaped rocks in the search area this is the only one that is definitely unique, cannot be missed, and is within the travel distance identified in his letter. And these are the only two rocks on the entire bench.

No marks have been located or identified on either the "Jackson" rock or the tent shaped slabs. However, the inside of the slabs unfortunately were not examined. Jackson literally wrote that there was a mark cut out "in" the rock not "on" the rock. It has been suggested that the mark may actually be on the inside of the slabs. Only a re-examination of the site can determine if Jackson literally meant "in" or "on" the rock.

Nicholson then makes this intriguing revelation: "I have been independently advised that the ashes from the fire-pits were carbon dated a few years ago. The carbon dating results identified the ashes as being circa the very early 1800s."

On the matter of the curse, Nicholson courts controversy with a different interpretation from those generally accepted. He suggests the translation of Slumach's "*Nika memloose, mine memloose*" is "No man who finds the gold will live long enough to bring it out." This is much longer than the "When I die, mine dies" translation usually offered. We sought input on this discrepancy from Indigenous people who know the languages involved. Their conclusion is that Chinook Jargon contains similar words. "*Nika-i*" means "my" or "mine." "*Memloose*" means "to die" or "dead." The word "mine" was judged to be an

A gold seeker views a glacier from a precarious perch. The outlook over Slumach country is magnificent. MICHAEL COLLIER COLLECTION

English reference to the mine. Thus, "When I die, mine dies" appears to be correct.

In his travels in the upper reaches of the mountains northeast of Pitt Lake, Nicholson came across a ruined cabin and, later, a crumbled campsite that had an old stove, a mortar and pestle, and some food tins dating to the early part of the 1900s. These findings led Nicholson to believe that this site might well have been that of Volcanic Brown's last camp, where gold supposedly was found in a glass jar by his would-be rescuers. That report is legendary and has never been confirmed.

Nicholson also speculates about Fire Mountain in the Lillooet area, noting that gold was discovered there in 1880. He writes:

Fire Mountain has been identified as being of significant interest to Game Warden Stevenson during the 1931 search for R.A. Brown. The history of Fire Mountain is not only interesting in the context of R.A. Brown, it is also significant to Jackson.

The initial discovery on Fire Mountain was during the early 1880s and Jackson's time period in question was between 1891 and 1906. It is distinctly probable, as previously mentioned, that Jackson was one of the countless prospectors drawn to the upper Harrison Lake country in search of their fortunes.

Nicholson tells of Stu Brown, who wrote to the provincial government in 1974 claiming to have discovered rich gold deposits inside a provincial park. As recounted earlier, Brown felt that he discovered Jackson's find, but not Slumach's, nor that of Volcanic Brown. Nicholson says this about Stu Brown's find:

The location itself is exactly like Jackson described it, except the canyon is shorter than a mile and one half. Seeing it from the same ridge that Jackson once stood on was an exhilarating experience. Brown describes a pool . . . about twenty feet across and "ankle deep in gold" . . . full of small nuggets.

Nicholson confirmed in our conversation that Brown had indeed brought out a 2.2-kilogram (5-pound) nugget from the site. Trips back in to further prove the claim were thwarted by challenges of weather and illness. Then Brown came up with a plan:

Stu offered to hike into the site with me so that I could both see it for myself and independently document his discovery . . . Stu's plan was for both of us to take two empty packsacks into the site. We would fill one of the packsacks with nuggets, walk it out a short distance and leave it at a predetermined location. We would then walk back in and fill the second packsack, bringing it out to where the first one had been left. The object was to leapfrog the two packsacks out to the location of our vehicle.

Brown and Nicholson arrived very late in the day in the Fire Mountain area, and were about to embark on a two-day hike into the Terrarosa Glacier when they awoke to a heavy rain that had not been forecast. The downpour was so intense that the trip had to be cancelled. Nicholson writes, "Due to Stu's age and his progressively worsening Parkinson's disease, a planned trip the following year had to be cancelled." Readers will appreciate Nicholson's disappointment when he says, "I have not had the opportunity to return to the area."

Nicholson suggests that, given the different kinds of gold that the main protagonists in this story reported finding, there must have been multiple gold finds. He notes that reports of Slumach and Volcanic Brown having gold chipped out of a vein, Jackson finding "colours" (placer gold) and then nuggets, and Stu Brown also finding nuggets, all point to at least two and perhaps three different locations:

The identification of two different types of gold circumstantially identifies two different locations of gold. In my opinion, there is a high probability that there are three separate gold deposits, independent of the other, that have been erroneously

Greg Henderson (left) and Don Waite hold the "lost and found" Waite binder, previously thought irretrievably missing with its irreplaceable documents. COURTESY OF DONALD E. WAITE

interconnected through the generality of the legend itself.

The lengthy time spans between the different finds also make it less likely that all were in the same place:

Slumach brought a substantial quantity of gold into New Westminster on at least one occasion during the 1880s. Jackson wrote his infamous letter claiming . . . to have found a creek, literally full of gold, sometime around the turn of the 19th century. Shotwell and Harrington are on record as returning to civilization with an undetermined quantity of gold in 1911. Gold was found in R.A. "Doc" ["Volcanic"] Brown's last known camp in 1931. In 1974, G.S. "Stu" Brown documents his claim to have found billions of dollars worth of gold in a location that matches the description given in Jackson's letter.

Nicholson reports that some spoilers may have contaminated the area in order to dissuade competitors:

These individuals readily admit to marking several large rocks with either the letter X or the letter J. These unscrupulous individuals also claimed to have flown over several areas and scattered hundreds of pounds of melted brass nuggets in countless different creeks. It was their assumption that if they could not find the legendary gold, they would contaminate areas so badly that no one else would easily find it either.

Frequent correspondence and discussions continued between Nicholson and Stu Brown, focusing on future attempts to find the gold, but age and illness prevented these from taking place.

Nicholson's account wraps up with a collection of local myths, including one that says Slumach's ghost wanders the north Pitt Lake region, awaiting unwary searchers.

Finally, he believes it is unlikely Slumach had any connection to a lost mine or the legend.

With his active searching days over, Nicholson moved on to more writing. In 2009, he created the web-based *BC Prospector Magazine*. This ran for only three editions, but provided ample information on prospecting, gold prices over the decades, bush survival tips, and summaries related to the Slumach legend. The magazine remains available online.

Greg Henderson

There's a video clip online of Greg Henderson and Daryl Friesen charging through the bush north of Pitt Lake, believing that Slumach's gold is within reach. "I can smell it," says Friesen. "It's just around the corner." How those two ended up together on the quest to find the missing mine in the footsteps of Stuart Brown began with Waite's missing binder.

Henderson is a mechanic by trade and is now in his sixties. He'd been an amateur miner as a kid, never too seriously. Into adulthood, he prospected around the Lytton and Lillooet areas. Having heard of Slumach as a child, he admits to finding it "an enticing story" since his mid-twenties. But he had other ways to find treasures. He partnered up with a friend who had a penchant for finding heritage clothing ("jeans worth a thousand dollars") in antique shops or where they had been discarded. They started buying abandoned storage lockers, one of them looking for left-behind jewellery and clothing, and the other looking for things a mechanic could repair and resell.

One day in Maple Ridge, they got a preview look at a locker abandoned by its one-time owner. It was stacked floor to ceiling with old clothing. Plus a motorbike. "Three hundred dollars, and we'll get our money back when I fix the bike. We'll make money on the clothes," he told his partner. They bid. They got it.

The clothing was worthless.

At the very back was a shelving unit. "On top of it was a massive piece of quartz, loaded with iron pyrites. Fool's gold," Henderson says. "Taped to the bottom of it was a note: 'Terrarosa Glacier'."

Then, two items on the bottom shelf drew his attention: a binder and a yellow folder. First he picked up the folder, intrigued by a handwritten message on the cover: "Warning. If you look inside this your life will be in danger." He opened it and thumbed through it quickly. "Inside were geological studies of the upper Pitt River. First Canyon. Second Canyon. Third Canyon. There was a map of Terrarosa Glacier with several X marks. And walk-in points to get to them were identified."

And the binder? It was loaded with photocopies of handwritten notes, newspaper clippings, and copies of research. There was a name within it he'd never heard: Don Waite. "There was so much information in there, I thought I had a gold mine," he said. A thought flashed through his mind: "I'm going to be the guy who finds Slumach's gold."

His partner wanted to throw the paperwork away as they had with the clothing. The story splits in three from here on.

First, Henderson had heard of Friesen and his search for Slumach's gold, and called him. "I've got info here you'd die for," he said. Thinking mostly about the yellow folder and the map within it, he said, "I'm not sharing unless you show me all you have about Slumach." They became fast friends, prospecting and hiking together. "We were obsessed like anybody who finds an X marking the spot on a map." It was Friesen who explained who Don Waite was.

Secondly, and this order is important, Henderson showed up at Waite's bookstore event, as mentioned earlier. Waite's jaw dropped at seeing his long lost material. Soon after, Henderson and Waite met Fred Braches over coffee, and they discussed Waite's missing—now found—binder.

Thirdly, Henderson tried to track down the previous owner of the storage locker. No one with connections to the locker was still alive, but his search led to a Peter Velmore, who was known to have prospected up in the Pitt Lake area in the 1980s. Velmore once worked on a crew that was building the Pitt River Lodge, and one day Velmore had met Waite there. Henderson muses, "He may have taken Waite's binder as I think there's no way Don would have let go of that stuff." Henderson tracked Velmore's trail to where he once lived on the Katzie reserve, and where he had died.

Henderson admits, "I didn't show all of the material [in the folder] to Daryl until the TV show *Curse of the Frozen Gold* was being filmed." The map became a big part of one episode. But it's no longer in his possession. The producers of the show kept Henderson's yellow folder, and, at last report, he had not received it back.

Henderson believes Slumach had gold. "I don't think Slumach found gold anywhere near where everyone's been looking. It came from outside the area. Slumach was a nomadic person, and knew the Indigenous trade routes. Slumach may have been at a Potlatch of Hunter Jack's and been given gold." Henderson hedges his bets: "If it came from within the area, which I don't think it did, then Corbold Creek is the only place that makes sense."

Adam Palmer and Evan Howard

"I don't believe or disbelieve anything—that's why I'm looking." These are the words of mountaineer Adam Palmer, who has hiked the high points around the north end of Pitt Lake for over a decade and a half, much of the time with fellow adventurer Evan Howard, always on the hunt for Slumach's elusive hoard.

To say adventure flows in their blood is an understatement. Whether acting as a two-man team or operating with others, they seem unafraid of any challenge that any location can throw at them.

The duo first met via a post on the popular hiking site clubtread.com. Both wanted to explore the Terrarosa area, and it soon became clear they shared an interest in finding the lost mine. Palmer's interest had been sparked

as a youth; Howard's, too, had begun when he was "growing up in gold country," British Columbia's Fraser Valley. Books on lost gold mines caught their attention, and they gravitated to the one closest to home—Slumach's supposed find. Both combined an early love of climbing mountains with the quest for gold, and they focused that quest on the Pitt Lake area.

Palmer and Howard launched their first search together in 2009, and over the years, they have tackled the Terrarosa Glacier, the Stave Glacier, the Lillooet and Douglas mountain ranges, the Piluk Glacier, the upper Pitt River, the Misty Icefield, Fire Lake, and Harrison Lake. Both say the Stave area was the "most promising."

Palmer cites Volcanic Brown's repeated quests in the Stave Glacier area to support his focus on that search location. He says, "Brown was on the Stave Glacier for many years, exploring, and he is the only real-life prospector that had the most knowledge of the legend and geologically as well." Howard agrees, feeling the actual location could be "more Volcanic Brown's than Jackson's, if one believes the letter." Palmer and Howard have searched diligently for evidence of Brown's last camp, as well as indications of any "finds" he may have had.

Do they believe Jackson and his letter were real? Palmer says, "Prospectors came out of there with gold. Was one Jackson? I'm not sure." Howard joins in, "I'd like to believe he found gold and that Brown followed in his footsteps."

Both adventurers have been thrilled to share their journeys with the world through their television work. Together, Palmer and Howard led the team of searchers who starred in the 2015 television series *Curse of the Frozen Gold* up to the lofty heights of the Terrarosa and Stave Glaciers, and other challenging locations where they believe gold will be found. Howard continued the quest with a new team in the 2022 series *Deadman's Curse*.

The challenge, of course, is that there's "never enough time." Palmer says "working with professional journalists and researchers helping to solve this legend" has been among his best experiences to date. He says most people will never really know what searchers go through when they're on an expedition in the search areas. "Words cannot describe the vastness of the territory." Howard's assessment cites "working with an entire team" as a highlight. Both clearly embrace the teamwork involved in such searches.

Does Palmer believe significant amounts of gold will be found in the broad search area? His answer is short and to the point: "Yes!" On the other hand, Howard smiles as he says, "I hope not"—he wants to continue the search as long as possible.

Their energy, enthusiasm, and obvious competence in tackling the challenges of searching in the higher locations are contagious, and one has only to view both television series to gauge that. And they'll continue searching. Howard notes, "The bad, sad, and dark sides to history and this story and legend can be really heavy," but with new information coming to light frequently and people digging deeper into Slumach's story, the mountains remain compelling for both adventurers.

Kru Williams

"Speaking as a prospector, there is gold out there, plain and simple."

Kru Williams is one very stoked and energetic prospector—an intriguing aspect of this competitive martial artist who trains fighters in his Port Moody gym.

Williams was sixteen years old when his uncle regaled him with an enticing legend involving a "crazy Indian" who lived in the woods. "Oh yeah," the uncle added, "There's a curse to consider, too!" He warned Williams that if he went up there to look for gold, there was going to be trouble.

The hopped-up teenager was determined to prove his uncle wrong. He couldn't understand how someone like Slumach, who according to some Indigenous Peoples lived off the land and cherished the earth and its people, could be a murderer. "I started to feel a kinship with Slumach, and that's when I started doing my own research," recalls Williams, whose very heart and soul reside in nature, especially in the wilds around Pitt Lake.

Williams believes that Indigenous people had no use for gold. But, he says, Slumach was around miners in town. He saw who had money and who didn't, and then he figured out how they got it.

> Slumach was aware of the European settlers' ways, and he saw how they gained riches to get their alcohol or women. Once you're in the bush and you continually go out hunting and fishing— it's the only place you want to be. It made sense to me why Slumach lived out where he lived. If you're in the Pitt, you fall in love with the Pitt. If you're on the river, mountains out here, you're the richest man alive because you can't pay for paradise like this.

Driven to immerse himself in Slumach country, Williams moved to the Pitt area and then to Harrison Bay, where he lives today.

When COVID-19 hit and mandates to isolate were issued, Williams seized the opportunity to get back out in the bush and start prospecting. "I figured if gold is in the Pitt, it's got to prove itself in the Pitt River. The problem is that the Pitt is full of so much silt. Prospecting is perseverance. Nobody goes out there just 'getting' gold. You have to prospect for it and try, try, try again." Williams prospected on the Fraser River, with little luck.

Then, a chance encounter in Chehalis territory with Adam Palmer (another martial-arts enthusiast) and a memorable four-hour conversation with him about Slumach re-ignited his enthusiasm. "Adam was young, cool and knew how to get out in the bush and move. I'm a physical guy and Adam is extremely physical. I've got the prospecting; Adam's got the mountaineering, a "'no-brainer,'" he quips.

They promised each other early on that they would search together for—and find—that elusive shiny gold. It was the occasion that set the two of them on difficult and dangerous missions in search of the legendary gold, as recounted in the then soon-to-be-filmed History Channel series *Deadman's Curse*.

Top Adam Palmer and Taylor Starr take a break at the Misty Icefield in search of a legend as much as in a search of lost gold. DARYL FRIESEN

Bottom David Muise, shown here with Adam Palmer on the right, is the only gold seeker to claim, on record, "I found Slumach's gold." GREAT PACIFIC MEDIA

David Muise

It's a statement for the ages, at once brash and unbelievable, but on the public record: "My name is David Muise, and I found Slumach's lost gold mine."

Muise is part Tom Sawyer and part Sherlock Holmes—and perhaps part Peter Pan. He showed up as a surprise to almost everyone at a Lost Mine of Pitt Lake Society meeting in 2022, the same year he appeared in *Deadman's Curse*. He'd been looking for the lost gold forever. Who knew?

Muise's confidence comes across as a mixture of naiveté and experience. His story is one of climbing and seeking and a preoccupation with defeating any curse, while at the same time being scared off by it. His belief is that the gold exists, though he's got none in his pockets. His tale is exasperating to listen to but sure to gain followers, if they can figure out where he went.

He saw the gold in the creek—"I stood two feet away, and there's lots." He shied away from taking it: "I left it. That's where the curse came in." Now, he's going back to get it. He knows the odds are against him—both for getting the gold out and for living to tell about it.

Acknowledging that dozens if not a hundred adventurers go in search of the mine each year, he says there are "probably one or two that perish."

Muise figures that paying with one's life is one of the curse's costs of finding Slumach's gold. A run-up investment is losing all that you own in pursuit, and that is a cost he has paid. "It cost me everything I had. Plus thirty-three thousand dollars," he says. Not quite everything—he kept his car and lived out of it for years. The lesson sobers him, but not to the extent of giving up his quest: "Why would I give up now?"

His site—and he's the only one attempting it—is just east of Pitt Lake's more likely legend locations. He has settled on Stave Lake, actually just to the north of it. He's excitable, often talking like his mouth and mind are on fast-forward. "I know what is there. What to expect. How to get in. How to get out," he says confidently.

And getting in is tough, with the usual access challenges searchers find in this area, given the rough and often vertical terrain. He got there once. As he posted on a community forum, "When I arrived at the large tent-shaped rock, I found it had a pile of stones placed on top

Gail Starr is a recognized authority on Indigenous culture and married to Don Froese, who appears in the TV series *Deadman's Curse*. INDIGENOUS CULTURAL AND HERITAGE MONITOR

of it. These stones were independently chosen and placed in a way to mimic the cliff that is just west of the rock."

He made at least one return attempt. On that occasion he fashioned a raft to reach the north end of the lake. He made his way to the foot of an immense waterfall that he says "guards" the hidden site. Getting up alongside the tumbling water is a forbidding task, and cannot be achieved easily. Claiming that the waterfall was sparse and friendly at another time of the year, he says he once made it to the top and that's where he said the gold is.

He's written,

> I know that many have searched and some have even said they found it but I will tell you that nobody has seen this place in decades. The markers spoken about in the stories are all there but the directions are off. Probably meant to keep people away from its true location. I have documented it all. Such as the 2 mile valley, creek with no outlet, tent rock, the mark cut into it, the 3 peaks on a lower ledge, the water coming out of the rock just below the dam, you have to make a circle to get to the mine . . .

Defeated not by fear but by the reality of a difficult climb to where "it's four thousand feet up," Muise says he will persevere. "I want to be known as the man who found Slumach's gold mine."

Taylor Starr and Don Froese, the Spirit Catchers

Slumach followers agree: the allure of finding gold is compelling, and unravelling a legend is fun and challenging. But there are some different, important perspectives around the man and his legend that deserve equal attention.

In 2023, Don Froese, his wife, Gail Starr, and their daughter, Taylor Starr, graciously shared with us their deep connections to Slumach. Fortunately, readers can discover more about these connections in television programs such as *Deadman's Curse* and the popular *Deadman's Curse: Slumach's Gold* podcast.

Froese, whose Halq'eméylem name is Peq Yexwela (meaning "white eagle"), is a hunter, fisherman, Elder of the Sq'éwqel (Seabird Island) Band.

He first became aware of the Slumach story through his long-time friendship with Adam Palmer. Froese's interest deepened during one of his careers when, as a census worker, his job brought to light how the Euro-Canadian legal system treated (or mistreated) Slumach and his people.

"What really interested me was not so much Slumach finding gold, but just his story as a person living in Katzie on that particular reserve, and how he was a man of the land. He was very much connected to the land and connected to the water," says Froese.

"My content spirit, my peace of mind and heart come from the land. People like Slumach remind me a lot of my Elders and my relatives," reflects Froese.

Any excitement searching for gold on *Deadman's Curse* is tempered by poignant glimpses into the history of Indigenous Peoples in what is now known as Canada. "It's opened our eyes to where people once walked on these traditional trade routes thousands of years ago, and up to the early 1900s. Today, nobody walks those paths."

Froese isn't concerned that viewers will want to check out the show's locations for themselves. Fortunately, the show doesn't reveal specific locations, which Froese says are protected by ancestral guardians.

"We're treading very carefully . . . we have to go in and use a lot of our traditional teachings to walk these paths, otherwise we're going to get in trouble. We don't want anyone to get hurt."

"The real gold is just having the opportunity to be in these locations."

Gail Starr, whose Indigenous name is Kwelaxtelotiya (meaning "to be close to"), is a cultural elder with the Sq'éwqel and is connected to Slumach through her maternal grandfather. They are descendants of John Halim, who came to British Columbia in 1858 from the Big Island in Hawaii, looking for gold. She believes that Slumach would have been of mixed Hawaiian and Coast Salish heritage.

Kanaka Creek flows down from Maple Ridge to join the Fraser River at the eastern end of what is now the "Haney Bypass" route for the Lougheed Highway. The name is a reference to the Native Hawaiians who came to the Pacific Northwest in the mid-1800s to work as labourers aboard Hudson's Bay Company vessels during the fur trade. They were referred to as "Kanakas," derived from kānaka in the Hawaiian language, which is used by Native Hawaiians to refer to themselves. They first settled next to Fort Langley, and then moved across the river to establish a settlement where the creek named after them meets the Fraser. Jason Allard felt Slumach may have been born on Vancouver Island; his daughter was living in Cowichan at one point.

The TV series *Deadman's Curse* exposed some of the wrongdoings that occurred in the past, she says. Information found in paper clippings and other documents painted Slumach as a villain or "this wild man of the woods, and a very not-so-nice person."

This incorrect information is why, according to Starr, the Katzie people are reluctant to talk about Slumach. Elders say that in truth, Slumach was a community person; he liked to be up in the mountains; he had a family; he provided for the community.

Their perspectives convey Slumach as a man of the land, and as such, living in his traditional Katzie territory and looking after it. He encountered people who didn't belong there, and developed a reputation as a crazy man up in the mountains.

"He was a loner, but he was just protecting his land and (the) rights of the Katzie First Nation," affirms Starr. "The Katzie community never talked about the gold; they only talked about the land."

But, she adds, when Slumach found gold, his life as a Katzie community member changed. People (including Louis Bee) wanted to know where he found it. Because the federal government made changes to reserve boundaries, many of the community members were displaced, and moved from their original community down toward the Fraser River. The Katzie Reserve today is on the north bank of the Fraser, around the north end of the Golden Ears Bridge.

"Katzie are still dealing with the history from the 1800s and their separation."

Taylor Starr, Slumach's great-great-grandniece, carries her grandmother's traditional name, Falmouqtelotiya.

Until she was about twenty-three, Taylor Starr knew little about Slumach; she then began learning about his family, on her grandmother's side. "Why hadn't I heard about Slumach?" she recalls. "Why don't people talk about him?" Her curiosity took hold.

Participating in *Deadman's Curse* was an enticing opportunity for Starr to discover more about Slumach. "I'm loving every second of it because I'm going to the archives, and going out on the land where Slumach could have walked. So how better to learn about my ancestor than to actually follow in his footsteps?"

Starr believes a treasure exists . . . somewhere. "Even though we walked in his footsteps, we could be walking right over it, or thousands of miles from it."

On collaborating with the *Deadman's Curse* team, Starr says, "Our connection to our ancestors is something that can't be written down, and when that's shown to us on an expedition or on location somewhere, the production pivots pretty quick, and they do it with a lot of respect . . . "

On their spirit quest, she says, "From an Elders' view, they say this is good medicine for people; it gives them hope."

Jason Ovid Allard, interpreter at the Slumach trial, and possibly Slumach's jailer.
FRED BRACHES COLLECTION/PUBLIC DOMAIN

Fred Braches, the Skeptic

Little did we know when we first met with Fred Braches that he would become the dean of Slumach investigators, bringing all that was known and claimed about the legend as close to an academic impartiality as we'd meet in our research.

Braches was at Don Waite's place on a drizzly Saturday morning in February 2007 when Rick dropped by for a visit and to meet Braches.

"I heard you'd be here, so I came," Fred said to Rick. "First, I read your book from 1972. I saw you treated Slumach with respect. I'm looking for Slumach, facts first. Not looking for gold. Nice to meet you." Fred handed Rick a coffee, and the three sat down and began an easy conversation that laid the ground for strong friendships among the authors as the years evolved; stories were swapped, and respect earned.

Braches was to become infamous as "the skeptic" in all things Slumach, questioning and out-researching others, documenting minutiae, and holding tellers of tall tales accountable. While some might have seen him as curmudgeonly, others saw him as avuncular. Where some came to see him as intransigent, others saw a historian relying on details. That he was the resident guru as well as a confident questioner during the *Curse of the Frozen Gold* TV series seemed a natural outgrowth of his reputation for preferring fact over fiction. With his hugely informative website, slumach.ca, he became as close to a "Slumach scholar" as there is.

Braches was clear from the outset: "British Columbia, between the Fraser and Klondike gold rushes, was a world full of prospectors, fortune seekers, and speculators, and even blather about gold would have triggered a stampede to the Pitt Lake area." And nothing of the sort ever happened.

Notes from the conversation with Waite that morning are interspersed with observations by Braches. When talk turned to Slumach's hanging, he sat forward on the couch and gave his opinion that the half-day trial was "exceedingly short." He opened a leather case that held two photocopies of a document. "I brought you each one of these. It's a copy of the judge's procedure notes and the hanging certificate. I finally tracked them down in the Ottawa archives."

Spidery handwriting filled the white spaces around the printed document's framed words:

Department of the Secretary of State, Canada.
Address: New Westminster B.C.
Name: Hon. Mr. Justice Drake
Date: 15/24 Nov. 1890
Heading: Capital Case of Sumah (or Shumah)

Among the pages in Fred's leather case was a copy of a Canadian Pacific Railway Company telegram that read: "Your letter . . . in reference to the execution of the Indian Sumach received this day . . . " Waite and Rick flipped through Braches's research while he added his observations.

"You know, there's no record of Bee's death certificate. And Bee's wife, Kitty, is the only one to speak about him at the trial," said Braches.

"Slumach should have pleaded self-defence," he continued.

Waite and Rick nodded in agreement.

"And the sketch in your book from 1972 shows four people in the canoe when Slumach shot Bee. Change that. There were only two—Bee and an Indian from Harrison River named Seymour."

Braches sat quietly as Waite reminisced about his trips to Pitt Lake seeking the lost gold. When Waite was done, Braches reverted to debatable details. He said he thought that Slumach should have been spared capital punishment because of his old age.

To back up his assertions that the Slumach story has been wildly distorted, Braches was compiling copies of as much original 1890s material related to Slumach's time before the murder, arrest, and trial as he could put his hands on. He wanted to concentrate on the people and the time, rather than the legends that grew, unaccountably in his view, from Slumach's hanging. It was his intention to ferret out every document tucked within archives or found, copied, or kept by scholars or fellow researchers.

"The Slumach story has grown to a collection of legends of epic proportions, and it is time that we go back to the source and the simple facts," he said.

Braches posted a set of primary sources online regarding Slumach, the man, and his trial, adding some commentary to those. These formed the core of his award-winning slumach.ca website. He explained, "I'm sharing the records I've found and will add to the collection as new material comes to me. That information is there for all to use and appreciate. There's no commerce in binding this information for resale, although I am planning to make a desktop version available."

Braches wouldn't let us go without talking about the speculation that Slumach had gold, of a sort.

"We've heard rumours the Harrison Indians [Sts'ailes People] told Slumach where the mine was," he began. "That accounts for stories he had half a sugar bag filled with nuggets. Slumach had let them use his canoe. So if he did have gold, he'd likely have gotten it second-hand from them. In that case, it wasn't even Pitt Lake gold. It was Harrison Lake gold."

Not that such a "what if" scenario means he believed Slumach actually had anything to do with gold: "You already suggested in your book from 1972 that the newspaper people at the time of the crime would have had a field day if there was any reason to connect Slumach with gold findings—there is nothing of that kind in the 1890s records."

As the coffee and the morning both ran out, Braches prepared to leave. He did so with an admonition: "You're writers. Often, not all the facts go through as truth. Readers deserve to know the difference between healthy skepticism and fabricated stories. That motivates me to seek what was behind the man behind the legend."

BRACHES'S CONCERNS AND COMMITMENT strengthened our own commitment to sort through the rubble of rumours and layers of facts once more before our 2007 edition went to press. As our research work continued, he provided views on a variety of topics he had uncovered in his search for the truth. Fred ensured that other researchers knew the need to be impartial and to see the lure of the legend that evolved around Slumach as based upon false stories, self-aggrandizement by unreliable witnesses, and allegations about as-far-from-known "facts" as they could be. That, however, did not keep these "facts" from being repeated by newspapers with a willing, gullible audience. Braches alluded to one of many examples of mistruths, in the August 8, 1926, edition of the Sunday *Province*, which published an interview with Jason Allard about Slumach. Braches wrote as follows, later identifying such instances as "creative journalism":

Jason Allard, "who knows everything there is to be known about Fraser Valley Indians," according to the *Province*, knew Slumach "the desperado" by repute, and he claimed to have been one of Slumach's jailers. Allard believed that Slumach and his brother were born in Nanaimo, although their father came from the Pitt Lake and Pitt River area. Living up the Nanaimo River, Allard suggested Slumach murdered any stragglers coming his way for the only reason that he "liked to be monarch of all he surveyed." Caught in the act of killing "an Indian," he escaped by playing dead in his canoe and with his brother moved to Pitt Lake and there, living like hermits, murdered "everyone that ventured into their territory . . ."

"One can picture the wild terror of being hunted by this long-haired strange creature." Allard told the interviewer, "When Slumach was first captured, he behaved just as any wild creature would do." Allard remembered that the longhaired Slumach "had wonderfully large eyes which reminded of the eyes of a grey lynx." Later in the article, we read that Slumach "was not given to talk and never boasted about the number of scalps he had taken."

In the eyes of many in those days, Slumach was a savage. On the other hand, Allard described Slumach as a "most charming personality, with the manners of a French dancing master . . . [who]

This rifle is similar to the one Slumach used to murder Louis Bee in 1890. OP MEDIA GROUP

continued to exhibit the same good manners" during his time in jail. Slumach's name, according to Allard, was actually *Slough Mough*, which means "rain," and he also suggested that Slumach's brother's name was *S'mamqua* or "ceremonial undertaker," a name Allard thought very appropriate because this brother "always chose the graveyard to do his courting."

The surname Bee of the victim, "half-breed Kanaka" Louis Bee, is interpreted by Allard as *Poll-al-ee*, though records show it was *Boulier*. No evidence was ever presented to back up Allard's claims regarding Slumach's previous violence. About the "secret of a great gold mine" the reporter adds: "Had Mr. Allard only known that his prisoner knew of its existence, he might have become a very wealthy man, for the murderer, with his fine manners, would undoubtedly have told him where it was."

Braches went on to reflect on the person at the centre of the legend:

In her interviews, Aunt Mandy stressed that her parents (Peter and Katherine Pierre) said that Slumach was a kind old man, and that he was a crippled and harmless old widower who lived in a shack at the bottom end of Pitt Lake, on the abandoned Silver Creek Indian Reserve.

Why, then, did this kind, elderly man shoot Bee? Slumach reportedly also told Jason Allard "that the young man who he killed had tantalized him on every occasion." It was said that there was "bad blood between Slumach and Bee." Bee's words that day may have been the last straw, enough to enrage Slumach to the point that he shot and killed him with his old front loader.

There is some debate among well-intentioned historians over whether Slumach shot Bee in self-defence. Don Waite recalled that Aunt Mandy told him "Bee came at Slumach with an axe." Waite is inclined to "believe her version over that of Seymour's, being fully aware of what the police, etc., could have told Seymour to say at the trial."

Braches countered that Mandy's remarks about an axe-wielding Bee not only do not match testimony at the trial, they do not match descriptions of Bee's shot wound. He suggested an axe-wielding Bee would have suffered a frontal shot, and not one "at the shoulder, going down through the heart and lung," which was described by Dr. Walker, who performed the autopsy on Bee's body. Braches concludes that Dr. Walker's testimony "is consistent with Charlie Seymour's witness account of the murder."

Braches worked to put to rest other falsehoods, encouraging us to better define truths, avoid teasing with hearsay, and assiduously rid the tale of willful misstatements.

Wrote Braches,

There were rumours in the press at the time of his conviction that this was not the first time Slumach had killed, but as Aunt Mandy said: "It all started with all the lies they said about him.

He was this and that, you know, a cruel old man and all that." Indian Agent McTiernan believed Slumach, who denied that he had killed anyone other than Louis Bee.

Braches notes, "The buzz may have related to a number of reportedly unsolved murders in the area for which Slumach's hanging was meant to be a deterrent, aside from punishment for his own crime."

Whatever musings of the day were satisfied, one element of the legend is not disputed, as Braches notes: "With the hanging of this old man, the press's interest in Slumach died."

BRACHES DID NOT LET up over time. We had introduced coverage in the *Daily Columbian* of the Louis Bee murder by noting, "The most reliable information on Slumach is found in the press records of 1890–91." Fred later suggested that calling the *Daily Columbian's* information "reliable" was too strong an endorsement. He explained one notable discrepancy:

> The reliability of the press as a source of information is immediately put in question by the account of the murder in the *Daily Columbian's* first report in September 1890, a version repeated in January 1891 after the hanging of Slumach. What is reported in the press is quite different from what is recorded at the inquisitions and the trial. If, as reported in the newspaper story, there were "several other Indians" around when Bee was murdered, they all would have been called to witness. In truth there was only one witness to the murder, a man called Seymour, from Harrison, and it is on his pronouncement that Slumach was convicted. This Seymour lived in a fishing camp at Lillooet (now Alouette) Slough together with Louis Bee, their wives and an unnamed old man.

On that fateful day, Bee and Seymour set out to find bait for their sturgeon line. They heard a shot and went to see who was shooting and what the shooter was hunting. Sitting in their canoe alongside the shore they encountered Slumach, who was standing on the bank with a single-barreled muzzleloader in his hand. Some words were spoken, Slumach fired, and Bee's dead body dropped overboard into the river. Slumach went to his own canoe and started reloading his gun. Seymour fled over land, recovered his canoe later and reported the murder to the Indian Agent Peter McTiernan at New Westminster that same night.

The earliest printed reference of the search for gold in the Pitt Lake area that we found while researching our 1972 publication was in the April 3, 1906, edition of the *Province*. Braches critiqued it as we were editing our 2007 book—informing assertions we'd made with new facts or interpretations. Under the headline "Buried Treasure at Pitt Lake," the story says "that it would appear that some man Frazier secured information that an old man, who has ere [*sic*] this been gathered to his rest had some valuable placer grounds in the Pitt Lake country. He had recovered $8,000 in gold nuggets and these he had hidden under a rock. He had then passed away, but had left directions where the treasure and the placer ground had to be found."

To us co-authors, this sounded like the famous (if hard to prove he existed) W. Jackson, so where did the name Frazier come from? Was Frazier another prospector or another identification for the same story?

Reportedly, Frazier's news came to the knowledge of others who set out to find the gold "ahead of another party which was stampeding to the treasure ground." Of course, nothing was found. They all had a hard time, though: "The party had a very rough trip as the weather was rainy, and sleeping out did not remind one of the dreams between Dutch feathers."

Might the man who recovered "$8,000 in gold nuggets" and left it "hidden under a rock" be Jackson? This would be slightly later than the time of his reported trek into the rugged country northeast of Pitt Lake, but the verbal clues match those in his famous letter.

BRACHES CREATED HIS AWARD-WINNING slumach.ca site shortly after our 2007 book *Slumach's Gold: In Search of a Legend* was published, and it has grown to be *the* reference site for all who seek information on Slumach and the legend that surrounds him. An award of excellence from the annual conference of the British Columbia Historical Society was bestowed upon Fred and the slumach.ca site on May 25, 2009. Virtually everything ever written about the Slumach story, from early newspaper reports of Bee's murder, Slumach's capture and eventual execution, through numerous articles, fantastic tales, legal records, books, and other miscellaneous items are on the site. It excels at exposing falsehoods. The physical collection backing up the site's postings resides today with the Special Collections department at the Vancouver Public Library, but digital copies of everything are available online.

Braches also produced two Wikipedia pages that profile the story. They summarize the legend and are excellent repositories of almost everything that has grown up around these topics.

In 2017, Braches published his first book on the subject, *Fact and Fiction: Slumach and the Lost Creek Mine.* Then, in 2019, he released *Searching for Pitt Lake Gold: Facts and Fantasy in the Legend of Slumach*, dedicated to Slum.ook, the name recorded in an 1879 census of Indigenous Peoples, which accounted for various groups from Yale through Coquitlam, listing the number of dependents, population, etc.

Braches has numerous works to his credit on his community of Whonnock, BC, where he resided for decades. His writings are popular with residents and researchers alike who seek in-depth information on local history.

Sadly, Fred Braches passed away at the age of ninety-three on February 1, 2024. Around two hundred mourners attended his memorial service in early March: friends, family, fellow Slumach writers, admirers all.

Fred Braches, historian, researcher, author, television star, and consistent skeptic seeking the truth versus the fiction of the lost gold mine of Pitt Lake. GUILLERMO GARCIA

Overleaf A rainbow casts a beautiful glow over Fire Mountain and Fire Lake, along the route often taken by gold seekers. Is there a pot of gold at the end? ADAM PALMER

Chapter 13

Curse of the Frozen Gold

THE MEMO HEADER LEAPT off Brian's computer screen in March 2014: "Re: Slumach TV project."

It had been years since a TV production about Slumach had been aired, so Brian jumped at this new opportunity. Kristen Colle was connecting from a Toronto-based television production company called JV Productions. They were producing a documentary on the Slumach story and were using our 2007 book as "a valuable resource." Could we talk on the phone?

Moments later, Brian was hearing Colle's pleasant voice on the phone line. She said the company wondered if they could continue using our book as a resource with our blessing, and if we authors might be interested in more formal involvement on camera.

"We've been talking with Don Waite and Fred Braches. We know Daryl Friesen and Adam Palmer," said Colle. She also mentioned Danny Gerak and Evan Howard, all of whom had been part of the Slumach fraternity for some time, so Brian felt he was in familiar territory. He replied with a resounding "yes," and said he would confirm the willingness of his co-authors to be involved. Thus began our participation in *Curse of the Frozen Gold*.

Danny Gerak's Pitt River Lodge became the home of the cast and crew, and a log home upriver became the "location" for the crew's on-camera sessions. A poster board featuring visual items related to the various searches they embarked upon provided a busy backdrop to their meetings. Outside, a large helicopter pad was the base for easy airlifting in and out of the location for the crew, cast, and equipment. The upper Pitt River and its rich fishing opportunities flowed by just a few yards away.

In this production, various theories on possible locations for Slumach's supposed hoard were explored. The legend itself was analyzed as well. Palmer and Howard supported the concept of gold being found at the higher elevations where they had been searching for many years. Friesen favoured locations both up high and down low, and eventually they found a mining stake bearing the name of prospector Clayton Gadsby, long believed to have found a promising location. Waite pointed to locations actually near the upper Pitt River. Gerak pointed to locations further afield, up Corbold Creek to the lower echelons of the Terrarosa and Stave Glaciers, where Volcanic Brown was said to have searched.

The series positions Braches as the inimitable skeptic amongst a group of five unabashedly ardent gold seekers who passionately search for Slumach's hidden hoard. He maintains a calm, reasoning approach to all alleged evidence throughout the six episodes, repeatedly demanding "proof" beyond legendary information or "feelings" about promising locations.

One midway episode took Friesen, Waite, and Braches to San Francisco in a hunt for proof of Jackson's existence, given his reported return to San Francisco in 1901, where he allegedly deposited gold nuggets of a value between $8,000 and $10,000 in the Bank of British North America. A tip that ship passenger records might have survived the fire that destroyed the bank in 1906 led the trio searching for that evidence. While the name Jackson turned up, the timing was wrong, and thus the expedition failed to substantiate the man's existence, let alone his gold.

Brian and Rick figured in the third episode, brought in as "the guys who wrote the book with Mary Trainer" to talk about their own theories as to the reality of Slumach's legends and also the locations where searching might prove fruitful. Brian's penchant for the Sloquet Valley Creek area and Stu Brown's interest in the location led the producers to propose a separate trip there—one that never got made, thwarted by fog that kept the helicopter on the ground and rains that ruined the road access. Sloquet Creek flows out of the area below the Terrarosa and Stave Glaciers and had long attracted Brian as a location for Stu Brown's pond. Rick's fixation with Widgeon Creek being in "Slumach's back yard" was similarly thwarted as inclement weather lingered in the area.

The ever-candid Friesen told us that while he and the crew were near Stu Brown's reputed site, they had actually found a bit of gold, which he held up to show us. It was captured on video.

Having exhausted every search angle they could in the time and conditions available, the season came to a close without finding leads that could point to success. *Curse of the Frozen Gold* made it to the small screen on the History Channel in Canada and Animal Planet in the US in the fall of 2015. The producers hoped for a second season, but timing was not a friend: the American election of 2016 captured attention spans shortly after the first airing. The single season survives on repeats, but a second season has not been forthcoming.

Danny Gerak regrets that: "Too bad we didn't get a second season. We were just getting into serious work."

He told Rick of loggers finding an anvil ("An anvil!" he laughs) in the woods alongside Golden Road. This was a clear enough indication to him of mining close enough to a "hidden valley" to validate his theory. And the loggers had found caves dug into the mountains, large enough for a prospector to crawl through searching for something of value, like gold.

"And in one they found a cross. We were going in the right direction. We went to the creek, but never to the top end where you need climbing ropes. We only went for the show, not looking for gold in the nooks and crannies."

The flip side of his regret holds hope for other gold seekers. "With the proper resources, like a second season, we would have found gold. To me, there's something there," concludes Gerak.

Gold seekers as television stars frame the banner for *Curse of the Frozen Gold* promotions in 2015. Daryl Friesen, Danny Gerak, Don Waite, Fred Braches, Adam Palmer, and Evan Howard prepare for the first episode. COURTESY OF THE DISCOVERY CHANNEL

Overleaf ADAM PALMER COLLECTION

Chapter 14

To Stake a Claim

IT WOULD HAVE BEEN immensely helpful to future gold seekers if Jackson had formally staked a claim in 1901, leaving behind his preferred location registered with the provincial mining department. The seasoned prospector Volcanic Brown at least left his last campsite as a clue. However, few contemporary gold seekers have filed papers or banged markers into the ground and declared, "Here's where I think Slumach's gold is." So, when challenged to make good on location theories, Rick and Brian decided to stake claims.

They were at Pitt River Lodge with the television crew and exploration team filming *Curse of the Frozen Gold* in the summer of 2014. Outside the lodge's windows, the wind howled. Don Waite, wrapped in a sweater, nudged others to consult a topographical map on the table before them and declare "[their] best guess where to go searching for gold in our next episode." Lodge owner Danny Gerak claimed it must be in vicinity of his lodge, or else his years of hunting for gold while fishing for salmon may have been wasted.

Daryl Friesen, ever opinionated, ever be-hatted, ever rubbing his right hand on the scruff of his beard, was ready to boast about some remote site no one knew of when he instead turned to Rick and Brian and said, "You've just arrived today, what's your idea?"

Rick replied, "Widgeon Creek. It's close to where Slumach shot Bee. Near where Slumach lived. Rough enough territory to hide a gold creek. I've hiked there and sensed how easy it would be to get lost."

"Well . . . in as practical a sense," Brian countered, "I'd say Canyon Creek, given its proximity, is another possibility." Everyone knew Canyon Creek was to the northeast of where they stood that day in the warmth of the log-walled room. It flows into Corbold Creek, which drains from glaciers and flows into the upper Pitt River. Brian said, "When we first heard the story around the campfire in 1957, Canyon Creek was alluded to. It was only when researching our 1972 book that I found out I was actually thinking of Corbold Creek, which flows into the upper Pitt River. I'd been wrong about the name all these years."

Friesen pounced on Brian's comment. "You should stake claims at Canyon Creek. I've got one near where Canyon Creek feeds into Corbold Creek from the east, a mile and a half upstream from the Pitt. I know unclaimed sites near my claim."

The next morning at breakfast, Friesen unfolded a map showing the exact location of his claim. Logging roads crossed not far away. There were four spots noted on the creek, one showing a handwritten STAKED. "That's mine," he said. "I suggest you stake the two sites west from mine. The creek flows your way and there's a steep descent that might have fed gold there." Rick nodded, enthralled.

With Daryl's help, Brian and Rick staked a claim where Brian had long envisioned the mine may be—at Canyon Creek, which feeds into Corbold Creek. Their three claims were in close proximity, giving them a sense of confidence in the location, though it proved to be a challenging location. *VANCOUVER PROVINCE/PNG*

"I'll help you file the claim," offered Friesen, no doubt thinking company on the creek might enhance his own prospects. "At your age, it's free. There'll be maybe twenty bucks in related filing charges. And, it'll cost you a couple hundred bucks when you renew."

In a show of companionship, Brian took a twenty-dollar note out of his wallet and pushed it across the table to Friesen, who circled our sites on his map. Brian said, "Upper Pitt River, Corbold and Canyon Creeks, and

the possible location of the lost creek gold mine. I'm in."

The following week, back from the woods and with an air of excitement, Brian and Rick went to a government office on Dewdney Trunk Road in Maple Ridge, each with their "Free Miner Claim" papers downloaded from the website and filled in. True to his offer, Daryl Friesen had been walking us through the process over the phone and helped us both apply for a British Columbia electronic identification, which is free and begins the claim-staking process. The resulting account confirmation allows a period of ninety days to complete Mineral Titles Online (MTO), the provincial electronic registration form, which allowed us to receive a "client name" and proceed by "presenting yourself and supporting documentation" at a Point of Service office.

The website's admonition is enchanting: "With the issuance of your free miner certificate, you have become a valid free miner":

A Free Miner Certificate (FMC) gives you the right to:
• acquire and maintain mineral and placer title;
• access your title during exploration and development.

The certificate also clarified cautions that those exploring their staked claim need to keep in mind, among them:

An FMC does not authorize you to do certain things during the five years it's valid, including:
• to use a FMC for purposes other than activities directly related to mineral or placer exploration and mining;
• to place any structure (cabin, greenhouse, garbage) on your title;
• to conduct any mining activity (exploration, road building) without approval from a Regional Mines Office.

About the location of our claims, Friesen said, "I've been there, but never made it down to the creek. It's real steep. Maybe a couple hundred feet. Only way to get at the creek east or west from where your claims are is by climbing down. Where our claims are—yours are beside mine—it's a cliff. You'll rappel by rope. Your claims straddle the creek. Be careful crossing it." A claim, Rick and Brian would learn, covers 52 hectares, or 128 acres.

Brian had determined the following coordinates on Google maps: 40 degrees, 37' 24"N and 122 degrees, 37' 30.5"W. He also noted that the ridge elevation was 536 metres.

A few weeks after we had filed our claims, journalist Glen Schaefer wrote a piece in the *Province* about the lost creek gold mine. He began by quoting fellow reporter Jon Ferry from an October 1983 report about how people searching for Slumach's gold "go missing on land in some of this province's wildest, roughest terrain." Schaefer wrote about "the Antonsons . . . filing prospecting claims at two likely spots, based on their recent explorations," and asked, "Why would two grown men keep on with such a quest?" Rick replied to Schaefer in the article, "We can't shake it. We're tethered to the legend and the whole mystery, and that small possibility that there is gold up there."

Added Brian, "There are so many characters involved in this. As chroniclers of the whole thing, we have a lot of fun with it; this has been a great lark for us."

Schaefer wrote that Ferry's 1983 companion, photographer Gerry Kahrmann, was not among the believers after he had spent a week in the Pitt Lake and lower Pitt River area. Kahrmann said, "The most plausible explanation for Slumach's lost gold mine was that he was jumping gold prospectors coming back to New West and making off with their gold. That was his gold mine."

Soon after this article was printed, Daryl Friesen and the film crew explored Corbold Creek and made their way up to Canyon Creek. In the fourth episode of *Curse of the Frozen Gold,* there's a scene of Friesen rappelling down the cliffside, plunging toward the creek. Panning didn't show colours and there were no nuggets lying about in the creek. Friesen's customary stance came out once again: "I'll have to come back here."

As this book goes to press, Friesen says his claim at Corbold Creek lapsed, as had ours. Friesen said, "They're all open again. Mine lapsed because I was otherwise busy, not because there's no gold there . . . someone else can now stake them."

Chapter 15

A Bridge, an Inn, and a Map

TRIBUTARIES OF INFORMATION ARE crucial to researchers—they flow independently until they merge with the main story, their confluence bringing fascinating stories as amateur historians continue in search of a legend. Which brings us to the story of a bridge, an inn, and a map.

The bridge was built across the lower Pitt River in 1885 as part of the construction of a section of the Canadian Pacific Railway, from Port Moody eastward. It eventually joined the railway's westward construction at Craigellachie, BC—a place noted for being the site where the last spike was driven on the railroad that bound Canada together with a ribbon of steel. Slumach would have paddled under this bridge if he ventured to New Westminster by water. Importantly, on the day Slumach shot him, Louis Bee and his companion, Seymour, paddled north up lower Pitt River and crossed to the west side at what is today Addington Point, where the fatal shot was fired. After abandoning their canoe and fleeing the scene of the crime, Seymour ran down the west side of Pitt River until reaching the bridge. He then crossed it and trekked back to their camp. Slumach disappeared into the forest upriver. The stretch of river north of where the bridge crosses it is Chatham Reach, a name popularized by the band Tiller's Folly in a song of the same name, which speculates about Bee and Slumach.

The inn was the Wild Duck Inn in Port Coquitlam. Historian Chuck Davis tells in his book *Port Coquitlam: Where Rails Meet Rivers* that the "Minnekhada Land Company built the accommodation in 1912 as a two-storey bunkhouse for CPR workers, located on the Dewdney Trunk Road." Davis wrote that it "was also an inn for travellers on the Dewdney." In its day, it was called the Minnekhada Hotel. Not long afterward, the nearby railway bridge was converted to also accommodate automobiles, replacing a ferry service and serving that purpose until 1957. (Brian and Rick travelled across it in the family car as kids.) It was an indication of traffic growth brought about by increased interest in the area's produce and affordable land.

The inn became, in Davis's words, "a stopping place for hunters who came . . . to shoot waterfowl found in the Pitt Polder area, hence its third and final name"—the Wild Duck Inn. By the late 1940s, the lodge had become a sort of "exotic roadhouse," a destination resort for fishers, boaters, hikers, gold seekers, and honeymooning couples from Vancouver, including, in 1947, Al and Elsie Antonson, parents of Rick and Brian. The inn's proximity to the lost mine may have foreshadowed Al's father years later telling grandsons Brian and Rick, in his Norwegian accent, "Ja, I too vent to look for gold left by Slumach up Pitt Lake."

A 1972 photo of the Wild Duck Inn when it was located at the southwest corner property formed by the lower Pitt River and the CPR bridge. The inn was demolished in 2008. WAYNE LYONS

The map in question was on the wall of the Wild Duck Inn's bar for over fifty years and went missing when the inn was demolished after construction of the current Pitt River Bridge began in 2008. Murals had been added to the inn's decor around 1955 during an expansion undertaken by the owners, Rock Heron Holdings. The most prominent mural was recalled by one person as "a map larger than a 4 x 8 [foot] sheet of plywood." With a splash of gold lettering and a dollop of fake gold dust, it pinpointed an area as the APPROXIMATE SEARCH AREA OF LEGENDARY LOST SLUMACK MINE near Widgeon Lake, an affirmation of local rumours. When it went missing, the public and the gold seekers were uncertain if it was destroyed or taken away.

The quest to find the Wild Duck Inn's missing map began in earnest years later. On a windswept Pitt Lake one summer day in 2014, Brian and Rick were in Danny Gerak's boat after the three had been at Pitt River Lodge with the television crew filming *Curse of the Frozen Gold*. They were heading twenty-four kilometres (fifteen miles) from the lakehead to the south shore landing at Grant Narrows.

As the boat bounced on choppy waters in the middle of the lake, Brian said to Gerak, "I always wanted to get closer to Spindle Creek. I've thought that's where Slumach's gold might be ever since we saw the 1958 television show *Treasure*."

Gerak said, "Let's head to the west shore and take a look."

They didn't get close to shore in the chop, but they reached the outlet of DeBeck Creek. Higher up the mountain, Spindle Creek joins the DeBeck. And that is the location of the scene from *Treasure* that enthralled Brian.

All that was missing was creeping fog and a mist of mystery.

"We remember a wall map at the Wild Duck Inn showing the lost mine near Widgeon Lake," said Rick.

"That map has gone now," said Gerak. "I've heard that when the inn was demolished, someone bought the map at an auction. We don't know who, but I've an idea where to start tracing it."

In a follow-up discussion, Garth Dinsmore (who had introduced us to helicopter pilot Dean Russell) said he would work on Gerak's suggestion to contact Valley Towing, a company that did barge work and knew the inn well. The trail sent him looking for large paintings by someone named Peter Carter-Page who had worked for Disney in California and reportedly painted several murals for the Wild Duck Inn.

Fred Braches posted a description on his blog: "We're wondering if the map survived and is perhaps in someone's basement." A disappointing eyewitness reply came shortly thereafter, dashing all hope when we read it: "I was there the day the Wild Duck Inn sold everything off. The map was painted on the wall from my recollection, so it was torn down."

Adding to this disappointment one day a month later, Braches passed along some information to us from Greg Henderson, who confirmed the map had been "painted on the wall, which means it's likely gone, as the walls were all torn down. If so, it's in pieces in a dump somewhere."

Happenstance is a dedicated researcher's friend. Braches soon determined, "The map was *not* painted on a wall but on sheets of fibreboard and we know it was purchased at the final auction at the Wild Duck Inn by a resident of Whonnock." Serendipitously, the current owner of the large map and Braches had connected. In fact, they were neighbours! "The map is in excellent condition," said Braches.

In 2018, Dinsmore, Braches, Brian, Waite, and photographer Terry Marshall went to a house two doors west of Braches's home in rural Whonnock to, as Braches described it, "see this map in the back of Wayne's garage."

As it turned out, Braches's neighbour, Wayne, bought the map and a couple of other Wild Duck Inn signs as they were tearing the place apart. He told Brian he had "paid around $1,200 for it." According to Wayne, the painting was created in 1955. Braches determined, about the painter, "There's no indication who it was, no signature on the map or on the back." Could it have been Carter-Page? And, one might ask, why, of all the landscapes, did the painter pinpoint Slumach's gold at Widgeon Lake?

When the Wild Duck Inn's wall map of Pitt Lake was finally found, Garth Dinsmore, Brian Antonson, Don Waite, and Fred Braches showed their delight at the discovery. TERRY MARSHALL

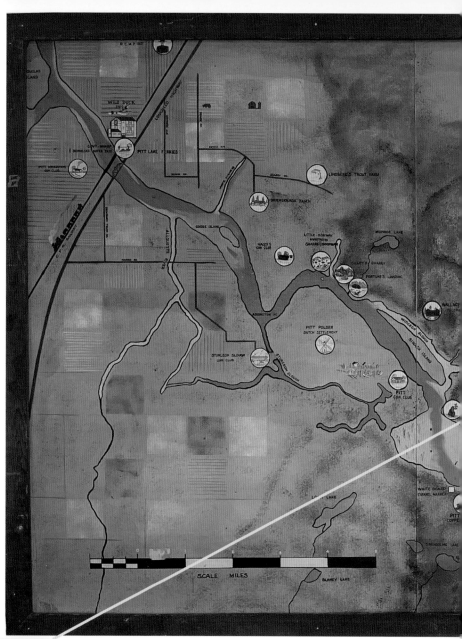

APPROXIMATE SEARCH AREA
OF LEGENDARY LOST SLUMACK MINE

Map K: Wild Duck Inn mural map—For years this map graced a wall in the bar at the Wild Duck Inn along the lower Pitt River in Port Coquitlam. When the building was demolished, the map went missing, setting up a hunt for it decades later. It was a search that ended happily. COURTESY OF WAYNE MCKEAN/GREAT PACIFIC MEDIA

Inset This mark on the Wild Duck Inn map sent many a gold seeker in search of the treasure near Widgeon Lake. BRIAN ANTONSON

Overleaf Stave Glacier country, prime searching area for many seekers of the legendary gold. ADAM PALMER COLLECTION

Chapter 16

Deadman's Curse

"I'M ACTUALLY WORKING ON another series already." This was Adam Palmer speaking with Brian over lunch at the venerable Sasquatch Inn, located on the Lougheed Highway in Harrison Mills. The Sasquatch Inn has been operating since 1954, and is a popular stop for locals and travellers alike, a perfect place to swap news about Slumach's lost mine.

"Tell me more," said Brian. Talking "Slumach" with Adam Palmer was never dull. He had been one of the featured gold seekers of the 2015 television series *Curse of the Frozen Gold*. He and his hiking partner, Evan Howard, have searched high and low—mostly high—for evidence of gold. They believe the treasure likely lies around the 2,130-metre (7,000-foot) level in the mountains north of Pitt Lake.

And now, in the midst of Covid days in 2021, Palmer was developing another series that would feature him and a new cast of gold seekers as they delved deeper than ever into the legend, exploring the facts and fiction built up since Slumach's death in 1891.

Just before the pandemic hit in early 2020, Brian had been approached by Great Pacific Media's Michael Francis to discuss the legend. They had been working with Palmer, and wanted to explore our work.

Tim Hardy and Francis were executive producers for what became the series *Deadman's Curse*, which debuted in September 2022. Great Pacific Media has a track record for "factual television." One of their successes is *Highway Thru Hell*, which chronicles the never-ending adventures, challenges, high drama, and crises encountered by emergency crews dispatched to deal with accident scenes on British Columbia's Coquihalla Highway.

Deadman's Curse would rank in the top five Canadian reality television series in 2022.

Adam Palmer was Hardy and Francis's first connection with the legend. The other stars of the series, Kru Williams, Taylor Starr, and Don Froese came on to the cast and soon became compelling performers, each playing to their strengths in front of the cameras. Longtime gold seeker and Slumach authority Don Waite is featured, along with skeptic Fred Braches, maintaining his guiding principle that facts matter more than fiction.

Together, and apart, Palmer, Williams, Starr, and Froese became "intrepid searchers," exploring the background of the legend, as the series delved into the deeper significance of its subtitle, *Legend of the Lost Gold*.

It opens with chilling voiceovers with words and phrases such as "eerie" and "hidden" and "walking into a death trap," and Palmer's willingness to "go to places no one will go." Williams claims, "There is no better motivation than gold" before adding that their gold seeking requires "bravery, guts, and a little bit of stupidity."

The stars of the hit television series *Deadman's Curse*, gold seekers. Left to right: Taylor Starr, Adam Palmer, Kru Williams, and Don Froese. GREAT PACIFIC MEDIA

DEADMAN'S CURSE

Best Information Lifestyle or Reality Series

Best Direction & Best Screenwriting

LEO AWARDS

LEO AWARDS
WINNER
2023

However, the narrator offers a more succinct take on the Slumach story. "It is a legend of greed and adventure."

The first episode sees the opening of an old box of Slumach material collected by West Vancouver's Ian Carter, whose grandfather, Dick Carter, had searched for the mine in the 1940s. In the box is a tattered, faded, torn piece of paper: the Jackson letter. This is the same item Ian's father, Jim Carter, had shared with Brian in 2007, saying at the time he believed his father, Dick, had made the copy from an unknown source. That contrasts with the *Deadman's Curse* episode, in which Ian introduces it to Palmer as "the original Jackson letter" that was passed down from his grandfather, Dick to Jim, who in turn passed it down to Ian. Are the conflicting claims a simple misunderstanding between father and son as to the letter's provenance? Or is it the result of positioning for the drama of reality television? No matter, it serves the purpose of the series, adding to the intrigue. This letter is longer than the more common version so often seen, and suggests Jackson's search location is *northwest* of the head of the lake instead of *northeast*, where most seekers focus their searches.

There are plentiful admonitions for would-be gold seekers. Williams boasts, "The curse is for quitters," while Palmer, cautious of Williams's obsession, warns, "You can't go looking for this lost gold mine with gold fever. That will get you killed."

One excursion takes Williams, along with Katzie artist, Rain Pierre, to the BC Archives in Victoria in 2021. Rain is the great-great-grandson of Slumach's catechist, Peter Pierre. When Pierre was twenty-eight, he was gifted with the name Slamuk. "I am honoured with the ability to carry it," he said, and has it tattooed on his arm.

In this episode they resurrect the judge's bench book, the record kept during Slumach's 1890 trial by Judge Montague Tyrwhitt-Drake. It was Drake who condemned Slumach to hang in 1891. The cast read Slumach's words that "Bee bullied" him.

Injustices against Indigenous Peoples will not fade. While the series and books are beginning to scratch the surface of Truth and Reconciliation, the lack of forceful statements still taints any storytelling on Slumach. What part will these works play in current Truth and Reconciliation discussions?

On screen, Pierre spoke about his reaction while reading legal documents from the trial at the BC Archives.

There are a lot of emotions reading this. It really is parallel to what my dad's been saying, and the stories are true from my end. My family's been telling the truth, and it's crazy because it was all happening in 1890 and I was born one hundred years later.

We're now just uncovering the real story. Injustice that happens to our people isn't new.

I feel pain for him and my people, because this is how we were treated, but we're getting to the bottom of this, and we need to bring it to light.

He [Slumach]deserves justice, and he needs to have his picture painted with the right brush, and that's with our people, and our stories and our truth.

Father and daughter Don Froese and Taylor Starr have a more direct familial connection to Slumach. Taylor calls him her "great-great-grand uncle," making him Froese's great-grand uncle. Throughout the series, Taylor's stated goal is to find the truth behind the legend of her forebear. For his part, Froese is experienced in the outdoors, and readily embraces any opportunity to be in nature.

When Kru Williams met Adam Palmer, both were leading outdoors classes for youths and young adults near Harrison Mills. Palmer recognized Williams's potential onscreen "presence" and suggested he be a part of the team that was being built by Great Pacific Media. Williams, already a weekend gold prospector, plays an important role in the series as someone who has been attracted to the Slumach legend since his youth and now has a chance to live his dream of actually searching for the gold.

In creating an episode, Palmer and Williams struck out into the Mamquam Mountain area, northwest of Pitt Lake, hoping to find some promising returns, but they found nothing. Mamquam Icefield? Palmer said, "I put that landmark to rest. There's no gold there."

Palmer takes up the story of Bernard Rover, from the 1960s, seeking the ground he worked and finding what they believe to be the remains of his cabin. He explains why people like Rover chose locations where the geography may reveal gold. "Prospectors always look for where water has done the job for them." And sometimes that leaves nuggets or exposes a vein. Here he talked of "flour gold," a term we authors were unfamiliar with. Palmer explains it is very-fine gold, wee flakes. The "small bits" as one wag puts it.

Rob Nicholson says he knows where the gold is, yet has qualms as he was warned to stay away by an eerie experience as he approached what he believed was the likely site of Stu Brown's find. "Retreat and live, or proceed and die," said an apparition. "There is definitely something strange going on in the upper Pitt," he says. "I will not go back to find out."

Of Brown himself, Nicholson says, "He's a very credible man." And, Nicholson's search encouraged the cast and crew to seek the location he had visited. The "pool" described by Brown as being just a few feet across is actually a small lake these days, was held back by a rock wall similar to that described by Brown, and was much more than Brown's description of "ankle deep." Palmer dons a wet suit and diving gear and moves into the frigid waters to seek some evidence of gold, but finds none. At a pensive moment, as he looks over the site and the mountains in the distance, Palmer says to Friesen, "I'm glad you're here. That's the real gold."

Froese clarifies what viewers are sensing. "This is not about Slumach and his gold. This is a lot of stories." Episodes see them working with veteran gold seeker Friesen to explore a target location. Despite high hopes, disappointment reigns. Friesen is adamant, "Throughout the legend, this has been the time to go searching." And new gold seeker, David Muise, leads cameras up Stave Lake to a location up a tributary that feeds the lake—again, with no positive result.

Two episodes take the team to Jack Mould's search location near Bute Inlet, on the traditional lands of the Homalco First Nation. It is 300 kilometres (around 220 miles) northwest of Pitt Lake, and the remoteness is intended to register with the audience and those acting out prospecting ambitions. They find the once floating, now grounded barge home Mould lived in while exploring the local area. Palmer and a marine biologist dive to a shipwreck in Bute Inlet that Mould had inferred was

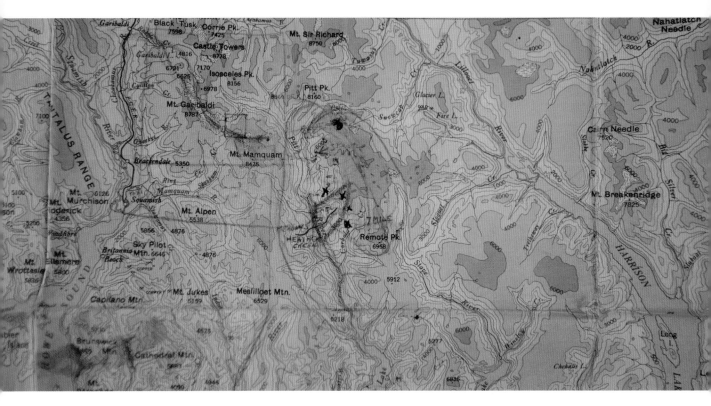

Map L: Dick Carter Search Area—Dick Carter hiked the areas of Garibaldi and Golden Ears Provincial Parks searching for Slumach's legendary mine. In the 2022 television series *Deadman's Curse*, participants followed Carter's map in their search for gold. We present it here digitally edited to protect sensitive information. COLLECTION OF A.W. (DICK) CARTER. COPYRIGHT IAN W. CARTER. USED WITH PERMISSION

a Spanish galleon, but it turned out to be a much more recent sinking.

Suggestions are that if Mould found any gold in the Bute Inlet area, it certainly was not Slumach's gold. Said Palmer, "It's an illusion like everything else in Jack Mould's story."

The episode also visited the riverbank where Mould disappeared. It appears to be almost like quicksand, with a muddy surface that cracks and crumbles as Williams walks on it. Could Mould have slipped into the muck and fallen into the water at that point?

Judith Williams's book *Cougar Companions: Bute Inlet Country*, published first by Raincoast Chronicles and more recently by Harbour Publishing, includes more rollicking tales of Jack Mould's adventures while searching for gold. Williams talks about his larger-than-life

character, about his ever-optimistic attitude about finding gold, along with convincing investors to provide their support. She also covers an incident, chronicled in a *Deadman's Curse* episode, where Mould dynamited a Homalco burial site while searching for the mine. This arrogant affront was of great concern to the Homalco, and almost anyone who heard of it. Mould's discovery of human bones drew attention, but he ignored the Homalco's concerns about his lack of respect for their ancestors and their ancient Indigenous burial practices. Mould had desecrated sacred ground. This episode of *Deadman's Curse* expresses disgust at this behaviour. Williams says, "We're not just here for the gold. We're here for the truth." And the truth intended for viewers is that Mould's behaviour toward Indigenous culture was reprehensible.

In the end, none of Mould's claims held up to scrutiny, and the series casts aspersions on his behaviour. Waite and Braches dismiss Mould's activity as unrelated and tangential. Equally dismissive, Palmer said, "The legend of Pitt Lake is not the legend of Bute Inlet."

TO SOME VIEWERS, THERE was no more eccentric character than David Muise, who is unabashedly a captive of Slumach obsessions. We were surprised to encounter his eccentricities through the series, yet it was impossible to dismiss his escapades, having earned his fuller profile as a tenacious, avid, bewildering, and bewildered gold seeker.

Importantly, in the final episode, we learn that the Carter family has been reframing one of Dick Carter's paintings, and they found hidden and stuffed behind it a stash of papers, photographs, newspaper clippings, and a map from his Slumach-gold-seeking escapades of the 1940s. The Carter map enters the Slumach story as a reliable source for potential locations as Dick explored various areas he'd determined and marked with an X. The cast follows a route sketched on this map to see if anything promising showed up. They determine that Carter was in the vicinity of where Volcanic Brown was only ten years after the prospector had been there. One of the cast whispers, "Carter found gold." At Heather Creek, they find some of the claim posts, explaining that there are four posts for each claim, and they are lucky to have found any of them. Palmer says of Dick Carter's gold-seeking expeditions, "This guy's the real deal." While they encounter evidence of earlier prospector presence in the area, no gold is found.

No disappointments dissuade the team from its goal to keep searching. "If we find the gold, we find Slumach's story," said Taylor Starr.

As the season comes to a close, Slumach's gold still unfound, one of the characters questions the motives of other gold seekers they've been following. Don Froese warns of a real danger for seekers of Slumach's gold: "The curse is the greed."

No matter, perhaps, as the voice-over and screen both fade with the one question that remains on everyone's mind, despite those dangers:

"Where's the gold?"

Overleaf Ancient pictographs show human activity prior to the arrival of European settlers and adventurers. ADAM PALMER COLLECTION

Chapter 17

Slumach's Last Day: Baptism, Death, and an Unmarked Grave

THE COMFORTING PRESENCE OF his nephew and catechist Peter Pierre in the early morning hours; one last breakfast; baptism as the sun rose, and then—the ominous arrival of the hangman at the jail. These comprised Slumach's final hours before 8 AM on Friday, January 16, 1891.

A simple piece of paper documents his solemn baptism, saying it occurred "immediately before execution."

Were his family and friends weeping nearby? We think so.

Now lifeless and cold, Slumach's body was cut down from the rope, and taken away for burial. Only a few people knew where, until more than a century later, when a discovery was made.

Slumach's Unmarked Grave

Fred Braches laid the small, freshly cut cedar bough carefully on the close-mowed grass. The bough joined two others that were laid moments before. Braches, his wife Helmi, and Brian stood with their heads bowed, taking in this solemn moment on this sacred ground.

The three were gathered at Slumach's grave to recognize his interment on a crisp winter morning. A chickadee chirped in the distance. A passing car purred along a nearby street. Otherwise, silence prevailed, and the three absorbed that silent moment into their memories.

This gathering occurred in December 2008, almost 117 years after the mortal remains of "the murderer Slumach" had been lowered into a grave later covered by this patch of grass in St. Peter's Roman Catholic Cemetery in the Sapperton area of New Westminster. His grave had been left unmarked and unknown for more than a century.

How had Slumach's unmarked grave been found? The search had taken twists and turns. Rumours of the location had circulated since his hanging. One rumour suggested Slumach was buried on the grounds of the British Columbia Provincial Gaol, where he was hanged, at the corner of 8th Street and Royal Avenue. Another suggested he had been moved off to a long-time Indigenous graveyard, which existed on the grounds of the modern-day New Westminster Secondary School. Still others suggested he could have been buried in one of two cemeteries in Sapperton.

Finding the grave was the result of solid research by Archie and Dale Miller. From 1973 to 1999, Archie was the curator, and later also the archivist, of New Westminster's Museum and Archives, operating out of the Royal City's Irving House, the oldest completely intact building in BC's Lower Mainland. In retirement, the Millers continued their work as local historians.

Fred Braches points to Slumach's unmarked grave in New Westminster, British Columbia. BRIAN ANTONSON

Originally, the Millers were not searching specifically for Slumach's grave. They were looking for details of the possible burial of Slumach and others in the prison yard after their executions.

"We were interested to see if some or all of the remains stayed in that location or were removed to the city cemetery or elsewhere. That research led us to the references to Slumach, his execution, his baptism, and his burial directly in St. Peter's Cemetery," recall the Millers.

Two cemeteries sit across a street from each other in the Sapperton area of New Westminster. St. Peter's Roman Catholic Cemetery is on the west side of Richmond Street, while the larger Fraser Cemetery is on the east. The records of burials in these two cemeteries are not kept in chronological order, and thousands of people have been buried in both locations over many decades. The Millers undertook a painstaking review of the record books, line by line, suspecting that Slumach might be found within one of them.

And then, there it was: "Petrum Slumach," buried on January 16, 1891, following his execution. At baptism, Slumach had taken a Christian name, Peter ("Petrum") from his uncle, Peter Pierre.

Unmarked graves have no headstone, but they are numbered and easily located. The ardent researchers walked across the street from the small hut where they had found Slumach's final details recorded and then across the grass to his grave. Located between two marked graves, it was easy to discover.

In a touch of irony, Slumach is buried just a short distance away from Captain George Pittendrigh, who presided over securing Louis Bee's body and ultimately presided over Slumach's preliminary hearing following his arrest.

We recall that in an interview with Don Waite in 1971, Aunt Mandy (the daughter of Peter Pierre, and Slumach's grand-niece) claimed that Slumach's daughter had tried to get possession of his body for a proper burial.

"There is no evidence in the cemetery files that such [a] request was ever made, and no logical reason for it to have been denied if it were made," claim the Millers. "Other disinterments were approved at that time and, to the Church, this would be no different."

Could there be a more appropriate burial site? There are no known plans for a disinterment today. A poignant visit to the snow-covered grave was made in January 2009 when Katzie members Garnett, Willie, and Cyril Pierre, together with Fred Braches gathered to honour Slumach's legendary status.

Fred Braches recalled Cyril Pierre's comment as he walked up the slope at St. Peter's Cemetery in Sapperton: "This has been a long time coming." Apparently, finding Slumach's grave had been one of his lifetime goals.

What does the future hold in terms of justice for the man at the centre of this legend? Nothing can change what happened to him. But could an initiative to have Slumach exonerated or provided an amnesty of sorts be appropriate? Would a move to find him guilty of the lesser charge of manslaughter be successful, more than 130 years after his conviction and hanging?

Here are two relevant definitions: An exoneration "occurs when a person who has been convicted of a crime is officially cleared after new evidence of innocence becomes available." A pardon "occurs when a government decides to "forgive a person convicted of a crime." There have been periodic discussions at meetings of the Lost Mine of Pitt Lake Society about whether Slumach's conviction for murder could be changed to a conviction for manslaughter, given that Slumach's shooting of Bee appeared to be in self-defence.

Perspective can be gained by hearing the Métis leaders' response to Canadian musings about pardoning Louis

Archie and Dale Miller, whose diligent research finally located Slumach's unmarked grave.
COURTESY ARCHIE AND DALE MILLER

Slumach was interred in St. Peter's Catholic Cemetery in New Westminster. Decades of searching finally identified his unmarked grave.
ARCHIVES OF THE ROMAN CATHOLIC ARCHDIOCESE OF VANCOUVER

Riel, almost a century and a half after his hanging. Jean Teillet, Riel's great-grand-niece said, "The Métis Nation has always rejected moves to exonerate Riel. You can't give him back his life . . . You cannot fix something after you've exacted the worst punishment that we could grant. It will achieve nothing. I prefer to leave history the way that it is."

Could there be a process to formally and/or emotionally return Slumach to the fold of his family? Could a "naming" of a street or a park or some other permanent memorial to him be created so his name lives, not in infamy, but in full recognition of the injustice of the day?

Many have pondered actions that could occur—or not. Such moves are not for us to initiate. That said, we stand ready, along with other interested parties, to support any initiatives that might be taken to rectify the supreme wrong that was perpetrated against Slumach on January 16, 1891.

Registrum Baptizatorum in Ecclesia

55

Diœcesis

milia.	A. D. Die Mensis.	REGISTRUM BAPTISMORUM.	Observanda.
...och	Jan 16 1891	*Ego infrascriptus baptizavi* Petrum (Slumach, Indian). nat _____ ex _____ ex loco _____ et _____ ex loco _____ *conjugibus* Patrini fuerunt _____ W. M. J. Morgan O.M.I	In gaol immediately before execution, New Westminster (Catery Indian)

Slumach was baptised as Peter ("Petrum") Slumach an hour before his death in 1891. This certificate attests to that event, saying he was baptized "in gaol immediately before execution, New Westminster." ARCHIVES OF THE ROMAN CATHOLIC ARCHDIOCESE OF VANCOUVER

Overleaf ADAM PALMER COLLECTION

Afterword

On How Firm a Ground?

THE CASE OF SLUMACH and his gold is not closed, nor is it likely to ever be. Any legend has its roots in some truth—but just where the truth lies in this particular legend will remain a cause for conjecture years from now.

When *Slumach's Gold* was published in 2007, the three of us had been in search of a legend for thirty-seven years and yet felt it was unresolved, perhaps permanently so. After all these decades, no one has found the legendary Pitt Lake Mine gold. With this book, after fifty-four years, the three of us are putting our quest to rest. In doing so, we're aware of our own shortcomings. Agatha Christie's admonition to historians could well apply to our efforts: "The contemporary historian never writes such a true history as the historian of a later generation. It is a question of getting the true perspective, of seeing this in proportion." Time may yet uncloak this legend with truth.

Slumach and Volcanic Brown will always maintain their places in this fascinating tale, as given them by historical fact. Yet there are also characters who unwittingly slipped into the legend with suspect names like Jackson and Shotwell and Harrington.

We hear of dozens who have died in the attempt to find Slumach's lost mine; have they died chasing a wild dream fabricated by a fertile imagination or two, or have they died with the secret cache only metres from their fingertips?

At this point, we can recognize that Jackson thought gold to be in the mountains north of Pitt Lake, as did Wilbur Armstrong. Rikk Taylor thought it was on the east side of Harrison Lake. When Daryl Friesen asked Bill Barlee, "Do you think that the lost mine of Pitt Lake exists?" Barlee replied, "Yes, but not where most people think it is. Most people think that the mine is somewhere past the head of Pitt Lake." Barlee thought the mine is "somewhere west of Harrison Lake." Stu Brown was convinced it sits in the upper Sloquet area.

Pilot John Lovelace's beliefs were clear: At the end of his first episode of *Wings Over Canada*, on Slumach, a relaxed Lovelace is shown sitting alone on a riverbank. Looking out over the water, he asks no one in particular, "Is there gold in the Pitt River Valley?" He pauses for just a moment before answering his own question. "You bet there is—beyond your wildest dreams."

Michael Collier said, "If I was giving advice, I'd say think about the route that the rescue party looking for [Volcanic] Brown came, which would parallel Brown's route."

WHAT ABOUT SOME OF the other gold seekers we've written about? What are their best guesses? Here's what we know.

Don Waite claimed, "The only person I think has any credibility in this story is Aunt Mandy. Her father got it directly from Slumach, and then Peter told it to his daughter Mandy. And I'm pretty sure that some of it got lost in translation, but it's all coming from First Nations people being handed down. I believe what she said, that she said it with all honesty. Slumach found gold up in this, we call it Third Canyon."

Over the years, Waite came to bolster the prospect of Third Canyon with this: "Pierre, her father, he went looking for it so there has to be something to that story."

We asked Waite more recently, "What do you think that something is? Do you think Slumach actually told him?"

"Oh, yeah. He told him exactly where to go."

"So if you believe that, do you believe Slumach himself actually had gold?"

"He had gold, but he got it from the Port Douglas people."

Daryl Friesen said, "Too many people are rolling all the dice on one guy. Slumach had slivers of placer gold when he went to the store to trade it in. And Volcanic Brown clearly had gold from a vein. W. Jackson's gold was placer nuggets the size of walnuts. They all found gold but in different spots."

Greg Henderson said he strayed away from the film crew while they were shooting scenes for *Curse of the Frozen Gold* near Corbold Creek. "I found gold at Corbold Creek while we were filming. Nice gold in the lower pool. No nuggets, but if Slumach found gold nuggets that would be where."

Mike Boileau said, "No. The legend will generate tourist dollars, but that's all you'll ever get out of it."

Danny Gerak said, "It's a true story. People just aren't using their heads. Some are going too far, flying around in helicopters to places these old timers never would have gotten." Homing in on the nameless creek that flows into Corbold Creek, he's convinced that's where Slumach, Jackson, and Volcanic Brown found their gold, in what

he still calls the "hidden valley." "I've been to the creek numerous times. There's got to be gold there. There's still time to find it."

Rob Nicholson said, "No doubt the mine exists in the area"—in fact, he believes there are at least two locations: one with placer gold and the other with vein gold. He suggests these locations are close to the "Jackson rock" and the pup-tent-shaped slabs in the Iceworm Creek area.

Adam Palmer said, "The gold mine's truth, sometimes it's a little sloppy."

Evan Howard, in response to the question of whether Slumach's gold will ever be found, said, "I hope not." He wants to continue the search for as long as possible.

Taylor Starr believes a treasure exists . . . somewhere. "Even though we walked in his footsteps, we could be walking right over it, or thousands of miles from it."

Don Froese said, "There's definitely gold, for sure. I'd have to say that after shooting Season Two [of *Deadman's Curse*], we're getting close to a motherlode. We're getting close to what Slumach could have found."

Kru Williams has mused about the possible locations as much as the dangers of going looking for them, saying, "There's plenty of room for more tombstones."

David Muise said, "It's still there. Still laying there."

Fred Braches said, "It was in one of those streams up north of Pitt Lake that, some 150 years ago, a nameless Indigenous man, likely a member of the Katzie First Nation, found that 'good prospect of gold' and that turned out to be the fabulous placer deposit spawning a legend of epic proportions." Braches wrote, "It seems that Aunt Mandy did not want to shatter the legends of Pitt Lake gold, which were so dear to the Katzie. On the other hand, she sought to diminish Slumach's role as the discoverer of a bonanza at Pitt Lake by reducing his find to a realistic value in gold for any rich accidental find." Never shy about a balancing view, Braches has been fond of quoting long-ago Vancouver archivist Major J.S. Matthews who, he says, "lost patience with the number of inquiries he received about Slumach's gold and called the story 'pure rubbish.'"

THERE'S ANOTHER IMPORTANT FACTOR at play today. It was John Lovelace who had contemplated the effects of climate change on the landscape, and we agree that it has probably shifted the terrain over the last century. Notable shifts of the territory in search areas since Slumach's death 130 years ago are to be expected. Rock falls, changes in vegetation growth, wildfires, receding glaciers, record rainfall, along with water-level changes and flow route carve-outs all affect the landscape, sometimes drastically rearranging geographical features. When Adam Palmer was shown under an ice-roofed cave under a glacier, he said, "That's a by-product of global warming. It's revealing things that have been hidden for so long." Kicking the ground, he said, "This is the last frontier on earth. He called it "virgin dirt."

Consider an American item by reporter Stephen Sorace following catastrophic rains in California: "Treasure hunters are again combing the loosened rocks and soil of California for gold . . ." 175 years after that state's gold rush, noting as "snowpack build up during the winter storms . . . begins to melt . . . the rushing water pushes gold in the mountains down the rivers." The same could be said about climate-change effects in the Pitt Lake area. As one Californian, Jim Eakin notes in an April 22, 2023, *New York Times* article, "Anytime you can stand next to a river, and you hear the boulders tumbling, you know the gold is moving, too . . ." That sounds like Slumach country.

READERS MUST DECIDE FOR themselves on how firm a ground the various theories concerning the mine stand, and in that same vein, we feel we ought to share *our* individual feelings about the truth behind the legend. In 1972, at the risk of eating our words at some future date, we summed up our views. We refreshed them for our 2007 edition and now share our 2024 perspectives.

No doubt new information will come to light that will support or supplant the material found in this book. Until then, we trust our book fulfills its intended purpose to present an interesting, informative, and realistic look at one of the most intriguing legends over three centuries—certainly an outstanding chapter in British Columbia's history.

In 2024, Brian recalls that more than five decades ago, we individually pondered the question "On how firm a ground is this legend?"

I stated that while Slumach certainly did live and certainly did die a murderer's death, "it would seem the legend of Slumach's Lost Creek gold mine is just that—a legend." I whimsically created this limerick:

Unwitting hero he,
Who murdered Louis Bee,
But all the rest,
Is just pure jest,
A joke on you and me.

In our 2007 book, I wrote about those now associated with the quest in finding the gold—failed quests in each case—and wrapped up my observations by saying "And I want there to be reason one day for a follow-up book titled *We Found Slumach's Gold!*"

That was not to be, unfortunately. Despite 133 years of searching for any supposed lost gold involving Slumach or Jackson or Armstrong or Brown or the second Brown, that compelling quest has yielded no results.

Thus, it would be easiest to say "nothing's changed," but that would be inaccurate. We have learned much more about Slumach, about his times, and about those who have searched for his supposed hoard over the past decades. We have new insights into the man and into what led to his murdering of Louis Bee, indeed even into the location of that sad act.

And so, almost seven decades after we first heard that captivating, if inaccurate, tale of Slumach and his lost creek gold mine around a crackling campfire, I believe this: that Slumach lived and was hanged in 1891 for the murder of Louis Bee is simple fact, but that is the only factual element to be found in all of this. Did he have gold? There is no evidence of that. Did he throw nuggets the size of walnuts around saloon floors in early New Westminster? No evidence there, either, and surely, local media would have been alive with such occurrences. Did he put a curse on his mine as he stood on the gallows? No evidence there, because newspaper reports of the time said he went to his death without saying anything.

For some reason, by 1897, a scant six years after his death, Slumach's name was associated with a mining venture designed to find gold. Was this because of some unwritten history involving him? Or was it because of pure conjecture from a time when stories of conspiracies and rumours of wealth spread differently but much like they do today? Did Jackson live and write a 1904 letter that has compelled searchers to seek his tent-shaped rock, lo these many decades? Again, no evidence. Did Volcanic Brown leave eleven ounces of raw gold in a jar in his tent? No evidence whatsoever. And what of the myriad others who have searched for Slumach's supposed but elusive gold? Again, no evidence whatsoever has been presented to confirm it even existed in the first place,

Is it possible to find gold in the various areas that have been searched over for so many decades? Certainly. The old line goes, "Gold is where you find it," so there's no evidence that any of this cannot be true. But lacking any clear evidence to the contrary, my summation is that the ground upon which more than a century of tales about Slumach's gold are based is not firm at all.

Mary writes:

Over the years, much of the research into the legend was conducted through traditional sources, such as the occasional documentary film, archived documents, magazines, and newspapers. But newspapers are businesses, and in the last 133 years some editors strove to attract readers by crafting and printing sensational stories, including the search for gold in BC. Sometimes, the stories were filled with discriminatory words, racism, and opinions that couldn't be substantiated.

Nowhere, over the past five decades, did I come across stories about Slumach written by Indigenous writers. Now in my seventies, I'm very heartened that the next generation of researchers will have greater access to information and perspectives about the legend now emerging in a variety of media and created by Indigenous People, including Slumach's relatives.

These are significant, valuable, new resources. Because of them, I'm most happy and grateful to say that I now know more about Slumach as a person.

I believe that future researchers and gold seekers will encounter two new potential challenges. What impact will the emergence of artificial intelligence (AI) have on their work? Will climate change in southwestern BC require rethinking on where to search for the motherlode?

I'm convinced based on all we've learned over the decades that Slumach found gold, but where? Geologists say it is doubtful that gold could be found in the Pitt Lake area. However, during the Cariboo gold rush, a miner or miners returning south to New Westminster and carrying precious gold cargo could have passed through Slumach's territory.

Or, had Slumach come upon a mine discovered by some gold-seeking Spaniards, who are known to have visited coastal and Interior areas in the late eighteenth century?

Some gold seekers claim they know the mine's location. But think about it: If you were one of those intrepid folks, why would you *ever* tell anyone or share a map? It just makes sense that you would want to keep your information to yourself. What better way to obscure the trail than by falsifying and publishing your findings.

We'll never know if any one gold seeker has actually found the motherlode and has quietly packed out their prize without saying a word—a much more likely scenario, in my view.

Rick writes:

I believe gold may have been found near Pitt Lake.

In 1972, we had done only two years of research; with no evidence proving Slumach had a mine. Now, over fifty years later, we're sure he didn't have a mine, but perhaps he had stumbled upon a little bit of gold? And if so, where was it from? I'd say it would have come from the Widgeon Creek or Widgeon Lake area, where he was known to frequent. As to the legend, have dozens of people been fools, searching for gold and dying in the quest? Did they not heed the lack of evidence about Slumach's mine? Now, after fresh starts and false starts by a host of diligent gold seekers who have shared their findings, I arrive at a more solid conclusion.

Unless you believe Aunt Mandy's story that Slumach scrawled a rough map on his death cell's bench and showed it to Peter Pierre, no person's words link Slumach to gold. If the story was true and Pierre believed Slumach, it is certainly likely that Pierre could have slipped, fallen, and broken his hip while in Pitt country, as Aunt Mandy said, maybe or maybe not looking for gold. Regardless,

it is a short leap of faith for me to imagine his laughter at the circumstances of his mishap. One can almost hear his words, "Ol' Slumach must've placed a curse on this area."

That scenario, with its thin thread to facts, ties Slumach to the curse and to the gold. I want to believe in that linkage because it is fun and tenable and is the root of a legend. It sits well beside the available evidence that suggests Slumach never had gold in sufficient quantity to arouse suspicion, let alone in amounts to prompt press coverage. Yet it also squares with the possibility that he found slivers of gold to pry out of a rock with his knife—at least once.

I believe Rikk Taylor's words: "They found gold—and there was lots."

Now, if I could only find the plastic bag Rikk gave me with the gold ore and assay reports . . . did I gift it inadvertently in an unopened box of books and materials donated to the SFU Library Archives? Might it have been in one of the boxes of old books I donated to the Vancouver General Hospital Foundation's bookstore—and if so, where did it go? Who has it?

Rikk had reconciled a legitimate gold find in the Harrison Lake area with gold from a century-old legend that he loved as much as we do. And he said what he wanted to believe was true: "They found Slumach's lost mine." Frankly, I don't hold that statement to be correct—I don't believe it was Slumach's gold they found.

Unless . . .

Overleaf ADAM PALMER COLLECTION

Appendix A

A Slumach Timeline

1808	Explorer Simon Fraser descends the river that would be named after him.
c. 1810	Slumach is born, perhaps on Katzie lands, perhaps elsewhere.
1858	Fort Langley becomes the birthplace of the Colony of British Columbia.
1859	New Westminster becomes the capital of the Colony of British Columbia.
1868	Victoria becomes the capital of the amalgamated colonies of Vancouver Island and British Columbia.
1869	The *Mainland Guardian* newspaper publishes an account of an "Indian" with gold from the Pitt Lake area.
1871	British Columbia becomes Canada's sixth province.
1879	A federal census records Slum.ook.
1890	Slumach murders Louis Bee and the first media mention of him appears in the *Daily Columbian*.
	Slumach is arrested, tried, and convicted for the murder of Louis Bee.
1891	Slumach is hanged for the murder of Louis Bee.
1890s	Peter Pierre may have searched for gold belonging to his uncle, Slumach.

| 1897 | An offering for shares in Slumach Mining Co. Ltd. appears in local papers. |

| 1898 | New Westminster's great fire, when many court, newspaper, and police records are destroyed. |

| | W. Jackson, whose existence is unproven, allegedly finds gold north of Pitt Lake. |

| 1901 | Jackson allegedly deposits gold in the Bank of British North America (now the Bank of Montreal, or BMO) in San Francisco. |

| | Prospector Clifford Wellington claims Slumach had told his nephew of his mine's location. |

| 1902 | Indigenous man exchanges gold for cash in New Westminster three times (as later reported in a 1905 *Province* article). |

| 1903 | George Moody says, "Pitt Lake may be next of the great goldfields" after reportedly finding $1,200 in gold dust in the area. |

| 1904 | W. Jackson allegedly dies in San Francisco, after writing a deathbed letter to Shotwell. |

| 1906 | The first article on the gold legend appears in the *Province* on April 3. The find is attributed to an old man who reported this to a prospector named Frazier (the latter sounds very much like the legendary character Jackson). |

| | The San Francisco earthquake destroys bank and records that could have confirmed Jackson's existence and the claims made about him. |

| 1911 | Shotwell and Harrington reportedly arrive at the Ruskin train station and general store with gold, having come down the Stave River, perhaps from the Stave Glacier. Both reportedly die shortly after returning to Seattle. |

| 1915 | Wilbur Armstrong reports his last search after a decade of seeking for the "Slumagh" mine (which would mean he started in 1906, perhaps along with Frazier). |

| 1925 | The *Province* article by E L. Purkins appears about "The Lost Mine of Pitt Lake," citing Shotwell as the character some researchers now speculate was a mixup with the legendary Jackson. |

| 1928 | Volcanic Brown fails to return from searching for the mine and is rescued by a volunteer search team. |

1928	Ragnar Bergland and Louis Nelson prospect in the Widgeon/Spindle area, far away from where Shotwell and Harrington had searched in the Stave area.
1931	Volcanic Brown again fails to return from searching for the mine. A volunteer search team finds only his last camp.
1939–1956	Lurid, concocted images of Slumach's purported victims Molly Tynan and Susan Jesner are included in magazine articles by C.V. Tench.
1940s	Various newspaper articles appear about searches for the "lost mine."
1947	An article by Clyde Gilmour about "Hoodoo Gold" appears in the *Province*.
1950	Alfred Gaspard disappears while searching for the mine. Various newspaper articles about searches for the mine continue to appear. Duncan McPhaden searches for gold.
1952	Slumach Lost Creek Mine Ltd. shares are issued.
1955	The Wild Duck Inn map is created, showing the approximate location of Slumach's mine near Widgeon Lake.
1958	An American network television program, *Treasure*, brings the Slumach legend into the spotlight, featuring a search for the mine near Spindle Canyon. An article titled "Lost Gold and Murdered Maids," by Thomas P. Kelley, appears in *Cavalier* magazine in July.
1960	Lewis Hagbo's death is reported in various local papers such as the *Maple Ridge-Pitt Meadows Gazette*, suggesting he may have been the twenty-third person to die while searching for the mine.
1961	The *Columbian* launches a series of weekend searches—prompted by the dreams of Wally Lund—by hundreds of gold seekers at Sheridan Hill in Pitt Meadows.
1960s	Tiny Allen finds a tent-shaped rock and then dies before returning to the site where he found it.
1966	Allen Jay's article appears in *Canada Month*, April 1.

1968	*RCMP Quarterly* includes a story about "Old Slumach" by S/Sgt. R. Harding.
1970	Bill Barlee tells the Slumach story in *Canada West* magazine.
1972	In June, the first book about the legend is published: *In Search of a Legend: Slumach's Gold.*
	In August, Don Waite tells the Slumach story in his book *Kwant'stan.*
1973	Charles Miller's book, *The Golden Mountains: Chronicles of Valley and Coast Mines* is published.
1975	*Beautiful British Columbia* magazine features an article on the lost mine by Rick Antonson.
1976	"Legend of the Lost Creek Mine" by T.W. Paterson appears in *Canadian Treasure Trails* magazine.
	"Slumach's Glorious Gold" article by Brian Antonson appears in *Canadian Frontier Annual.*
1981	Heritage House publishes *Slumach's Gold: In Search of a Legend*, edited by Art Downs, a compilation of earlier works by Rick and Brian Antonson, Mary Trainer, and Don Waite.
1983	The *Province*'s Jon Ferry and CKVU's Dale Robins report on a weeklong search for the mine in the Widgeon Creek area at the southwest corner of Pitt Lake.
1985	Gold seeker Norm (whose last name is withheld by family request) searches northeast of Pitt Lake and photographs a tent-shaped rock around which he claims he found gold-bearing rock.
1987	The first meeting of the Lost Mine of Pitt Lake Society.
1991	A German television series *Treasure Hunters*, by Sylvio Heufelder, tells the Slumach story and searches for the mine northeast of Pitt Lake.
1993	Elizabeth Hawkins's book, *Jack Mould and the Curse of Gold* is published by Hancock House.
1994	Michael Collier's docudrama, *Curse of the Lost Gold Mine,* airs on Canadian TV network Canwest Global.

| 1995 | Gold seeker Donna (whose full name is withheld at her request) and husband search for the mine. A *Vancouver Sun* article about it says they found the mine site, but it had already been worked out. |

| c. 2000 | Rikk Taylor, former publisher of the *Columbian*, claims gold has been found and mined near the east shore of Harrison Lake. |

| 2001 | Daryl Friesen publishes an e-book, *Spindle Quest*, about his lifelong search for the lost mine. |

| 2002 | John Lovelace produces a *Wings Over Canada* episode on the Slumach legend and the search for the mine.

Rob Nicholson publishes an e-book, *Lost Creek Mine*, about his lifelong search for the mine. |

| 2005 | Edgar Ramsey's novel, *Slumach: The Lost Mine* is published by Ramsey Books.

German filmmaker Anton Lennartz makes a first visit to the Pitt Lake area, seeking the story of the lost mine. |

| 2007 | Heritage House publishes *Slumach's Gold, In Search of a Legend,* the thirty-fifth anniversary edition, and a four-page article is printed in the *Province*.

Fred Braches launches his websites slumach.ca and slumach.blogspot.com |

| 2008 | Slumach's grave is located. (Brian and Helmi and Fred Braches visited the grave shortly after the discovery.) |

| 2009 | The Katzie Band hosts the Lost Mine of Pitt Lake Society at the Katzie longhouse near the Golden Ears Bridge.

An American magazine, *Treasure*, and *Swedish Press* magazine publish articles on Slumach. |

| | *The Essentials:* 150 *Great BC Books & Authors* by Alan Twigg names *Slumach's Gold* among 150 great BC books. |

| 2010 | German filmmaker Anton Lennartz is rescued on the second filming visit to the Pitt Lake area.

Lennartz's film *Auf Slumachs Spuren* (*On Slumach's Trails*) is released in Germany. |

2011 — Two Wikipedia entries are created by Fred Braches: Slumach, and the Lost Mine of Pitt Lake

Daryl Friesen publishes *Seeker of Gold* (formerly *Spindle Quest*): *Chasing Lost Creek Gold.*

2014 — The *Province* publishes five articles in the *BC Mysteries* series by reporter Glenn Schaefer, including one on Slumach.

2015 — *Curse of the Frozen Gold* TV series is broadcast on the History Channel in Canada, and Animal Planet in the US.

2017 — Fred Braches publishes *Fact and Fiction: Slumach and the Lost Creek Mine.*

2018 — Reporter Robin Gill's piece, broadcast on Global's *Global National*, keeps the legend alive.

The Wild Duck Inn map is tracked down by Fred Braches and Garth Dinsmore.

The Slumach research archives of Brian and Rick Antonson and Mary Trainer are acquired by Simon Fraser University.

2019 — The Slumach story is told to a Canada-wide audience on CBC Radio's *The Doc Project.*

Searching for Pitt Lake Gold: *Facts and Fantasy in the legend of Slumach*, by Fred Braches, is published by Heritage House.

Fred Braches's Slumach research archives are acquired by the Vancouver Public Library's Special Collections department.

2022 — The *Deadman's Curse* TV series on the History Channel begins.

2023 — The *Deadman's Curse: Slumach's Gold* podcast begins.

2024 — *Slumach's Gold: In Search of a Legend—and a Curse* is published by Heritage House.

Appendix B

The Setting:
Katzie First Nation,
Slumach's home, and Pitt Lake

PITT MEADOWS IS PART of the Katzie First Nation's traditional territory. European settlers began to explore the area between 1837 and 1858, and it was officially organized on September 12, 1847. It was incorporated on April 23, 1914.

The city of Pitt Meadows is situated to the west of Maple Ridge, and is bounded by the lower Pitt River on the west, Pitt Polder on the north, the Katzie Reserve and the Fraser River on the south, and Maple Ridge on the east. Its elevation varies between 7.6 metres and 91.4 metres (25 feet and 300 feet) above sea level.

In the area's early development, young Dutch farming couples immigrated to Canada and purchased rundown dairies from the Mennonites, who were occupying the area at the time. The Dutch began a drainage project and reclaimed the flat land between the Pitt and Alouette Rivers

that was formerly known as Alouette (or Lillooet) Slough.

An island located about halfway up Pitt Lake was inhabited by settlers early last century was known variously as Wright Island, Goose Island, or Pen Island. In 1906 it was the site of a prison camp that was later abandoned. The island contained excellent quarry stone and timber that was used to build the BC Penitentiary in New Westminster.

Today, civilization has crept farther up the lake. Logging operations are carried on at the head of the lake, and there is a fish hatchery at Alvin—near where Corbold Creek meets upper Pitt River. Numerous vacation homes dot the shores of the lake.

Overleaf ADAM PALMER COLLECTION

187

Appendix C

Fact-Checking the Slumach Story

IN TODAY'S WORLD, WE'VE come to expect news media to acknowledge, indeed retract, errors in reporting. For the Slumach story, some of that "fake news" type of information continues even till now, and merits some clarifying notes here. The duel between fact versus fiction should be an informed one, so here goes:

Fiction: *S*lumach threw gold nuggets the size of walnuts around saloons in New Westminster.
Fact: There is no record whatsoever, either in the popular press of the time or in the court records, that Slumach ever had any gold.

Fiction: Slumach took women into the bush with him and then murdered them to protect his secret.
Fact: There is no record of Slumach having taken any women into the bush with him or having murdered anyone other than Louis Bee.

Fiction: Slumach cursed mine seekers on the gallows.
Fact: There is no record of Slumach having uttered a curse as he stood on the gallows.

Fiction: Dozens of searchers have disappeared as a result of Slumach's gallows curse.
Fact: There is no accurate way of tallying deaths resulting from searching for gold. Hikers and prospectors frequent the area. Reports earlier in the twentieth century said thousands of people headed up into the Pitt Lake area seeking gold every year. There's no way to account for how many returned.

Fiction: Jackson's letter points to the search area for the mine.
Fact: There is no evidence that Jackson was or was not an actual person. No original copy of his supposed "letter" exists, though various versions have appeared over the years.

Fiction: Jackson found gold and deposited an amount of it worth $8,000 in the bank of British North America in San Francisco:
Fact: There is no evidence Jackson existed or that the so-called "Jackson letter" is authentic. All bank records were destroyed in the 1906 San Francisco earthquake, so there is no way to confirm his existence or that of his deposited gold.

Fiction: Jackson's letter was accompanied by a map.
Fact: There is no evidence a map exists or ever existed, and there is no confirmation that any copies of the alleged Jackson letter were authentic.

Fiction: Slumach waylaid miners returning from the Cariboo mines and stole their gold.

Fact: There is no evidence that this occurred. There is no evidence that Slumach had any gold, and there are no reports of murdered miners on the routes down from the goldfields near Barkerville and Wells.

Fiction: Volcanic Brown's last camp was found with eleven ounces of raw gold in a glass jar in his tent.
Fact: There is no evidence Brown's camp had any gold in it. Newspaper reports recounted the search for Brown, but no reports stated that any gold had been found in a glass jar.

Fiction: Slumach was railroaded in his trial with poor legal representation, a short sequestering of the jury, no presentation of necessary witnesses, and a rushed execution.

Fact: Slumach's trial did not last long, and a request to delay it to allow relevant witnesses to be located and brought in to testify on Slumach's behalf was ignored; though witnesses were present in the courtroom the following morning, they were never called to testify. The jury was out for only a few minutes, and the decision to execute Slumach came immediately. Whether those witnesses could have changed the outcome is pure speculation.

Fiction: Molly Tynan's body was found in the Fraser River by a fisherman whose nets dragged her up, and Slumach's knife was found in her body.
Fact: There is no evidence that any of Slumach's purported victims ever existed, even less that they were murdered by him. Slumach was hanged for the murder of Louis Bee.

Appendix D

Remnants of Research

IN CONDUCTING RESEARCH, WE uncovered bits of information incidental to the Slumach story and related elements that don't smoothly fit into the main narrative, and collected them here.

LOGGING COMPANIES HAVE CARRIED on operations over many decades at various locations in the Pitt Lake area, and some still do. There have been suggestions that Slumach once worked for one of those companies as a hunter and that he would leave camp and return from an unknown location in an hour with fresh meat and a handful of gold nuggets, though this was never confirmed.

ANOTHER STORY CONCERNS AN old prospector whose home was on a well-used trail between Squamish and Pitt Lake. Travellers would frequently tell him of a gold mine to the northwest of Pitt Lake. The trail into the mine was fairly well marked for quite a distance, and then suddenly disappeared. Those familiar with the trail knew it picked up again just a few feet from this point, but its beginning was obscured by heavy brush. The second trail continued for a time until it, too, disappeared, only to pick up in a third trail nearby. This frustrating situation repeated itself all the way to the mine, and the few people who knew of the deliberate tricks in the trail found it easily, whereas others, of course, became befuddled and gave up.

Apparently, this old prospector began to frequent the area. He once came across another prospector who had broken his leg and was near death because of a gangrenous infection. The dying prospector had with him a bag of gold nuggets, and told of the fabulously rich find he had made. He described it as being "up so high that nothing grows. As you stand by it you can see in the distant southeast Pitt Lake." He gave directions to the old prospector, and mentioned that the first person to find the gold had been an Indigenous man. The old prospector died without ever finding the mine. This tale lends credence to the searches in the Mamquam area.

SLUMACH'S EXECUTIONER, DESCRIBED AS a tall, thin character wearing a hood, is alleged to have been the same person who executed Louis Riel, the nineteenth-century Métis leader who led two resistance movements in Manitoba against the Canadian government. This may be unfounded rumour, with no confirmation available.

SLUMACH'S AXE WAS OF the type traded by the Hudson's Bay Company in the 1880s. A Dr. R.I. Bentley, who attended at his hanging, reportedly took it from Slumach's possessions. It was last known to belong to a collector in Chilliwack, BC.

ON SEPTEMBER 10, 1898, a three-hour fire destroyed much of the residential and business districts of frontier New Westminster, turning to ash many records that might have shed light on the legend of Slumach's mine, including records belonging to Captain Pittendrigh, who figured in the search for and eventual charging of Slumach.

THE *DAILY COLUMBIAN* REPORT of Slumach's trial on November 14, 1890, mentions that defence counsel asked for Slumach's case to be adjourned on the grounds that two important witnesses for the defence, "Florence Reid and Moody," could not be "obtained" in time for the trial. It has been suggested that this Moody may have been an illegitimate offspring of Colonel Richard Clement Moody, but Colonel Moody left British Columbia in 1863, and a George Moody, thought to be the witness in question, was born in 1875, the son of an Indigenous woman and Sewell Prescott Moody, the first large-scale lumber exporter in BC, thus calling into question the Moody claim. Although both witnesses were present at Slumach's trial, the defence counsel did not call them.

OVER THE YEARS, THE Slumach legend has provided fodder for screenplays, short stories and novels, most of which were never published—with one exception. In 2005, more than twenty years after author Edgar Ramsey began to write it, *Slumach: The Lost Mine* weaves together two threads: an anthropology professor's interest in writing a book on the legend, and two miscreants' plan to get rich quick with a trek into the Pitt Lake wilderness to find the

gold. Some sex, gore, and mysterious happenings from an unknown source are thrown into the mix, and when the two teams converge at the head of the lake, this pulp-fiction telling sheds a different light on the Slumach legend.

COLUMBIAN NEWSPAPER JOURNALIST ALAN Jay started but never finished a novel about Slumach. He wrote 30,000 words before declaring he couldn't take it any further. He gave it to Rick. Jay has since passed away, and his story now rests with the Simon Fraser University Library Special Collections (along with the Slumach research papers donated by us).

EXHIBIT EH! WAS A fun television escapade shown on the CTV Travel Channel and hosted by Todd Macfie and Frank Wolf, who roam the country "exposing Canada, one mystery at a time." Slumach's story was an inevitable lure, and their twenty-three-minute episode, created for the 2006/2007 season, begins with them hunkering down in the New Westminster Public Library, apparently engaged in diligent research—all aimed at finding a "stash of gold" that no one has been able to locate.

They report that "forty people have succumbed to the curse," and hedge their own bets by going to Pitt Lake country under the guidance of two known prospectors, who take them to the "golden mountains" and caution that "gold is usually in the worst spot." Bravely, they don headlamps and enter a long, deep mineshaft. They chisel away as instructed, but leave empty-handed.

Finally, the hosts caution other would-be prospectors with sage, if peculiar, advice about the rugged topography: "What is not straight up, is usually straight down."

FROM THE FIRST PADDLEWHEELER on the Fraser River in 1863 through to their demise in the early 1920s (much of the period storied by "King of the Fraser" William Irving, whose residence is today a museum in New Westminster), the vessels were the river's signature. Today, a

This photograph purports to show Slumach's axe, taken from his possessions after his hanging, and is displayed with other items to show its relative size. While the veracity of this claim can't be confirmed, it is rumoured to be in the possession of a Chilliwack collector. In any case, this axe is typical of those in use in Slumach's time. (PART OF THE CREDIT) R. HARDING, "SHOULDER STRAP," *RCMP QUARTERLY*, JULY 1968

family-owned enterprise offers tours on the *M.V. Native*, a handsome remake of those earlier boats. While it features historic tours and commentary on the way to Fort Langley, it has on occasion taken groups (it holds one hundred passengers) to Pitt Lake. Another such trip, with Brian on board for commentary about the lost mine legend, entertained river trip enthusiasts. The views of the Golden Ears are stunning, the geography remarkable for variety, and the history comparable only to stories in which others have sought elusive gold.

YES, THERE'S A SONG about Slumach's lost mine, which shouldn't surprise anyone who knows American actor Walter Brennan, who sang about the lost "Dutchman's Gold Mine" in Arizona. Actually, there are two, including a German label release in 2018 called "Slumach's Ghost," but the one of note is from Bruce Coughlan and the band Tiller's Folly. The song title is "Chatham Reach," where the famous murder of Louis Bee happened:

> And ever steeped in mystery your legends would unfold
> Of stalwart men to reach their end in search of Slumach's Gold
> And ever still, I'm haunted by the ghost of Louis Bee
> Sweet mystery, and it calls to me.
> Now winter brings it's bitter chill
> My breath hangs in the air
> The frost has turned the tall grass
> To the colour of my hair
> My life is done, my race is run
> But with a longing I am filled
> To linger still, down on Chatham Reach.

THE SLUMACH STORY HAS long seemed destined for the stage, and that finally occurred in 2021 under the auspices of the Emerald Pig Theatrical Society's *A Night of the Macabre*. One of three vignettes performed by two actors was the original play by C.L. Young, *Slumach's Gold and the Widow's Curse*. It is the story about the widow of the last miner to work the lost mine—and of course has twists for the female journalist in the tale.

SOME FACTS ABOUT GOLD: its atomic number is 79, and it appears on the periodic table in that position. Gold is measured in ounces or troy ounces. It is classified in "carats": 24 carat (24k) gold is pure gold, 14k gold is 58.3 percent gold. Gold often is found with copper, silver, iron, lead, calcite, tellurium, zinc, and quartz. It is found as placer gold, quartz vein gold, "glory holes," and nuggets. The largest gold nugget ever found is the Welcome Stranger nugget, found in Australia in 1869, weighing 2,520 troy ounces (78 kg., or 173 lb.) Gold is found worldwide. A "motherlode" is a "principal vein," a main source of a large amount of the metal.

CANADA POST ONCE CONSIDERED issuing a set of stamps in 2018 or 2019 involving possible Canadian hidden treasures, one of which was Slumach's gold. We received correspondence from them during their consideration process. Unfortunately, the Stamp Advisory Committee did not retain the suggestion on *Hidden Treasures*.

This pictograph is on the west side of Pitt Lake. One source claims it profiles the legend of "Slumack" or "Shumack," but this has not been proven, and is open to interpretation. Another source claims it is a warning that the lake is violent and cold, windy and dangerous.
OP MEDIA GROUP

PRIOR TO THE CREATION of Canada's first criminal code in 1892, English criminal law applied in BC. Between 1871 and 1892 someone charged with murder would be charged under federal legislation. Generally, there was simply murder and manslaughter. Murder carried a mandatory death penalty; manslaughter did not. Slumach was charged with murder. Had he been charged with manslaughter, he might have avoided the hangman's noose. Section 232(1) of the code states that culpable homicide that would otherwise be murder may be reduced to manslaughter if the person who committed it did so in the heat of passion caused by sudden provocation. Additionally, the accused could not give sworn testimony until 1892.

FRED BRACHES SUGGESTED IN his blogspot: (https://slumach.blogspot.com/) that both Louis Bee and Charlie Seymour were involved in the illegal liquor trade with Indigenous people. Seymour was arrested and sentenced to six months of hard labour in 1882; Bee had been similarly charged and similarly incarcerated in 1887. Speculation arose that, on the fateful day of Louis Bee's murder, the two may have again been participating in that line of work, rather than fishing. That may have been the reason for their presence at the location where Slumach shot Bee, though no evidence for this has ever been presented.

PODCASTS COVER A WIDE variety of topics and personalities and are available from various online sources at any time. In keeping with the times, the developers of the hugely successful *Deadman's Curse* TV series created their own podcast, *Deadman's Curse: Slumach's Gold*, in 2023.

Host Kru Williams dove deep into the Slumach legend with guests from relevant backgrounds. Some were his co-stars on the TV series, while others were researchers, gold seekers, experts in different fields, and Slumach enthusiasts who could all shed some light on the legend and its characters.

Episode by episode, the podcast reveals new information from the voluminous files available on Slumach—some factual, some rumoured, some legendary, some contradictory, all swirling around the stories chroniclers have shared for more than 130 years. Were gold nuggets thrown around saloons in frontier New Westminster? Was there a gallows curse? Did Slumach have gold? And if he had gold, was it from a secret mine? Did he have an ongoing grudge with Louis Bee? Or was he just a simple hunter and fisherman who lived a subsistence existence on the shore of lower Pitt River?

These questions and more were the meat in the Slumach podcast sandwich.

Some information in the podcast was gleaned from conflicting accounts from interviews with Amanda Charnley (Aunt Mandy). There was speculation Slumach found some gold and sold it to a New Westminster shopkeeper for twenty-seven dollars, but there was also erroneous information that Bee was killed at Lillooet Slough, across the lower Pitt River from the actual murder site at Addington Point.

There is an account that Slumach drew a map to where he found some gold for Aunt Mandy's father, Peter Pierre, the day before he was executed. Aunt Mandy provides different accounts regarding how Bee's murder occurred, and what was said between the two men. And she states that Slumach was baptized the day before his hanging, when newspaper reports say that occurred at 7 AM on January 16, one hour before his execution at 8 AM. She also states that he was buried in the "prison cemetery," when the actual interment record shows he was buried in St. Peter's Roman Catholic Cemetery later on the same day he was hanged. Might her conflicting accounts cause concern for the accuracy of other things she said to her interviewers?

Overleaf ADAM PALMER COLLECTION

Words of Appreciation

IN 1972, WE WROTE:

Hidden in every legend is the first person that ever told the story. Were it not for them, we would be without the parts of our history that are the cornerstones of our heritage. We're unsure who to thank for that regarding Slumach's gold.

This book is the work of many people. It is the people who supported us in our hopes of publishing a study of Slumach and his legendary mine. It is the people who called us to say, "I have something you might be interested in . . . " It is the people who helped out by making necessary trips here and there when the authors couldn't. It is the people who willingly shared their knowledge, advice, and experience to make this whole thing possible. And it is the people who stood patiently by and allowed us to pursue our research at the risk of neglecting other important duties. And we thank them sincerely for all their help.

Those words stood the test of time. Many ventures and more than five decades later, many other people have also earned our sincere appreciation. The authors thank all of the individuals who willingly shared their knowledge, advice, experience, and material to help us create this edition. We are especially grateful to Don Waite and Fred Braches, who made significant contributions by providing interesting input and angles that added to our book's thoroughness and credibility.

"First readers" and "reviewers" make important contributions to a book by reading early material. We thank folks who kindly gave of their time and talents for these purposes: Janice Antonson, Jess Ketchum, Garth Dinsmore, Jeremy Antonson, Darren Johner, Jeff Rudd, John Cherrington, Terry Marshall, Ken Mather, and Don Waite.

The three of us have enjoyed years of support, help, input and guidance from our respective spouses in our search for the legend, Sue (Brian), Neil (Mary), and Janice (Rick).

Our respect to Rodger Touchie and Lara Kordic for taking the decision to publish this work. Our writing once again benefitted greatly from editor, Karla Decker, who was with us on the writing journey for our 2007 edition as well as our book Whistle Posts West.

Sincere appreciation to Setareh Ashrafologhalai for our stunning cover design, to Sara Loos for the book's captivating layout, and to Nandini Thaker for savvy editorial management and shepherding our work along. And to Monica Miller, Kimiko Fraser, and Wendy Underwood for their creative leadership and promotional support of our work.

And we acknowledge the support of the late Wendy Antonson for her support over many years.

To Wil and Tom and Al and Steve, because one evening in the fall of 1969, stories were shared and one sparked what became a quest that culminated in this book . . . just sayin' thanks.

We greatly appreciate cartographer Eric Leinberger's work in bringing the area alive for readers via his map work, and it was wonderful to reconnect with Fred Bosman for new maps fifty-two years after we first worked together.

And our book is much the better with the work of many photographers and their partners and spouses who contributed excellent visual material to help us all actually see the various activities and wonderful countryside where the legends and realities have unfolded.

Special recognition is due to James Wheeler, Adam Palmer, and Don Waite who provided dramatic photographs that have contributed hugely to the overall visual impact of this work.

Sources and Permissions

We thank those who have provided information and been our sources over the years for our three books: The *Columbian, The Native Voice,* the *RCMP Quarterly, B.C. Digest, Canada West, Enterprise, Canada Geological Survey,* the *Daily Colonist,* the *Vancouver Sun, Shoulder Strap,* the *Province,* the BC Archives, the New Westminster Library, the Vancouver Public Library, and Wayne Lyons, Frebo Studio, and R. Harding, who helped to supply photos:

Books

Braches, Fred. *Fact and Fiction: Slumach and the Lost Creek Mine.* Whonnnock, BC: Whonnock Books, 2017

———.*Searching for Pitt Lake Gold: Facts and Fantasy in the Legend of Slumach.* Victoria, BC: Heritage House Publishing, 2019.

Davis, Chuck. *Port Coquitlam: Where Rails Meet Rivers.* Madeira Park, BC: Harbour House Publishing, 2000.

Friesen, Daryl. *Seekers of Gold.* Self-published e-book: Langley, BC: www.bc-alter.net/dfriesen/mineintro.html, 2006.

Hawkins, Elizabeth. *Jack Mould and the Curse of Gold: Slumach's Legend Lives On.* Vancouver, BC: Hancock House Publishers, 1993.

Historical Society of Pitt Meadows. *Pitt Meadows Through a Century of Progress as Told in Part by Mary A. Park to Edith M. McDermott.* Pitt Meadows, BC: Canadian Confederation Centennial Committee of Pitt Meadows, 1967.

Miller, Charles. *The Golden Mountains: Chronicles of Valley and Coast Mines.* Mission, BC: *Fraser Valley Record,* 1973.

———.*Valley of the Stave.* Surrey, BC*:* Hancock House, 1981.

Nicholson, R.W. *Lost Creek Mine.* Penticton, BC: Self-published e-book, 2003. www.rhistory4u.com/pittlakelegend.htm. Accessed February 2007. Not accessible online at our 2024 publication date

Paterson, T.W. "Legend of the Lost Creek Mine," in *Lost Bonanzas of Western Canada,* Garnet Basque, ed. Surrey, BC: Heritage House Publishing, 1999, 2006. Originally published in *Canadian Treasure Trails.* Langley, BC: Stagecoach Publishing, 1976.

Ramsey, Edgar. *Slumach:The Lost Mine.* Sonora, California: Ramsey Books, 2005.

Twigg, Alan. *The Essentials: 150 Great BC Books and Authors.* Vancouver, BC: Ronsdale Press, 2010.

Waite, Donald E. *Kwant'stan.* Self-published: Maple Ridge, 1972.

———.*The Fraser Valley Story.* Vancouver, BC: Hancock House Publishers. 1988.

Interviews

Our writing reflects many phone interviews, personal interviews, and discussions. Those have ranged from active gold seekers to people who contacted us with their theories about where the lost gold might be found. Rather than track them individually here, we've endeavoured to put the salient points and rumours into our narrative, yet we thank all who made their time available to further our quest.

Magazines and newspaper articles

Barlee, N.L. "The Lost Mine of Pitt Lake," *Canada West*, Winter 1970, pp. 10–15.

Antonson, Rick A. "Slumach's Curse." *Beautiful B.C.*, Spring 1974, pp. 1–16.

———."Gold in Them Thar Hills." *This Week*, January 19, 1976.

Antonson, Brian. "Slumach's Glorious Gold." *Canadian Frontier Annual.* Surrey, BC: Nunaga Publishing, 1976.

Ferry, Jon. "Gold Fever! Looking for the Lost Creek Mine." The *Province*, October 9, 11, 12, 13, and 14, 1983. This information also appeared nightly that week on CKVU with reporter Dale Robins along for the trip.

Hume, Mark. "Alberta couple survive 'curse' tracking legendary gold mine." *Vancouver Sun*, October 10, 1995.

Alan Jay provided us with his 1960s/70s manuscript of a novel-in-the-works about Slumach, which we understand to be the only copy available, and it rests with our Archives at SFU Library.

Television and Audio Sources

"Lost Slumach Mine." Bill Barlee's *Gold Trails & Ghost Towns*.

"The Sinister Plots," Episode 10: Delta: Big Red Barn Productions, 2007.

Curse of the Frozen Gold. Toronto: JV Productions, 2015. YouTube has portions of episodes.

Curse of the Lost Gold Mine. Vancouver, BC: Yaletown Productions Inc., 1994. Available on YouTube.

Deadman's Curse. Vancouver, BC: Great Pacific Media, 2022 and 2024. YouTube has portions of episodes.

Deadman's Curse. Vancouver, BC: Great Pacific Media, 2022. podcasts.apple.com/ca/podcast/deadmans-curse-slumachs-gold/id1685897099

Exhibit Eh! Exposing Canada, One Mystery at a Time. Hosted by Todd Macfie and Frank Wolf, CTV Travel Channel.

Treasure Hunters. "Episode 10: The Mystery of Old Slumach." Sylvio Heufelder. Germany: Tandem Films, 1991. Also on YouTube.

Treasure, syndicated American television series with Bill Burrud, 1958.

Wings Over Canada, Episode 507. Vancouver, BC: ATV Productions, 2002.

Websites

www.yaletownentertainment.com

en.wikipedia.org/wiki/Slumach en.wikipedia.org/wiki/Pitt_Lake's_lost_gold_mine

Beringseapaydirt.com, Monica, March 1, 2023

www.slumach.ca

(Note: in 2021, Fred Braches turned over ownership of and responsibility for slumach.ca to the three Slumach's Gold authors, who will host it henceforth. Anyone seeking any information on Slumach can continue to obtain it at this website. The authors of this book can be contacted at info@slumach.ca.)

slumach.blogspot.com

SLUMACH

A Web site for all who prefer facts over fiction

In 1891, an elderly indigenous man (whose name today is mostly spelled Slumach) was hanged in New Westminster, British Columbia for murdering a man called Louis Bee. Myth links Slumach to a fabled bonanza known as Slumach's Gold, Lost Creek Gold, the Lost Creek Mine, or the Lost Mine of Pitt Lake. Click here to read a summary of the story of Slumach and his supposed connection to the legendary gold of Pitt Lake.

Around 1900, stories started emerging in the press about gold found by an indigenous man in the impenetrable mountains around Pitt Lake. In 1915, an American prospector named Armstrong connected Slumach to this legendary Pitt Lake bonanza. Armstrong's story is the archetype of the Pitt Lake gold legend repeated ever since by oldtimers, journalists, and authors in their versions of the tale.

This site, created by Fred Braches in 2007, provides source material on Slumach and other real or imagined characters and features of the "Lost Creek Mine" stories. There are, for instance, transcripts of legal records, and newspaper and magazine articles about the Pitt Lake bonanza.

For the results of Fred Braches' research on the Pitt Lake legends, read his book *Searching for Pitt Lake Gold*. For other information read *Slumach's Gold: In Search of a Legend*, by Rick Antonson, Mary Trainer, and Brian Antonson. Both books were published by Heritage House Publishing, Victoria, British Columbia.

As of September 2021, slumach.ca is owned and managed by Brian Antonson, Mary Trainer, and Rick Antonson. If you use information from this site, we would appreciate your acknowledging slumach.ca as your source. Your contributions, messages, comments, corrections, and recommendations are very welcome. Feel free to put a link to this site on your website.

Contact: info@slumach.ca

Available at bookstores or Amazon.ca

Slumach's GOLD

IN SEARCH OF A LEGEND

RICK ANTONSON
MARY TRAINER
BRIAN ANTONSON

Newspapers 1800s

Newspapers 1900s

Publications 2000s

Aunt Mandy's Interviews

Legal Records

Books & Videos

E-books & Links

Miscellanea

Go to Blog

WIKIPEDIA

Slumach

Pitt Lake's Lost Gold Mine

Slumach.ca has become the most authoritative web source of information on almost everything ever published about the legend. SLUMACH.CA

Archives

All Fred Braches's original research material has been deposited in the Special Collections section of the Vancouver Public Library and it is also available at the 'slumach.ca' website.

The Antonsons/Trainer archives from researching and writing the 1972 and 2007 books were acquired by Simon Fraser University Library's Special Collections in 2018. May someone open it one day and find Rikk Taylor's plastic bag of gold ore and the assay report?

Overleaf ADAM PALMER COLLECTION

Index

New Westminster, BC, 13, 16, 25, 37, 40, 41, 42, 47, 49, 51, 87, 98, 117, 121, 134, 169, 178, 181, 189

New Westminster Museum and Archives, 87

Nicholson, Rob, 44, 113, 131–35, 165, 176, 185

Norm's tent-shaped rock, 84–86, 89, 107, 131, 184. *See also* gold; clues

q̓

q̓ic̓əy̓ (Katzie) First Nation, 33, 38, 42, 86–87, 118, 140, 141, 164, 176, 185, 187

Q

Queensborough. *See* New Westminster, BC

P

Palmer, Adam, 114, 115, 136–37, 138, 149, 163, 164, 165, 166–67, 176, 177

Patterson, T.W. "Tom," 73

Pierre, Chief Joachim "Joe," 118, 123

Pierre, Peter, 7, 26, 33, 40, 76, 119–21, 122, 169, 179, 181

Pierre family, 113, 118, 164–65, 171. *See also* Charnley, Amanda *and* Pierre, Chief Joachim "Joe"

Pitt Lake, 1–4, 7, 8, 9, 10, 11, 14, 15, 16, 28, 30, 38, 39, 40, 41, 42, 44, 47, 53, 54, 55, 63, 66, 70, 71, 74, 84, 86, 97, 109, 127, 128, 130, 136, 138, 143, 145, 163, 176, 187, 191

Pitt Meadows, BC, 42, 53, 72, 187

Pitt River, 9, 10, 11, 14, 15, 17, 24, 27, 28, 37, 40, 42, 68, 71, 72, 94, 95, 128, 129, 136, 137, 154, 157

Pitt River Lodge, 94, 129, 149, 153. *See also* Gerak, Danny

Pittendrigh, Captain George, 25, 27–28, 33, 171

Port Coquitlam, BC, 66, 72, 157

Province (newspaper), 47, 51, 53, 54, 55, 56, 61, 62, 66, 67, 68, 71, 76, 82–84, 99, 105, 123, 143, 155, 182, 183, 186

R

racism, 17, 19, 20, 23, 26, 27, 28, 29, 30–31, 37, 41, 61, 64, 72, 74, 86, 93, 118, 122, 137, 140, 143, 144–45, 164, 166, 171–72, 190

Reed, Florence, 20, 23, 32

Rhodes, Donnely, 97–98, 99, 100–101

Robins, Dale, 84

Rover, Bernard, 73, 165

Royal BC Museum and Archives, 19, 164

Royal Engineers, 37

Ruskin, BC, 53–54

Russell, Dean, 107, 159

S

San Francisco, CA, 47, 53

Scooch, Danny, 113

Seattle, WA, 49, 53, 55

sensationalism, 19, 20, 23, 26, 27–31, 34, 38, 44, 61–65, 88, 94, 105, 145, 190

Seymour, Charlie, 24, 26, 27, 28, 119, 142, 144, 145, 157

Sheridan Hill, 53, 72

Shiles, Bartley Willet, 40

Shotwell (prospector), 16, 42, 47, 48, 49, 51, 57, 134, 175, 181. *See also* Jackson W. (prospector)